AGENTS *of* BABYLON

What the Prophecies of Daniel Tell Us about the End of Days

DR. DAVID JEREMIAH

Tyndale House Publishers, Inc.
Carol Stream, Illinois

Visit Tyndale online at www.tyndale.com.

TYNDALE and Tyndale's quill logo are registered trademarks of Tyndale House Publishers, Inc.

Agents of Babylon: What the Prophecies of Daniel Tell Us about the End of Days

Copyright © 2015 by David Jeremiah. All rights reserved.

Designed by Jennifer Ghionzoli

Edited by Stephanie Rische

Published in association with Yates & Yates (www.yates2.com).

Library of Congress Cataloging-in-Publication Data

Jeremiah, David, date.
    Agents of Babylon : what the prophecies of Daniel tell us about the end of days / Dr. David Jeremiah.
        pages cm
    Includes bibliographical references.
    ISBN 978-1-4143-8052-0 (hc)
    1. Bible. Daniel—Prophecies.   2. Bible. Daniel—Criticism, interpretation, etc.   I. Title.
    BS1556.J465 2015
    224'.5015—dc23   2015026384

Printed in the United States of America

ISBN 978-1-4964-1123-5 (International Trade Paper Edition)

21   20   19   18   17   16   15
7   6   5   4   3   2

To the members and friends of Shadow Mountain Community Church,
whom I have had the honor of serving for thirty-four years

CONTENTS

Introduction

WHY A BOOK ABOUT BABYLON?

IN 1859, CHARLES DICKENS wrote his famous novel *A Tale of Two Cities*, which was set in late eighteenth-century Paris and London. This was the time of the French Revolution, when the streets of Paris ran with blood spilled in the country's reign of terror.

The Bible could also be termed a tale of two cities: Jerusalem and Babylon. Jerusalem, of course, is the historical capital of God's chosen nation, Israel, and the future capital of His eternal Kingdom. Babylon, on the other hand, is the city the Bible uses as a recurring symbol for the world's evils—decadence, cruelty, abuse of power, and especially rebellion against God.

Babylon began as Babel, the city established by the ambitious Nimrod in his attempt to organize the first worldwide government in opposition to God (Genesis 11:1-9). Centuries later, it was the armies of Babylon that conquered Jerusalem and the city of Babylon that held the exiled Jews captive.

Babylon fell more than five centuries before Christ, but its spirit survived in subsequent world empires, including Rome, the society that executed Christ and persecuted the first Christians. Despite its strength, the Roman Empire eventually fell. We know from biblical prophecy, however, that it will revive in the end times. But as Revelation makes clear, its spirit will be that of Babylon, because it will continue what Nimrod began—humankind's attempt to usurp the authority of God.

The other city, Jerusalem, has fallen several times and has been occupied or oppressed throughout much of history. It might seem, therefore, that Babylon, the city of man, has been stronger than Jerusalem, the city of God. But that's not the case. Yes, Jerusalem has been persecuted, but for a good reason: its persecution has been a form of discipline designed to prepare it for its future role. The book of Revelation makes it clear that in the history-long struggle between these two cities, Jerusalem will be the ultimate victor. Revelation tells of Babylon's final destruction and the ascendancy of Jerusalem as the permanent capital of God's eternal Kingdom.

The natural question, then, is why I would choose to write a book about an evil city that will eventually suffer an eternally crushing defeat. The answer is that we are living in a time marked by the spirit of Babylon, and we know from biblical prophecy that this force will continue to rise until it dominates the entire world. I wrote this book to help us prepare for that time, which I am convinced is close at hand.

* * *

BABYLON FROM THE INSIDE

Nowhere in the Bible do we get a clearer picture of the nature of Babylon than in the book of Daniel. The book bears the name of its author, one of the prominent exiles forced to march to Babylon when King Nebuchadnezzar conquered Jerusalem almost six centuries before Christ. A study of Daniel is relevant because it portrays a period of history that is much like the culture we find ourselves in today. The first half of the book gives us a picture of the kind of people we must be to remain strong in the face of the future God reveals in the last half of the book.

I have chosen to focus this study of the book of Daniel on the personality portraits it presents to us. These are the "agents" of Babylon. In Daniel we meet two kinds of human agents. First, we see people of prayer and firm conviction who know who God is and refuse to compromise their faith by giving in to the demands of a corrupt and godless culture. Second, we see people who are filled with pride, given to debauchery, and have no respect for any god but their own glory and appetites. Most important, we meet the Agent of agents—the Most High God, who exercises His sovereign control at every twist and turn of the story.

As we encounter these agents, we will explore the prophetic visions described in the book of Daniel. These visions show us two futures. The first is a future that had not yet occurred when Daniel wrote of it but has now been explicitly fulfilled in history. It's the story of four world empires that have risen and fallen exactly as Daniel predicted. The second future is one that is yet to come—a dark and foreboding future describing what we call the end times, which will occur before the glory of Christ fills the world forever. The explicit accuracy of the prophecies that have been fulfilled gives us absolute confidence in those that are yet to be fulfilled.

Both of these phases of Daniel's prophecy have immense value to us today. They bring to light the cyclical nature of history and project it into the future to show us how we must live in the present so we can prepare for the time yet to come. In fact, the entire book of Daniel—both the personal portraits and the prophecies—demonstrates why the courage, conviction, and devotion to prayer portrayed by Daniel are as critical today as they were in his time.

Daniel himself lived in a time of rampant godlessness in an empire that wallowed in opulence, debauchery, arrogance, blasphemy, and pleasure—an empire that brought devastation to God's people. Those with the discernment to read the signs of the times today (Matthew 16:2-3) recognize that the similarities between Daniel's Babylon and today's Western culture are signs that Daniel's dark prophetic visions loom close on the horizon. The only way to endure is to rely on God's strength, as Daniel did, and commit ourselves to standing up for principles of righteousness.

Years ago, Francis Schaeffer, concerned about the increasing godlessness of Western culture, wrote a book titled *How Should We Then Live?* That question can be answered vividly with the examples of courage and conviction in the book of Daniel.

Good men such as Daniel and his three godly associates didn't prevent the fall of Babylon. That wasn't their purpose. But they did prevent their own fall into compromise that would have swept them into perdition along with Babylon. Standing up for their faith wasn't easy. It took enormous courage, conviction, faith, endurance, and prayer. That's what it will take today for us to remain faithful to our God in an increasingly godless generation that is bent on following the way of Babylon into destruction.

* * *

THE STRUCTURE OF THIS BOOK

In my previous book *Agents of the Apocalypse*, I opened each chapter with a fictional narrative about the subject of the chapter and ended with an exposition of the Scripture behind the story. That structure seemed to help people engage with and understand the book of Revelation in a new way, so I decided to repeat the approach in this book.

If you have not read *Agents of the Apocalypse*, let me explain my rationale for this approach. The fictional section of each chapter is designed to whet the reader's appetite for scriptural truth by showing the drama and excitement inherent in biblical narratives. The second section is designed to separate fact from fiction and make relevant applications to our lives. To put it another way, the fiction drives the truth into our hearts, and the Scripture behind the fiction drives it into our minds. My prayer is that this book will accomplish both of these objectives in your life.

Dr. David Jeremiah
FALL 2015

Chapter 1

THE HOSTAGE

Daniel 1:1-21

The young man—hardly more than a boy—no longer bothered to brush away the flies that buzzed around his face. His tunic of fine linen was now caked with dust and sodden with sweat. The once-sturdy soles of his sandals, crafted by the finest cobbler in Jerusalem, were worn so thin that his feet were purple with bruises from treading the stones on the long, dry road.

He was dead tired, hardly able to lift a foot to take another step. Yet he and his companions kept walking, as they had every day for the past four weeks, beginning at dawn and not stopping until sunset. His only relief came when it was time to eat the meager ration of dried bread and drink the tepid water his captors provided. But it wasn't long before the hostages were prodded to get moving again, herded down the seven-hundred-mile road to Babylon.

The young man's name was Daniel. He was fourteen years old, tall and well built before the march reduced his muscular limbs to skin and bone. As miserable as the conditions were, he hardly noticed the flies, the bruises, the blistering heat, or even the mind-numbing exhaustion. Those challenges paled next to the horrors he'd witnessed before the march—images that were now seared into his fevered brain. The pounding of Babylonian battering rams against the walls of Jerusalem. The stream of Babylonian soldiers pouring into the city. The screams of panicked citizens as they raced through the streets. The Babylonians in their chariots, striking down men, women, and children. Worst of all, his final glimpse of his parents as they were brutally slaughtered before his eyes.

He groaned inwardly as he remembered his beloved Leah, the beautiful girl he was betrothed to, being wrenched from his arms and dragged away screaming. When he fought to free her, a Babylonian soldier knocked him unconscious and threw him onto a cart with other wounded Jews.

Daniel shuddered as he remembered the sickening feeling that came over him when he awakened in the cart. Everywhere he looked, the streets of Jerusalem were strewn with bloodied bodies. His tears flowed when he recalled passing the Temple and seeing enemy soldiers piling the sacred worship utensils onto wagons to be hauled away to Babylon. He remembered his shock as the cart carried him through the Eastern Gate, where he joined the other Jews who had been selected to march to Babylon. He looked around and noticed that all of them were young. Those who were old or middle aged or ill had been slaughtered or left in the city.

These images haunted Daniel's mind every waking hour as he made the grueling march, and they ravaged his sleep every night.

Someone behind Daniel spoke, pulling him out of his painful memories and back to the miserable present.

"I think I know you," the voice said.

Daniel turned and looked into the first familiar face he'd seen on the road to Babylon. "Hananiah!" The words cracked through his dry throat. "You survived."

"Yes, but I'm not convinced that's such a blessing. The dead ones may be better off than we are. Have you seen our friends Mishael and Azariah?"

"No," Daniel replied. "Have you seen Leah? She and I were taken at the same time, but I don't know whether she—"

The searing pain of a whip shot across his back.

"No talking!" a soldier bellowed. "You know the rules. Speak again, and it's ten lashes for both of you."

The relentless march continued for weeks. Many Jews died along the way, their bodies left by the roadside for the vultures. The first hole appeared in Daniel's sandal, and the stones of the road began to cut through his skin. The more raw his foot became, the more he struggled to keep pace. More than once he stumbled and fell, but each time he managed to get up and continue walking. He was growing delirious, no longer fully conscious of his surroundings. Yet his body kept staggering forward.

One day he was vaguely aware of a fellow journeyer saying he could see the walls of Babylon. Within hours, they passed through the gate of the city. The march came to a halt, and Daniel, more dead than alive, collapsed to the ground, unconscious.

* * *

Daniel awoke in a darkened prison cell crowded with other young men from his hometown, including Hananiah. He looked around and spotted his missing friends, Mishael and Azariah. His body was raging with a fever, and when he tried to move, he was seized by a searing pain. For the next few days, he wandered in and out of consciousness. When the pain finally subsided and he became aware enough to realize its source, he groaned with an agony that went even deeper than the physical pain. He and his three friends had been tragically mutilated. He would never be a husband. He would never be a father.

As the prisoners healed, they were allowed to rest and were given bread and water. A few weeks later, when the captives had regained sufficient strength, their overseers began assigning them tasks. Some of the men were sent to clean stables and groom horses; others were put to work as porters, carpenters, or janitors. Daniel was ordered to the wagon yard to repair chariots and oxcarts.

The female prisoners were also put to work, washing clothing, cooking, and mending garments. Some of the women served the men at lunchtime, brought weekly changes of clean clothing, and carried drinking water to them in the heat of the day.

One day several weeks after he had begun his labor for the Babylonians, Daniel had just finished remounting a heavy wheel onto a wagon when he saw a young woman approaching with a flask of water. Her head was covered by a hood to protect her face from the sun, and Daniel, in his eagerness to drink, didn't give her a second glance.

When he lowered the flask and wiped his mouth, he caught a flash of recognition in the woman's eyes.

"Leah?" he exclaimed. "Is it you?"

"Oh, Daniel," she cried through joyful tears. "I've looked everywhere for you. I was afraid you'd been killed."

"I'm so glad you're alive! I had no idea what they might have done to you."

"We can't keep talking." She looked over her shoulder as she spoke. "They watch us at all times. Keep drinking while I tell you what I've learned."

Daniel again put the flask to his lips.

"They are getting all the young women healthy again after the march. Soon the most elite Jewish women will be pressed into the service of noblemen and officials, and the most beautiful will become the king's concubines. The rest will be free to marry, though we will remain slaves. So there is still hope that you and I may have a life together."

Daniel stared hard at the dusty ground. "No, Leah, we have no future together. I am no longer the man I used to be. You must count me as dead and find another husband." He handed the flask back to her and turned away to hide his tears.

"But, Daniel—"

"You there, water girl!" the voice of a guard boomed. "Cut the talk and get on with your rounds."

Leah stifled a sob as she walked away. Daniel returned to the carts, his vision blurred by bitter tears.

That night in his cell, Daniel writhed on the straw. He would never know the joys of marriage. He would have no descendants. His name would be cut off forever in Israel, which for a Jew was almost worse than death. *God,* he prayed silently, *what will fill this emptiness in my soul?* Finally he fell into a fitful sleep.

At dawn, however, Daniel arose calm and serene. He had received the answer to his prayer. God Himself would fill the emptiness in his life. God would be his friend, his purpose, and his comfort. That morning in the darkness of his cell, Daniel made a solemn vow that he would be faithful and true to God, just as he would have been to a wife. He wouldn't allow anything to come between him and his God.

Bolstered by his newfound dedication to God, Daniel committed each day to the Lord and to the task before him. His health returned fully, and his body grew strong from the physical labor.

One day as Daniel was replacing the damaged spokes of a chariot wheel, a guard approached and called him from his task.

"You are wanted in the food galley," the guard said. "Stop what you're doing and report immediately."

A dozen other male slaves were making their way to the galley when Daniel arrived. More streamed in, until the room was filled with about thirty Jewish men. Among them were his friends Hananiah, Mishael, and Azariah.

When everyone was assembled, two Babylonian men entered the

room and stood before them. The first was a middle-aged, dark-skinned man dressed in the robes of a Babylonian official. The second, also finely dressed, stood slightly to the side, obviously an aide or assistant.

The official stepped forward and addressed the gathering. "My name is Ashpenaz. I am chief of the eunuchs in the palace of our great king, Nebuchadnezzar—may he live forever. You have been selected from among all the Jewish men as candidates for an exceptional honor. If you are chosen, you'll be trained for the king's service for the next three years. You'll learn the Babylonian language, literature, religion, philosophy, and astrology. You'll be well cared for and fed with the same food that is served at the king's table, including the finest meat that has been offered to the god Marduk."

Ashpenaz looked at the young men, pleased to see the hope reflected in their faces. "All of you were picked for your health, strength, and appearance. But before you are chosen, you must meet two additional qualifications: intelligence and discernment. To determine your fitness in these areas, I will interview each of you privately."

One by one, the young captives were ushered into Ashpenaz's presence. Some returned quickly; others had lengthy interviews. Some came out crestfallen or angry, while others beamed with obvious pleasure. When it was Daniel's turn, he was taken into the private chamber, where Ashpenaz sat facing him.

For the next hour, Daniel answered questions of almost every kind imaginable—political, religious, philosophical, scientific, and astrological. He solved riddles and mathematical equations. He unraveled problems of logic, named the constellations, and identified the major classifications of animals. With each answer, Daniel sensed Ashpenaz's approval growing. After an hour or so, Ashpenaz was actually smiling, nodding his head in approbation, and commending Daniel for his astute answers.

"You are amazingly well educated for such a young man," he said. "How do you feel about the prospect of serving in the court of the king?"

"It would be a great honor, sir. But my commitment to my God prevents it. I cannot, under the laws of my God, eat food sacrificed to an idol."

"Daniel, you must watch your tongue!" Ashpenaz said in a lowered voice. "Don't call Marduk an idol in the royal palace. You could be put to death for such sacrilege, and it would be a terrible waste to lose you. Yet there's no way I can allow you to eat any food other than what the king orders. To disobey him would mean my own death."

"But, sir—"

"Say no more, young man. This interview is over. You are chosen for training, which means I must give you a Babylonian name. From this day forward, you are to be called Belteshazzar. Now go, Belteshazzar. Report to my steward, and he will escort you and the others to the royal palace."

Eleven other young men were selected. The steward took them to the palace complex, where they were given baths, groomed, dressed in Babylonian robes, and assigned plush rooms. Among the men selected were Daniel's friends Hananiah, Mishael, and Azariah, who had been given the Babylonian names Shadrach, Meshach, and Abed-Nego.

At the call to the evening meal, Daniel walked with his friends to the dining hall. "You know we are about to face a crisis, don't you? We will be served food that we cannot possibly eat with a clear conscience before God."

"What will happen when we refuse?" asked Shadrach.

"We will be executed for disobeying the king's order. I don't know what you will do, but I will not eat that food."

The others affirmed Daniel's decision. "We will stand with you," they vowed.

The four young men were seated at a table with the other eight captives. As they awaited the food, they introduced themselves. Eleazar, the man seated next to Daniel, had been given the Babylonian name Malik.

Malik grinned broadly. "Men, our lives have suddenly taken a turn for the better. If we are careful, we can live out our years in luxury we never could have dreamed of in Jerusalem."

"But what about the food they will serve us?" Daniel asked. "We cannot eat anything sacrificed to idols."

"Don't you know that if we refuse, we will be executed?" Malik replied. "Since God put us in this place, surely He expects us to eat what is set before us. What choice do we have? He will understand our dilemma and not hold it against us."

All the men except Daniel and his friends agreed with Malik.

Daniel opened his mouth to respond, but just then the servers brought the food. It was even more extravagant and abundant than they had imagined: fish, pheasant, pork, and aromatic meats cooked in rich sauces, plus an endless array of fruits, vegetables, cheeses, nuts, and pastries.

The eight men did not restrain themselves—they plunged into the feast with great enthusiasm. Daniel and his three friends, however, sat silently, their plates untouched and their heads bowed in prayer.

When the meal was well underway, Ashpenaz's steward came in to check on the diners. When he saw that Daniel and his friends had not touched their food, he stormed over to them, his voice tinged with fury. "Why are you fools not eating? Are you trying to defy the king?"

"No, sir, not at all," Daniel replied. "We told your master that our God forbids us to eat food sacrificed to idols."

"Yes, yes, he told me that," the steward barked. "But he didn't believe you'd hold to it. He was sure that once the food was set before you, you would relent." He slammed a fist onto the table. "Now eat! If you disobey, it will mean your death."

"But sir, don't you see that we cannot betray our God?"

"I see that you will not," the steward retorted. "I won't allow you to defy the king and my master. Either you eat or you die."

"We understand, sir. You are under orders and you must carry them out, or your own life is in danger. But let us propose a solution— a test. Give us the foods we request, and if in ten days we are not as healthy as our companions, you may do with us as you will."

The steward resisted, but Daniel and his companions held their ground.

Finally, the steward threw up his hands. "Very well. You may try your diet for ten days. If your health, strength, or appearance wanes in any way, I will have no choice but to have you put to death."

When the steward left the room, Malik turned to Daniel. "You stupid fools!" he sneered. "Don't you know that you have just uttered your death sentence? There is no way you can flourish on the diet you are proposing. With no meat, you will waste away."

"We will see," Daniel replied. "In any case, we must obey the Lord's commands."

"Those laws were fine for those religious fanatics in Judah," one of Malik's friends jeered. "But only a fool would keep clinging to those ancient rules when times and circumstances change."

Over the next ten days, Daniel and his three friends stuck to their simple diet of water and vegetables. At the end of the trial period, the steward couldn't help but admit that Daniel, Shadrach, Meshach, and Abed-Nego appeared stronger, healthier, and more alert than their counterparts. He not only allowed them to retain their diet for the duration of their education; he encouraged it.

* * *

After three years of training, the twelve young Jews were dressed in the finest of Babylonian garments and presented to Ashpenaz, the chief of eunuchs. He inspected each man closely, instructed them in proper protocol, and led them into the presence of the great Nebuchadnezzar, conqueror of the known world and king of all the provinces of Babylon.

After looking over the candidates, the king called each one to stand before his throne. He posed questions, problems, and riddles similar to those Ashpenaz had posed at their initiation but even more complex. After the interviews were completed, the king sent the men away while he and his advisers deliberated.

The Jewish men were soon called back into the king's presence, where they lined up facing the throne. They stepped forward, one by one, to receive their assignments. One man was given the position of junior instructor in literature at the school for the children of Babylonian noblemen. Another became an aide to the master of numbers in the king's treasury. Others were assigned tasks as translators and tutors of children in the king's harem. One was appointed an aide to Ashpenaz.

Malik awaited his turn with eager anticipation. He was sure he would get a coveted assignment—one that would elevate him far above his peers. When his turn came, he faced the king with confidence that bordered on arrogance.

"To you, Malik," the king said, "I assign a place in the college of royal astrologers. May you serve me long and well."

It was the highest position yet given. As Malik returned to his place in line, he glanced triumphantly at Daniel, a smug smile tugging at the corners of his lips.

Then Nebuchadnezzar called Daniel and his three friends to the throne. "You four have proved yourselves to be scholars of the highest order. You possess knowledge, wisdom, and discernment surpassing any adviser or wise man in my empire. Therefore, I will retain you in my own personal service as advisers on all matters pertaining to the kingdom. May you serve me long and well."

Malik's smug smile evaporated into utter contempt. How could these four men who clung so blindly to outdated beliefs—who thought they were better than everyone else—be elevated above him? *This is not to be borne! Someday soon, by any means necessary, I will find a way to bring this upstart Daniel down.*

* * *

THE SCRIPTURE BEHIND THE STORY

When governments negotiate today, it's not unusual for this formula to be used: "If you will . . . then we will . . ." That formula is actually an ancient one—in fact, God used it when calling the newly redeemed Hebrew people to Himself at Mount Sinai. The covenant that God gave through Moses was conditional, an "if . . . then" covenant. *If* Israel walked in God's ways, *then* God would bless the nation. And *if* Israel abandoned God's ways, *then* God would curse the nation. The blessings for obedience are outlined in Deuteronomy 28:1-14, and the consequences for disobedience are laid out in verses 15-68.

While the nation of Israel exhibited brief periods of faithfulness and blessing, its overall history was one of spiritual decline and discipline. The book of Judges gives us the most appalling evidences of this downward slide, telling of one rebellion against God after another. When kings began to rule over Israel, more of them were wicked than righteous—many of them worshiping idols instead of the one true God.

The high point of Israel's faithfulness occurred under the leadership of King David, but even his story is tarnished with failures. His son Solomon began well as the nation's ruler, but in the latter days of his leadership, he "turned from the LORD" (1 Kings 11:1-13).

The idols Solomon brought into Israel to please his seven hundred wives accelerated the decline. After Solomon's death, the Lord carried out a severe act of judgment by wrenching the ten northern tribes away from the southern tribes, Judah and Benjamin.

The northern kingdom, which took the name Israel, was led by the wicked Jeroboam I and fell to new lows when they set up pagan altars at opposite ends of the kingdom to make idol worship accessible to the people (1 Kings 12:29). The southern kingdom became known as Judah. It retained Jerusalem as its capital and religious center and the lineage of David for its kings.

The northern kingdom of Israel descended rapidly into depravity until 722 BC, when it was overrun and assimilated by the Assyrians, never to be heard from again. According to the prophet Isaiah, Assyria was "the rod of [God's] anger" against His rebellious people (Isaiah 10:5).

The destruction of Israel should have been sufficient to jar the southern kingdom of Judah into serious rededication to God. But the impact of the disaster wore off, and the people of Judah fell into the same downward spiral that had doomed their northern brothers and sisters.

The prophets of God continued to sound warnings. They prophesied coming judgment for Judah if the people continued to follow Israel's rebellious example. One of these prophets was Isaiah, who gave the people this message from the Lord: "Behold, the days are coming when all that is in your house, and what your fathers have accumulated until this day, shall be carried to Babylon; nothing shall be left. . . . And they shall take away some of your sons who will descend from you, whom you will beget; and they shall be eunuchs in the palace of the king of Babylon" (Isaiah 39:6-7).

The Great Defection

> In the third year of the reign of Jehoiakim king of Judah, Nebuchadnezzar king of Babylon came to Jerusalem and besieged it. And the Lord gave Jehoiakim king of Judah into his hand.
>
> DANIEL 1:1-2

God's prophetic warnings to Judah went unheeded until finally, a little over a century after the fall of Israel, God's sword of judgment fell hard. The book of Daniel tells us how it happened.

Jerusalem fell to Nebuchadnezzar in 605 BC (2 Kings 24:1; 2 Chronicles 36:6), and the king deported his Jewish hostages to Babylon in three stages. The first group, which was taken immediately, included only the elite nobility. Two subsequent deportations occurred in 597 and 587 BC, leaving Jerusalem in ruins and only a few of the poor, aged, and infirm in the land.

Daniel 1:2 introduces us to the theme of the entire book: the sovereignty of God. The Lord *gave* Jehoiakim into Nebuchadnezzar's hand. "It was not Nebuchadnezzar's military might or brilliance that brought about the downfall of Jerusalem, but it was the sovereign will of God."[1]

Just as the Assyrians had been God's rod of anger against Israel, Babylon performed the same disciplinary action against Judah. God said He had ordained Babylon "for judgment" and that He had "marked them for correction" (Habakkuk 1:12).

For the next seventy years, the people of Judah would live in Babylon in a constant state of upheaval under the successive control of the Babylonian, Medo-Persian, and Persian empires.

The seventy-year duration of the Babylonian captivity was not a random number; it had a significant meaning. The book of 2 Chronicles explains that the Exile fulfilled "the word of the LORD . . . until the land had enjoyed her Sabbaths. As long as she lay desolate she kept Sabbath, to fulfill seventy years" (2 Chronicles 36:21; see also Jeremiah 25:1-14).

To understand what it means for the land to "enjoy her Sabbaths," we must go back several centuries to the time when Israel first entered the Promised Land. At that time, God instructed the people to observe the Sabbath of the land. *Sabbath* means "rest," and as a matter of good agricultural conservation, they were to allow their fields to lie fallow every seventh year (Leviticus 25:1-4). That year they weren't to plow; they weren't to plant.

Israel had failed to observe this one-in-seven Sabbath for 490 years. In that stretch of time, Israel should have observed seventy Sabbath years. So the Exile of seventy years, during which the Promised Land lay fallow, would make up for the deficit. If Israel would not give God the Sabbath He required, then He would take it from them by means of the captivity.

Ignoring this Sabbath law was by no means Judah's only sin. Like the country's northern counterpart, Judah had also fallen into idolatry under the reign of its kings (1 Kings 11:5; 12:28; 16:31; 2 Kings 21:3-5). Twenty kings ruled over Judah during the 345 years after its division from the northern tribes. Eight kings were good, and twelve were evil. Jehoiakim, who ruled when Jerusalem fell, was the seventeenth king, and history portrays him as one of the country's most wicked rulers, despising God's Word to the point of throwing it into the fire (Jeremiah 36:23).

The rebellion and idolatry of Judah and King Jehoiakim finally exhausted God's patience, and He chose the Babylonians—the most wicked and idolatrous nation on the earth at that time—to carry out His judgment. The irony of this choice is hard to miss: God turned evil against evil to accomplish His good purposes.

The Great Deportation

> The Lord gave . . . into his hand . . . some of the articles
> of the house of God, which he carried into the land
> of Shinar to the house of his god; and he brought the
> articles into the treasure house of his god.
> DANIEL 1:2

Soon after Nebuchadnezzar conquered Jerusalem, he received word that his father had died, so he returned to Babylon to take care of the affairs of the state. He left Jehoiakim on the throne but took several hostages with him, including Daniel and his three friends, to ensure the loyalty of the conquered people.

Along with the hostages, some of the "articles of the house of God" were taken to Babylon and placed in the temple of Marduk, Nebuchadnezzar's god (Daniel 1:2). These were the holy furnishings Solomon had created for the Temple, intended for the worship of God alone (1 Kings 7:48-51).

A century earlier, Judah's King Hezekiah had unwisely shown these treasures to a contingent of Babylonian visitors, and apparently their report was not forgotten (2 Kings 20:13). Isaiah the prophet warned Hezekiah that one day this nation would return and take away all the wealth he had accumulated (2 Kings 20:16-18; Isaiah 39:5-7). King Cyrus of Persia ultimately returned many of these articles to Jerusalem when the Jews' captivity in Babylon ended (Ezra 1:7-8).

Nebuchadnezzar's confiscation of these holy items was a gesture of religious dominance meant to demonstrate to the conquered Judeans that their God was too weak to save them from defeat. In that day, to conquer a nation was also to conquer its gods.

THE CONDITIONS FOR THEIR SELECTION

The king instructed Ashpenaz, the master of his eunuchs, to bring some of the children of Israel and some of the king's descendants and some of the nobles, young men in whom there was no blemish, but good-looking, gifted in all wisdom, possessing knowledge and quick to understand, who had ability to serve in the king's palace.

DANIEL 1:3-4

Did you know it's ten times harder to get accepted for employment at Google (one in 130 applicants is hired) than it is to get accepted to Harvard University (one in fourteen applicants is accepted)? With more than two million applicants every year, Google has an interview process that has become legendary in corporate America. On average, it takes thirty-seven days and many, many interviews to complete the job application process at Google.[2]

But how about a three-year application process? That's what Daniel and his friends endured when they were being groomed to serve in important roles in the Babylonian government (Daniel 1:5). The elite of Judah's young men were examined in three specific areas to see if they were qualified to serve.

The Physical Test

Those selected for service in the king's court were to be "young men in whom there was no blemish, but good-looking" (Daniel 1:4). The word for "young" in the original language usually refers to someone who is fourteen to seventeen years of age. Bible commentator Leon Wood characterizes these captives as "old enough to make the adjustment psychologically and young enough yet to learn easily and come to feel at home in the new cultural surroundings."[3]

The Intellectual Test

In addition to their physical prowess, the young men were to be "gifted in all wisdom, possessing knowledge and quick to understand" (Daniel 1:4). A high IQ was mandatory. Those who were to serve the king must be highly intelligent, knowledgeable, and quick to learn.

The Social Test

The king expected these men to "serve in the king's palace"—in other words, to serve in his presence (Daniel 1:5). They were to be young men of poise, social grace, and winsome personalities, because they had to function in a royal setting without causing embarrassment.

Further, only young men who had been born into royalty could qualify for this special assignment. They were selected from among the royal and noble families of the fallen nation. According to Josephus, Daniel and three of the young men chosen with him—Hananiah, Mishael, and Azariah—were from the royal family that produced King Zedekiah, the last king of Judah.[4]

The fact that Daniel was one of the young men who met these stringent qualifications tells us much about him at the outset. He was a young man of royal blood who was good looking, intelligent, and full of social graces.

THE CURRICULUM FOR THEIR SCHOOLING

Young men . . . whom they might teach the language and literature of the Chaldeans.

DANIEL 1:4

Nebuchadnezzar's three-year training course for these gifted young men included immersion in the extremely difficult Chaldean language and an introduction to Babylon's literature and learning, including astronomy, astrology, architecture, and religion.

At this particular time in history, Babylon was a recognized center of learning and knowledge. History tells of the famous Babylonian libraries that existed at that time, containing vast volumes of literature on almost every subject.

Another name for Babylon is Chaldea, a word often associated with magic and divination—arts that were highly valued in that culture. Daniel and his three friends were to be educated in a highly sophisticated but deeply pagan environment.

THE CAMPAIGN FOR THEIR SEDUCTION

> The king appointed for them a daily provision of the king's
> delicacies and of the wine which he drank. . . . The chief of the
> eunuchs gave . . . Daniel the name Belteshazzar; to Hananiah,
> Shadrach; to Mishael, Meshach; and to Azariah, Abed-Nego.
>
> DANIEL 1:5-7

The indoctrination of these young men into Babylonian culture
was by design. Nebuchadnezzar didn't want to simply educate them;
he wanted to disengage them from their previous cultural condition-
ing and transform them into full-fledged Babylonians. To accomplish
this, he did three things.

He Emasculated Them

Though the book of Daniel doesn't state explicitly that Daniel
and his friends were made into eunuchs, it is very likely they were.
After all, Ashpenaz, the man in charge of Daniel and the other
young men, is referred to as "the master of [Nebuchadnezzar's]
eunuchs" (Daniel 1:3). And the prophet Isaiah predicted that the
Babylonians would come and carry off the riches of Judah as well as
its sons: "they shall be eunuchs in the palace of the king of Babylon"
(2 Kings 20:16-18; Isaiah 39:7).

Young men who would serve King Nebuchadnezzar in his court
were allowed only one passion—the king's wishes. Therefore, it is
likely that Daniel and his friends were emasculated as part of their
preparation for service in the Babylonian kingdom.

He Obligated Them

Nebuchadnezzar "appointed for them a daily provision of the king's
delicacies and of the wine which he drank" (Daniel 1:5). He wanted
them to get accustomed to the good things of the palace so they

would never be satisfied to leave the king's service. Making them dependent on the bounty of the king's food and drink would place them in a position of obligation to him and tether them to a lifestyle only he could provide.

He Assimilated Them

When the young men arrived in Babylon, each of them had Hebrew names that had been given to them by God-honoring parents. In order to assimilate them into the Chaldean culture, Nebuchadnezzar commanded that their Hebrew names be replaced by names affiliated with various Babylonian gods (Daniel 1:6-7).

WHAT'S IN A NAME?

HEBREW NAME	BABYLONIAN NAME
Daniel "God is my judge"	**Belteshazzar** "Bel protect his life"
Hananiah "Yahweh is gracious"	**Shadrach** "The command of Aku"
Mishael "Who is what God is?"	**Meshach** "Who is what Aku is?"
Azariah "Yahweh is my helper"	**Abed-Nego** "Servant of Nebo"

- He changed Daniel ("God is my judge") to Belteshazzar ("Bel protect his life").
- He changed Hananiah ("Yahweh is gracious") to Shadrach ("the command of Aku"), after the Babylonian moon god.
- He changed Mishael ("Who is what God is?") to Meshach ("Who is what Aku is?").

- And he changed Azariah ("Yahweh is my helper") to Abed-Nego ("servant of Nebo"), after the second-greatest Babylonian god, Nebo.

Nebuchadnezzar wanted Daniel and his three friends to forget Jerusalem, their God, the Temple, and everything related to their Jewish heritage and culture. But Daniel and his friends didn't forget.

Almost seventy years later, we see Daniel in Babylon, still praying daily as he bows in the direction of Jerusalem (Daniel 6:10). Nebuchadnezzar could change their names, but he couldn't change their nature. Though much of Daniel's daily life was assimilated into Babylonian culture, his heart remained centered in Jerusalem.

The Great Decision

We see a steadfast commitment to the Lord budding early on in the lives of these four young men. Almost immediately after arriving in Babylon, they encountered enormous pressure to turn their backs on God and succumb to Nebuchadnezzar's indoctrination. It is both instructive and inspiring to see how they handled the crisis.

THE RESOLUTION

> Daniel purposed in his heart that he would not defile himself with the portion of the king's delicacies, nor with the wine which he drank.
>
> DANIEL 1:8

Early in his training, Daniel was confronted with the temptation to compromise his convictions. The first test came when food and wine from the king's table was set before him. To consume that food and drink would have been wrong for two reasons: first, many of the foods would not have met the health and ritual standards required by Jewish law (Leviticus 11). Second, much of the food and drink had almost certainly been previously dedicated as an offering to idols.

Daniel refused to defile himself by consuming the king's foods. It was a critical decision. Had he compromised, the book of Daniel might never have been written.

THE REQUEST

[Daniel] requested of the chief of the eunuchs that he might not defile himself. . . . And the chief of the eunuchs said to Daniel, "I fear my lord the king, who has appointed your food and drink. For why should he see your faces looking worse than the young men who are your age? Then you would endanger my head before the king."

DANIEL 1:8, 10

Daniel's refusal to follow the instructions of King Nebuchadnezzar placed him and his three friends in jeopardy. His decision also endangered Ashpenaz, the head of the eunuchs, who was charged with maintaining their health.

Daniel's appeal to Ashpenaz seems to have been rejected. But Daniel refused to give up. Ashpenaz placed a steward over the eunuchs in Nebuchadnezzar's court, and Daniel, still determined not to defile himself with the king's food, offered the steward a rational proposal: "Please test your servants for ten days, and let them give us vegetables to eat and water to drink. Then let our appearance be examined before you, and the appearance of the young men who eat the portion of the king's delicacies; and as you see fit, so deal with your servants" (Daniel 1:12-13).

Notice that while Daniel stood up for what he knew was right, he did it in a courteous and respectful manner. He didn't confront the steward with an insulting demand; he made a mutually beneficial request in a dignified way, which opened the steward's receptivity.

The steward agreed to allow Daniel, Shadrach, Meshach, and Abed-Nego to follow their own diet for ten days—water to drink and vegetables (literally, "that which grows from the ground") to eat. He would check them in ten days to see whether they were still as strong and healthy as those who were eating the king's delicacies.

The Great Demonstration

The result of Daniel's dietary experiment was conclusive. He and his three friends came out superior to the other hostages in every category of comparison.

THEY HAD GREATER IMPROVEMENT

> At the end of ten days their features appeared better and fatter in flesh than all the young men who ate the portion of the king's delicacies.
> DANIEL 1:15

When Daniel and his friends stood up at the end of their ten-day dietary trial, they looked healthier than any of the other hostages. They probably had better skin color, greater alertness, and stronger physiques. Their appearance was superior in every way to those who had indulged in the king's menu.

How could the appearance of these men have shown such exceptional superiority in such a short time? The answer, clearly, is that God's hand was in it. He rewarded their steadfast conviction by accelerating the positive effects of their diet.

THEY HAD GREATER INTELLIGENCE

> God gave them knowledge and skill in all literature and
> wisdom; and Daniel had understanding in all visions and
> dreams. . . . And in all matters of wisdom and understanding
> about which the king examined them, he found them ten
> times better than all the magicians and astrologers who were
> in all his realm.
>
> DANIEL 1:17, 20

At the outset, these four young men had a special affinity for learning—and for applying that knowledge. We can be sure they studied diligently, and God rewarded that diligence by greatly enhancing their wisdom and understanding.

At the end of the three-year program of study, the graduates were brought before Nebuchadnezzar to be evaluated. After interviewing Daniel and his three friends, the king was astonished at the scope of their knowledge and declared them to be "ten times better than all the magicians and astrologers" in all his kingdom (Daniel 1:20).

But Daniel was the valedictorian of the class. He was found to have even greater ability than the other three, especially in the realm of visions and dreams and their interpretations (Daniel 1:17). This revelation foreshadows the rest of the book of Daniel, which is filled with visions and dreams that reach far into the future of Babylon and, indeed, of the world.

THEY HAD GREATER INFLUENCE

> Now at the end of the days, . . . the king interviewed them,
> and among them all none was found like Daniel, Hananiah,
> Mishael, and Azariah; therefore they served before the king.
>
> DANIEL 1:18-19

Daniel's autobiography reads like a modern-day rags-to-riches story. From his lowly position as a captive, he was promoted again and again, ultimately rising to the highest echelons in the government of his captors. Nebuchadnezzar made him ruler over the province of Babylon and the chief administrator over all the empire's leading men (Daniel 2:48).

After Nebuchadnezzar's death, Daniel continued to serve the king's successors until finally, after Cyrus of Persia conquered Babylon and installed Darius as king, Daniel was made chief executive over the entire Babylonian empire (Daniel 6:3, 28). In today's terms, he was the Persian Empire's prime minister.

It's likely that Daniel influenced as many as thirteen kings and four kingdoms in his lifetime. As we will see in the following chapters, Daniel's influence on these kings was enormous. Wicked though most of the kings were, Daniel's counsel, courage, and absolute integrity often turned them away from idolatry and led them to recognize the power of the true God.

His influence in the lives of Nebuchadnezzar and Darius in particular is made evident by the fact that these great kings seemed to admire Daniel and think of him as a friend. Even though he often had to tell them what they didn't want to hear, they listened to him and respected his counsel because his honesty and loyalty were beyond question.

The account of Daniel's life is surely one of history's great success stories, a living illustration of Proverbs 22:29: "Do you see a man who excels in his work? He will stand before kings; he will not stand before unknown men."

The Great Devotion

Thus Daniel continued until the first year of King Cyrus.

DANIEL 1:21

The first chapter of Daniel would be beautiful even if we didn't have this last verse. But the last verse is a message in itself.

Daniel lived to see Cyrus, the Persian leader, conquer Babylon October of 539 BC, some sixty-six years after Daniel had been taken captive. By this point Daniel was probably over eighty years old and had lived a godly life in the public eye for almost seventy of those years. He'd outlasted some of the most powerful kings the world has ever seen.

For all the miraculous works God performed through and for Daniel, it's important to note that He never delivered Daniel from Babylon. Daniel lived nearly his entire life as an exile in a foreign land—as a hostage in a culture hostile to his faith. The message of Daniel, then, is not that God will remove all forms of oppression in our lives. Instead, this account serves as a promise from God that His people can find success and remain faithful to Him even in the most trying of circumstances.

Daniel lived in a culture that was utterly pagan, yet there isn't a negative word said about him in the entire Bible. When the leaders of Babylon tried to uncover some fault in his life, they found nothing worthy of mention except his faith in God (Daniel 6:4-5).

Through all the plots and intrigues that regularly lurked in royal courts, through all the jealousy that could only be expected toward a foreigner in high office, through all the volatility and capriciousness of the kings he served, through all of the envy, conspiracies, and persecutions, Daniel continued to serve his God without wavering.

In his classic commentary on Daniel, Dr. John F. Walvoord refers to this first chapter of the book as "an eloquent testimony to the power and grace of God in a dark hour of Israel's history when the faithfulness of Daniel and his companions shines all the brighter because it is in a context of Israel's captivity and apostasy. In every age, God is looking for those whom He can use. Here were four young men whose testimony has been a source of strength to every saint in temptation."[5]

* * *

DANIEL FOR TODAY

Welcome to Daniel's world! In studying the dramatic first chapter of this book, we can't miss its relevance to our own day—a collapsing culture, world chaos, egotistical rulers, and threatening tides driving us into the future. Yet God gave Daniel a long ministry, and the shadow of his life crossed thirteen kings, four kingdoms, and all subsequent prophetic history. Whether you're a child, a teen, or an adult, your legacy can influence the world until Christ returns. But in the meantime, here are some things we need to remember:

1. It takes conviction. Daniel made up his mind that he wouldn't be defiled. Though he was exiled from Judah, his heart was still under the control of the Lion of the tribe of Judah. Don't dilute your influence by compromising in a fallen society. Only those who plant flags in the ground of the Cross will exert influence for Christ.

2. It takes the right companions. We need friends we can pray with. Daniel had three such friends, and they had his back. God has friends like that in mind for you—in your dorm, at church, in your family, or in your neighborhood. Take the lead by finding a friend or two to pray for. Ask God to strengthen them with all power in their inner being by His Holy Spirit (Ephesians 3:16).

3. It takes calmness and courage. Notice that Daniel never panicked or overreacted in the face of opposition. Amid life-threatening situations, he remained poised and peaceful. He practiced Psalm 46:10: "Be still, and know that I am God; I will be exalted among the nations." We can remain calm when we have the deep, supernatural peace of knowing that God is our refuge and strength, a very present help in trouble (Psalm 46:1).

The devil doesn't know what to do with people of courage and conviction—people who cultivate godly companionships and spiritual calmness. But the Lord knows what to do with them. He uses them to change the world. He'll surely use you, too, if you'll determine to be a Daniel.

Chapter 2

THE INSOMNIAC

Daniel 2:1-30

KING NEBUCHADNEZZAR awakened suddenly and sat bolt upright in his bed, his body racked with tremors. He heard a scream slice through the night air, hardly aware that the noise had come from his own throat. When he looked down, he saw that his bedclothes were drenched with sweat and twisted around his body like a coiled snake. He looked around the darkened bedchamber, trying to steady his ragged breaths.

His chamberlain burst into the room, a cloak hastily thrown over his nightclothes. He was holding an oil lamp in front of him. "Your majesty! What's wrong?"

The king only stared into the distance, fixated on something the chamberlain couldn't see. Finally the king's eyes came into focus. "Light all the lamps," he rasped. "Send messengers to summon my counselors."

"Certainly, your majesty. I will have them here first thing in the morning."

The king glared at him. "You will summon them at this very moment."

"But sire, it is an hour past midnight."

"Did I ask the time? Call them now! I want them here before the moon moves another inch in the sky."

"Your majesty," the chamberlain pleaded, "they live in houses throughout the city. We cannot possibly get them here so soon."

"Then get whoever you can—those closest to the palace. For what little good they do, a handful is as good as thirty. Summon them now!"

The chamberlain hurried from the room and awakened servants to take the message to the king's counselors. Moments later, maids were scrambling to light lamps and manservants began dressing the king. A nervous valet dropped the king's outer robe onto the floor, and as he stooped to retrieve it, the king kicked him in the ribs. "We don't have time to waste!" he shouted.

Then a servant girl approached, bearing a silver tray with a pastry and a goblet of wine. One of the valets jostled her, sloshing wine onto the king's silk shoes.

"What were you thinking?" he bellowed. He slapped the tray from her hand, and the silver goblet clattered to the ground. The girl watched helplessly as the purple liquid splashed onto the polished floor.

As soon as the servants completed their tasks, they scurried from the room. The chamberlain escorted King Nebuchadnezzar to his throne, and moments later a sentry announced the arrival of the astrologers.

Eight men entered the throne room. All wore long robes blazoned with signs of the zodiac. Among them was Malik, the ambitious Jewish man who had recently become a protégé of Nimatar, the chief astrologer. It was Malik's first appearance before the king since his initial interview, and he held his head high, proud to be included.

When the astrologers reached the dais, they bowed low to the king. Nebuchadnezzar drummed his fingers on the arm of the throne, not even acknowledging their presence.

After a moment, Nimatar stepped forward. "O mighty conqueror of nations, ruler of all peoples, and greatly favored of the gods, what a delight it is for your humble counselors to be called to serve you. We stand eager and ready to do your will. Ask and we will—"

"Stop your babbling! Listen to what I am about to say, and listen well. This very night the gods sent me a vision that is critical to the future of Babylon and the entire empire. Like all visions, it was laid before me in symbols and images. I have called on you to give me the interpretation of the dream."

"O great king, may you live forever," Nimatar replied. "We will gladly do as you command. Tell us the dream, and we will interpret it for you."

"No. I will not tell you the dream. You will tell me the dream and then give me its meaning."

Nimatar and his colleagues stood silent. "O great king, surely you jest," Nimatar said at last. He gave a nervous chuckle. "The king knows it is impossible for anyone to see the unspoken thoughts hidden in the mind of another."

"I assure you, I am not jesting. After all, aren't you stargazers the great and wise possessors of mystic knowledge?" The king's words dripped with sarcasm. "I'm beginning to see, as I have long suspected, that you are merely charlatans buying your places at my table with lies and deceit. You ingratiate yourselves with high-sounding words that prove dry and empty as the desert wind. If you truly are messengers of the gods, they will reveal to you the dream as well as the interpretation. My decision stands: tell me the dream, and then give me its interpretation."

The astrologers stood mute. After a long moment, Nimatar opened his hands in a desperate plea. "O great one," he said, his voice quavering, "we are your most willing servants, eager to do your bidding in all things. We understand the signs and symbols by which the gods display their will to those they favor. Yet this request you have made is a difficult one. We humbly beg you to give us time to consult the gods before we reveal the dream to you."

"You're merely stalling!" Nebuchadnezzar shouted. "If I allow you to delay, any chance of influencing the wheels of fate will be lost. Yet I will be gracious and give you a quarter hour. But know this: if you fail, each one of you will be publicly dismembered and beheaded, and your houses burned to ashes. Now go babble your nonsense to each other and return to me with the dream and the interpretation."

The astrologers bowed as they backed out of the room. When they reached the hallway, they stared at each other, shaking their heads in dismay.

"Does anyone have any suggestions?" Nimatar asked.

After a long silence, one of the astrologers said, "The king says he is testing us, but I suspect that's merely an excuse. I think he has forgotten the dream."

"That could be true," another added. "For a monarch to forget a message from the gods is a terrible omen, and no king would dare admit to it."

"Are you suggesting that we make up a dream and he won't know the difference?" Nimatar asked. "That would be perilous indeed. Even if he has forgotten the dream, he's sure to know what he did not dream. Our deception would only anger him further."

"I wish Daniel were here," Shukura said. "On more than one occasion I have witnessed his pronouncements about the future come to pass."

"Daniel!" Malik spat. "What would we possibly want with that backward-thinking contrarian?"

"No, we don't want Daniel involved," Nimatar said. "He questions every decision we make and proposes alternatives that would be unthinkable in a kingdom like this one."

"That may be true," Shukura replied, "but right now I'm willing to listen to anyone with an idea that would save our lives."

"Surely you don't think Daniel could tell another man what he dreamed!" Nimatar scoffed.

After a quarter hour of futile discussion, the men were summoned again to face the king. They entered the throne room, pale and trembling. They reached the dais and bowed to the floor before the king.

Nimatar rose first. "O great glorious King Nebuchadnezzar, wise and just ruler favored by the gods of earth and sky, protector and—"

"Enough of your flattery! Tell me my dream or be silent."

"Your majesty," Nimatar pleaded. "What you demand of us is not merely difficult; it's impossible. No king on earth has asked a counselor to put himself inside the mind of another and reveal his unspoken thoughts. Only the gods can do such a thing, and they do not dwell in mortal bodies to be called on at will."

Nebuchadnezzar didn't dignify Nimatar with a reply. Looking beyond the doomed astrologers, he motioned to the armed soldier standing at the far end of the hall. "Arioch, get these imposters out of my sight! I want them cast into the palace dungeon. Then arrest every astrologer, magician, and sage in my service. By noon tomorrow, I want every one of them, including these fools before me, executed in the public square."

* * *

Daniel had finished his morning prayers and sat poring over one of the scrolls he'd brought from the king's library. It had been only a few months since his presentation to the king and his assignment to the royal college of counselors. He was essentially an apprentice, learning the intricacies and politics of the king's empire.

Daniel spent much of his time in the palace library and in sessions with the senior counselors. Thus he had come to know many of the high officials of the kingdom. He had been in the presence of

Nebuchadnezzar only a few times, and then merely as an observer. The king himself had never noticed or addressed him.

Daniel's concentration was broken by a loud knock at the door. Before Daniel could rise, it came again, louder and more urgent. He opened the door and saw the captain of the king's guard.

"Arioch! I don't know what brings you to my home, but your presence is a great honor. Please come in." He stood aside as Arioch entered.

"Thank you, my friend. Your welcome will not be so warm when I tell you my mission."

"What is it?" Daniel asked.

"The palace is in turmoil. The king had a terrible nightmare, and he called in Nimatar and his inner circle to interpret the dream. They couldn't do it, so he has condemned every astrologer and counselor in Babylon to death." Arioch paused, looking at the floor. "Daniel, as sorry as I am to say it, the sentence includes you."

"It seems unlike the king to react so strongly."

"Apparently he has forgotten what he dreamed, though the fear of it still clings to him. He demanded that the astrologers not only interpret the dream but also describe the dream itself. Of course, they couldn't do it. No one could do such a thing."

Daniel said nothing for a moment. Arioch waited. In the few short months Daniel had been in the palace, Arioch had come to respect the young Jew for his wisdom and humble demeanor.

Finally Daniel spoke. "I must ask a favor of you. Instead of taking me directly to the dungeon, take me first to Nebuchadnezzar himself."

Arioch shook his head. "Such a rash act would be fatal to both of us. You know that to enter the king's presence without invitation means death."

"Yes, but the king can waive the sentence if he chooses. You need not take the risk yourself. Take me to the door of the throne room, and I will enter alone."

"But why put yourself in such danger?"

Daniel gave a small smile. "Is it really a risk? If I don't go, my death is certain. If I do go, he may listen and I will be spared."

* * *

Within the hour, Daniel was standing before the door of Nebu-chadnezzar's throne room. Arioch instructed the guards to let him enter, and the young man walked down the pillared aisle toward the king's throne.

Nebuchadnezzar's brows furrowed as he looked at Daniel. "Who are you, and what do you mean by such defiance?"

"I am Daniel—Belteshazzar, in the Babylonian tongue. I am one of the recent initiates into your college of counselors."

"Are you one of the Hebrew captives?" the king asked. Without waiting for a reply, he went on. "Before I pronounce your death sentence, I will give you thirty seconds to explain your audacity in coming here."

"I have come in regard to your vision of last night. If you will give me one day to prepare, I'm confident that by this time tomorrow I can tell you both your dream and its meaning."

"You have more gall than brains. What makes you, an apprentice—a nobody—think you can succeed where my highest astrologers have failed?"

"My God will give me the answer you desire."

"Your God?" Nebuchadnezzar snorted. "Gods are just as useless as the whole lot of you so-called wise men."

"Yes, you are right, your majesty: so-called gods are useless. But not the one true God. Let me pray to Him for one night, and you will surely have your answer tomorrow. If not, you may put me to death."

Nebuchadnezzar studied the young man for a few moments. Then he lifted his golden scepter and extended it toward him. "Very well. I grant your life—until this time tomorrow. But if you fail, you will be the first of your colleagues to die. Now go!"

Daniel returned to his house immediately and called together his three friends, Shadrach, Meshach, and Abed-Nego. "Our lives are in grave danger," he said. "And so are the lives of the king's other advisers and astrologers."

"What happened?" asked Meshach.

Daniel recounted the entire story—the unspoken dream, the astrologers' failure to decipher it, and his own visit to the throne. "Arioch told me that when Nimatar was unable to describe his dream, the king went into a rage. He ordered all his counselors killed this very morning."

"Now we have one more day," Abed-Nego said. "What can we do?"

"We must pray. That's why I called you together. We must begin at this moment—fasting the rest of the day and not ceasing our prayers until bedtime. Then we can sleep and trust God for the answer."

The four men began their vigil and did not stop until the sun had set. Then they got up off their knees and went to bed.

In the silent hours before dawn, Daniel's sleep deepened, and a vision began to fill his mind. It was the most horrifying yet triumphant dream he'd ever had. He awoke at dawn, filled with awe. God had given him exactly what he needed to save his friends, the disgraced counselors, and himself. He had received exactly the same vision King Nebuchadnezzar himself had received the night before.

Daniel bathed and dressed in his finest garments. He opened the shutters of his eastern window and glimpsed the orange rim of the rising sun. He bowed to the floor, offering heartfelt thanksgiving to the God he loved.

After he got up off his knees, he bid a cheerful farewell to his companions. Then he strode confidently toward the lavish palace of Nebuchadnezzar, emperor of the known world.

* * *

The eight astrologers sat on the stone floor of the rank dungeon in the bowels of Nebuchadnezzar's palace. No one spoke. No one had slept, either—partly due to their wretched conditions and partly due to the doom that awaited them. Breakfast had been served, but they hadn't eaten anything. There was no room for hardened bread and gruel in bellies already filled with fear.

Shukura broke the leaden silence. "I wonder why they haven't come for us. Arioch said we'd be executed an hour after sunrise."

At that moment, a knock sounded at the door of the cell. Everyone tensed. At last Nimatar rose stiffly and shuffled to the door. A shadowed face appeared through the barred window. After a few minutes in subdued conversation, Nimatar returned to the others. "There is strange news from the king's palace," he said.

"Has the king given us a reprieve?" one of the astrologers asked.

"No, the news will not affect our fate," Nimatar said. "It seems that Daniel has talked the king into letting him try to describe and interpret his dream. He has given the fool a day to prepare."

"The imbecile!" Malik spat. "He's just stalling."

"At least he gained a day," Shukura said. "That's more than we could do."

"This only prolongs our agony," Nimatar responded. "Our informer told me that when Daniel fails, he will be the first one executed."

"But perhaps he will not fail," Shukura said. "He does seem to have some indefinable gift the rest of us lack."

"That gift is ignorance," Malik retorted. "Did you know he prays three times a day? The fanatic still follows the hollow rituals of our people's past."

"Sometimes I wonder if he's right. Perhaps we, too, should pray to his God. After all, our lives are in danger."

"Shukura! Listen to yourself," Malik cried. "You're drifting into his fantasy world. If his God had any real power, we Jews would still be in Jerusalem. The best we can hope for now is the pleasure of seeing that holy madman executed before our eyes."

* * *

THE SCRIPTURE BEHIND THE STORY

There are around two hundred "sovereign states" in the world today (there are currently 193 member states in the United Nations). Depending on how we define *nation* (according to most definitions, "a people in a place governed by a premier according to a paradigm of laws"), we can easily say there have been thousands of nations in the history of the world.

Today, national borders are fixed; in ancient times they were more fluid. Ancient nations were more like empires that expanded and contracted based on military strength. Victories meant expansion; defeats meant contraction.

The story of Daniel the prophet is set in the heart of one of the most powerful empires on earth in ancient times: the Babylonian Empire. Babylon had just expanded its borders westward from Mesopotamia to the Mediterranean Sea by conquering Israel and other small nations. When Daniel arrived as a captive, the ruler of Babylon was Nebuchadnezzar II, who, although he didn't know it, was about to play a part in outlining the future of the world's nations.

Here's why: while the rise and fall of nations may seem like historical coincidences to us, we learn from Daniel that it is God who "removes kings and raises up kings" (Daniel 2:21; see also Acts 17:26). This would have been a hard reality for a dictator like Nebuchadnezzar to face. He likely would have laughed at the idea of losing his grip on world domination. But it was true then, and it is true today: human kingdoms are weak, temporary, and imperfect imitations of the coming Kingdom of God, "which shall never be destroyed" (Daniel 2:44).

King Nebuchadnezzar II reigned over Babylon from 605 to 562 BC, and he is by far the most significant Gentile king in the Bible. He is mentioned about ninety times by the biblical writers. On three different occasions, God refers to Nebuchadnezzar as "My servant" (Jeremiah 25:9; 27:6; 43:10), yet he is also called "the lowest of men" (Daniel 4:17). Paradoxically, even the acts of the lowest of individuals can be used in the service of God.

It was Nebuchadnezzar who constructed the famous Hanging Gardens of Babylon, one of the Seven Wonders of the World. History records that he built these gardens to cheer up his wife, Queen Amytis, because she missed the green hills and valleys of her homeland in Media.

Secular history paints Nebuchadnezzar as a brutal, despotic king. All his subjects trembled before him; he trembled before no one and nothing—nothing, that is, except his dreams.

Daniel 2 tells the story of God speaking to King Nebuchadnezzar in a dream. Although the king was unaware of God's role in the dream, God was revealing to Nebuchadnezzar His plan for the Gentile nations. Bible teacher H. A. Ironside writes that this dream "contains the most complete, and yet the most simple, prophetic picture that we have in all the Word of God."[1]

When God gave His revelation to Nebuchadnezzar, He communicated by *dreams*. He never used *visions*, as He did in His revelations to Daniel. "In fact," writes commentator Leon Wood, "the Scripture shows God regularly employing a dream when giving a revelation to pagans. The reason seems to be that, with the dream, the human personality is neutralized and made a passive instrument for the occasion. With the vision, however, the person himself is often a participant and must be constituted to respond and react in a proper manner, something true only of a child of God."[2]

Many believe that Nebuchadnezzar's dream recorded in Daniel 2 is the most awe-inspiring dream in the Bible. It predicts the future of four successive empires: Babylon, Medo-Persia, Greece, and Rome. It outlines the reconstitution of the Roman Empire at the end of time and pictures the rise of Christ's Kingdom and His reign over the whole earth.

Yet the dream came in a strange form, using vivid symbolism that the king could not understand. It made him uneasy—and when the king was uneasy, the whole kingdom soon became uneasy.

Daniel 2 is divided into two distinct sections. The first thirty verses tell the story of the king's dream, and verses 31-49 record the interpretation of the dream. Daniel 2:1-30 is presented to us as if it were a three-act play.

Act I: Nebuchadnezzar Onstage

The events of Daniel 2 took place shortly after Daniel had become part of the king's court. In Daniel 1:18, we read that his three-year period of schooling had been completed and that he and the other young royals who were chosen for the course had graduated.

With that timetable in mind, Daniel 2 begins in a confusing way: "Now in the second year of Nebuchadnezzar's reign, Nebuchadnezzar had dreams; and his spirit was so troubled that his sleep left him" (verse 1). How could this be only the second year of Nebuchadnezzar's reign? We know that he was on the throne when Daniel and the other captives were brought to Babylon and that they'd been there for three years.

Scholars have proposed a variety of solutions to this question, but the simplest answer is that the Babylonians counted the first year of a king's reign as his "year of the accession to the throne." It may clarify the concept to compare it with our way of counting school years. A student graduates from public school after completing the twelfth grade, but he or she has actually been in school for thirteen years. The first year, kindergarten, is not numbered as a school grade. Similarly, in Daniel 1, we have Nebuchadnezzar in his year of accession after his father's death—in reality, his first year on the throne. Thus, in chapter 2, though by Babylonian reckoning he is in his second year, he has actually been on the throne for three years.

THE KING'S DREAM

> Nebuchadnezzar had dreams; and his spirit was so troubled that his sleep left him.
>
> DANIEL 2:1

By the time Nebuchadnezzar had his terrifying dream, he was secure on his throne. All his enemies had been subdued, yet he couldn't sleep. He was suffering from royal insomnia! The word for *troubled* in this verse is a strong term that describes a deep disturbance—one that causes apprehension. Nebuchadnezzar could conquer dynasties, but he couldn't conquer his own dreams.

British Bible teacher Geoffrey R. King writes, "As is so often the case, the cares of the day become also the cares of the night. . . . Nebuchadnezzar did a thing which no believer in God should ever dream of doing: Nebuchadnezzar took his problems to bed with him."[3]

A dream is different from a vision in that dreams always occur during sleep. God often spoke in Old Testament times through dreams. Perhaps the most graphic description of an upsetting dream in Scripture (like Nebuchadnezzar's) is the one related by Job's friend Eliphaz (Job 4:12-21). The dream, which Eliphaz describes as "disquieting," happened when Eliphaz was in a "deep sleep." He says, "Fear came upon me, and trembling, which made all my bones shake. . . . The hair on my body stood up." Eliphaz saw a "form," but he could not "discern its appearance." Then a voice spoke, delivering a message that became the foundation of Eliphaz's message to Job about the cause of his suffering (verses 17-21). Perhaps this is illustrative of what

Nebuchadnezzar experienced: a fearful dream that relayed a message. While Eliphaz understood the message he received, Nebuchadnezzar was confused about the meaning of his own dream.

It was by means of a dream that God warned Abimelech, king of Gerar, that Sarah was married to Abraham (Genesis 20). Pharaoh dreamed a dream, and God used it to show the wicked monarch what He was about to do (Genesis 41:1-36). God also spoke to a Midianite soldier by means of a dream (Judges 7:13-14). All these examples are instances of God speaking through dreams to people who apparently didn't worship the one true God.

Why would God speak to a pagan king like Nebuchadnezzar? The answer is that Nebuchadnezzar was the first ruler of the "times of the Gentiles" (Luke 21:24)—the period of human history when Israel's national life is dominated by Gentile nations, which will end when Christ returns. Nebuchadnezzar's rule began a time, still ongoing, when Israel was not at the center of world influence.

THE KING'S DETERMINATION

> The king gave the command to call the magicians, the astrologers, the sorcerers, and the Chaldeans to tell the king his dreams. So they came and stood before the king.
> DANIEL 2:2

After his terrible dream, Nebuchadnezzar called in his brain trust. His cabinet was comprised of four different groups: magicians, astrologers, sorcerers, and Chaldeans. This particular foursome is referred to several times throughout the book of Daniel (2:10; 4:7; 5:11).

The king gathered these consultants together, hoping they could interpret his troubling dream. When they were assembled, he announced his problem: "I have had a dream, and my spirit is anxious to know the dream" (Daniel 2:3).

The men replied in Aramaic, "O king, live forever! Tell your servants the dream, and we will give the interpretation" (Daniel 2:4). Aramaic was the language Daniel had studied for three years, as it was the language most commonly used in Babylon. In fact, from this point until the end of Daniel 7, the narrative is written in Aramaic instead of Hebrew.

THE KING'S DEMAND

> The Chaldeans spoke to the king . . . "O king, live
> forever! Tell your servants the dream, and we will give
> the interpretation." The king answered and said to
> the Chaldeans, "My decision is firm: if you do not make
> known the dream to me, and its interpretation, you shall
> be cut in pieces, and your houses shall be made an ash
> heap. However, if you tell the dream and its interpretation,
> you shall receive from me gifts, rewards, and great honor.
> Therefore tell me the dream and its interpretation."
> DANIEL 2:4-6

After the counselors had gathered and heard the account of Nebuchadnezzar's sleepless night, they asked him to recount the dream so they could interpret it for him. But he refused, demanding that his advisers tell him both the dream and the interpretation.

The king was unwilling to reveal his dream—perhaps he was putting his counselors to the test. After all, the only way he could be confident of their "divine" inspiration was if they were able to know not only the meaning of the dream but the dream itself.

Nebuchadnezzar told his counselors that if they failed to meet his demands, they would face the penalties of death, dismemberment, and disgrace: "The wise men would be dismembered either by being hacked to pieces or by being pulled apart. . . . In addition, their houses would be . . . completely destroyed and used for garbage dumps. This was no idle threat by Nebuchadnezzar, whose harsh treatment of King Zedekiah (2 Ks 25:7), two Jewish rebels named Ahab and Zedekiah (not King Zedekiah; Jer 29:22), and Daniel's three friends (chap. 3) proved that he would have no qualms about carrying out this cruel threat upon his counselors."[4]

On the other hand, if they were able to tell him the content and meaning of his dream, the king promised them three lavish prizes: gifts, rewards, and great honor—perhaps even marriage to one of his own daughters.[5]

The outrageous demand must have shocked the wise men. How could anyone interpret another person's dream without first hearing what it was?

THE KING'S DISAPPOINTMENT

The next few verses record a fast-moving interchange between Nebuchadnezzar and the wise men.

The Wise Men

> They answered again and said, "Let the king tell his servants the dream, and we will give its interpretation."
> DANIEL 2:7

The wise men responded in desperation by asking once more for the details of the king's dream. Since the king had no way of validating their interpretations, they could say whatever came to their minds and attribute it to their gods. Given the troubling nature of Nebuchadnezzar's dream, he apparently attached great importance to it. The only way to be sure of the counselors' interpretation was to demand that they tell him what he dreamed.

The King

> The king answered and said, "I know for certain that you
> would gain time, because you see that my decision is firm:
> if you do not make known the dream to me, there is only
> one decree for you! For you have agreed to speak lying and
> corrupt words before me till the time has changed. Therefore
> tell me the dream, and I shall know that you can give me
> its interpretation."
>
> DANIEL 2:8-9

Once again, we can't help but notice that Nebuchadnezzar didn't believe in his own system. He had an idea that these men were impostors, but it didn't bother him until it affected his future and peace of mind. Now it became crucially important to verify the integrity of their powers of interpretation.

John F. Walvoord writes, "It seems clear from the entire context that Nebuchadnezzar was not willing to accept any easy interpretation of his dream but wanted proof that his wise men had divine sources of information beyond the ordinary. He also sensed that they were attempting to gain time, hoping that his ugly mood would change. He wanted them to know that he had made up his mind."[6]

The Wise Men

> The Chaldeans answered the king, and said, "There is not
> a man on earth who can tell the king's matter. . . . There is
> no other who can tell it to the king except the gods, whose
> dwelling is not with flesh."
>
> DANIEL 2:10-11

Of this passage, Joseph Seiss writes,

It shows me, in one single sentence, that all the astrology,
necromancy, oracles, dreams, and mantic revelations of the
whole pagan world for six thousand years is nothing but
imbecilities and lies. It proves to me that all the religions,
arts, sciences, philosophies, attainments, and powers of
man, apart from God's inspired prophets and an all-glorious
Christ, are but emptiness and vanity as regards any true and
adequate knowledge of the purposes and will of Jehovah
or of the destinies of man. It demonstrates to me, in a few
words of sad despair, that all the learned theorizings of this
world's would-be wise, from Babylon's magicians down
to . . . the materialistic skeptics and pantheists of our own
day, are but rottenness, rubbish, and damning falsehood,
in so far as they conflict with the revelations which the
Almighty has given by His own anointed prophets.[7]

The wise men's evaluation was almost true but not quite—
there was not a *man* on earth who could reveal the king's dream.
But Daniel, who was on earth, had connections with Someone in
heaven who could reveal it. Daniel was a man on earth who was
in touch with heaven and therefore able to bring heaven to bear
on the things of earth. That's actually a pretty good definition of a
Christian today.

THE KING'S DECREE

For this reason the king was angry and very furious, and
gave the command to destroy all the wise men of Babylon.
So the decree went out.

DANIEL 2:12-13

Nebuchadnezzar was furious. He knew his men were just trying to buy time, so he gave them an ultimatum: either they would tell him his dream and its interpretation or they would be killed. When they were unable to comply, he gave the order to execute not only them but all the wise men of Babylon.

While the New King James Version says the king's slayers actually "began killing the wise men," most modern translations either state or suggest that the executions did not begin immediately. For example, the English Standard Version says, "So the decree went out, and the wise men were about to be killed" (Daniel 2:13). Scholar Stephen Miller confirms this interpretation, saying, "The wise men were being assembled for a formal execution [but] the slaying of these officials was not yet in progress."[8] This makes it likely that Daniel's plea for time and his correct rendering of the dream actually saved their lives.

On a deeper level, the king's decree was an attempt by Satan to rid the world of Daniel. A man who determines not to compromise his life usually gets Satan's attention. But Daniel's life was in God's hands, and Satan had no power to end it before God's sovereign time.

Nebuchadnezzar had no hesitation about ordering the death of these men. They seemed to be frauds in spite of their claims to have wisdom drawn from invisible spirits and pagan gods.

Unfortunately, this delusion of mystic power has not died in the ages since Nebuchadnezzar's Babylon. Today we see more and more people, starved for meaning beyond the empty materialism of the age, turning to mysticism, pantheism, and spiritualism to satisfy their spiritual hunger.

Act II: Daniel Onstage

DANIEL'S PROBLEM

> They began killing the wise men; and they sought Daniel and his companions, to kill them.
>
> DANIEL 2:13

Though Daniel and his friends were not a part of the failed attempt to recount Nebuchadnezzar's dream, they were counted among the king's wise men and thus included in the sweeping punishment. Arioch, the king's executioner, went to find and execute them.

DANIEL'S POISE

> With counsel and wisdom Daniel answered Arioch, the captain of the king's guard, who had gone out to kill the wise men of Babylon . . . and said . . . , "Why is the decree from the king so urgent?" Then Arioch made the decision known to Daniel.
>
> DANIEL 2:14-15

When Arioch came to Daniel's house to carry out the king's decree, Daniel asked why Nebuchadnezzar's orders were so urgent. Here Daniel illustrates how a great leader handles a crisis. *Don't panic. De-escalate the situation through sound reason.* Remember, Daniel had previously won over both Ashpenaz and his steward, and now he was about to influence Arioch to join his team as well. Daniel had such a charismatic personality that when he, a teenage boy, asked this high-ranking officer for an explanation, the man was willing to give it.

Securing Arioch's goodwill was a wise move on Daniel's part, for the captain soon played an important role in this unfolding drama. It's likely that no one else in Babylon could have so quickly introduced Daniel to the king.

DANIEL'S PERSUASION

> Daniel went in and asked the king to give him time, that he might tell the king the interpretation.
>
> DANIEL 2:16

Daniel received an audience with the king and asked for more time to fulfill the king's demand. Nebuchadnezzar sensed that unlike his other wise men, Daniel was asking for time not to stall but to seek from his God the solution to the king's dilemma. Surprisingly, Nebuchadnezzar granted Daniel's request. This was a highly unusual move for an imperial king who had just condemned his top brain trust for making the same plea.

DANIEL'S PRAYER

> Daniel went to his house, and made the decision known to Hananiah, Mishael, and Azariah, his companions, that they might seek mercies from the God of heaven concerning this secret, so that Daniel and his companions might not perish with the rest of the wise men of Babylon.
> DANIEL 2:17-18

Daniel and his friends petitioned God to spare them from the king's deadly decree. The Babylonian wise men sought the answer in the stars; Daniel and his friends sought mercies from "the God of heaven." One author has written that "this designation for God . . . was particularly significant when used in a country foreign to Israel, for it carried the thought that God was over the sun, moon, and stars, which were worshiped by the pagans."[9]

The best the astrologers could do was get to the stars, but Daniel knew the God who made the stars—the God in whom is hidden all the treasures of wisdom and knowledge.

While the wise men of Babylon were shaking in their boots, here were four young Jewish men on their knees before God. Daniel and his friends were certain that if they didn't lift up their voices in prayer, soon they might not have voices to lift up.

That night God revealed to Daniel not only the dream but also its interpretation (Daniel 2:19). More than one scholar has suggested that God let Daniel dream the same dream Nebuchadnezzar had dreamed!

DANIEL'S PRAISE

> The secret was revealed to Daniel in a night vision.
> So Daniel blessed the God of heaven.
> DANIEL 2:19

When God answered Daniel's prayer, he didn't rush straight to the king, as one might expect. The first thing he did was to gather his three friends and praise God in a private worship service.

Their words of thanks make up one of the most beautiful prayers recorded in the book of Daniel.

He first worshiped God for who He is: wise, powerful, sovereign, and all-knowing (Daniel 2:20). He worshiped God for His might and power, and then he expressed his confidence that no matter how powerful a ruler might be, God is still sovereign over the affairs of life: "He changes the times and the seasons; He removes kings and raises up kings" (Daniel 2:21).

This idea is in concert with other passages in the Bible:

- "Exaltation comes neither from the east nor from the west nor from the south. But God is the Judge: He puts down one, and exalts another" (Psalm 75:6-7).
- "The king's heart is in the hand of the LORD, like the rivers of water; He turns it wherever He wishes" (Proverbs 21:1).

Daniel also worshiped God for His knowledge. Daniel knew that the secret things belong to God (Deuteronomy 29:29). He recognized that God "knows what is in the darkness" and that "light dwells with Him" (Daniel 2:22).

Finally, Daniel praised God for the way his own life had been touched by God's character. He worshiped God for the wisdom he'd been given and praised Him because by that wisdom he would be able to reveal the king's dream: "I thank You and praise You, O God. . . . You . . . have now made known to me what we asked of You, for You have made known to us the king's demand" (Daniel 2:23).

With confidence in God's attributes, Daniel courageously approached Arioch, the very man enlisted by Nebuchadnezzar to destroy the wise men of Babylon, and asked to be taken into the presence of the king. Arioch agreed, and in the next scene we see the final interaction between Daniel and King Nebuchadnezzar.

Act III: Daniel and Nebuchadnezzar Onstage

> Daniel answered in the presence of the king, and said,
> "The secret which the king has demanded, the wise men,
> the astrologers, the magicians, and the soothsayers cannot
> declare to the king. But there is a God in heaven who reveals
> secrets. . . . He who reveals secrets has made known to you
> what will be. But as for me, this secret has not been revealed
> to me because I have more wisdom than anyone living, but
> for our sakes who make known the interpretation to the
> king, and that you may know the thoughts of your heart."
> DANIEL 2:27-30

Finally Daniel appeared before Nebuchadnezzar, confident of the dream's interpretation. He was careful, however, to let the king know that his ability came not from himself but from God. Daniel, on his own strength, never could have complied with the king's demand. But Daniel, as a servant of the Most High God, could.

What Daniel was about to reveal to the most powerful ruler on earth was that his days were numbered. If Daniel were alive today, he could very well stand before the ambassadors of all 193 member states of the United Nations and say, "Tell the leaders of your nations that their days are numbered. God has shown me a dream about the future of the kingdoms of this world. His Kingdom will be established on earth and will never end."

God has a plan for the nations of this world; He revealed that plan to the most powerful king on earth through His servant-prophet Daniel—and the plan has not been rescinded.

That is the power of God's prophetic Word—it gives us information upon which to build a life of hope and certainty. Instead of living in fear as the nations of this world compete with one another for power and supremacy, we can trust in the plan of God as revealed through Daniel.

* * *

DANIEL FOR TODAY

As we look over the record of the insomniac in this chapter, here are three things to consider:

1. **Since God will be awake all night, you can sleep!** Like Nebuchadnezzar, we often take our problems to bed with us. We lie down and think of the global threats engulfing society. But God wants to give His beloved children sleep, which means we can cultivate quiet, trusting minds and hearts that can rest in His sovereign control. "It is vain for you to rise up early, to sit up late, to eat the bread of sorrows; for so He gives His beloved sleep" (Psalm 127:2).

2. **You may not know what the future holds, but you know who holds the future.** Almighty God knows what we cannot know. He knows what is in the darkness. He knows what is in the future. And

He knows us and cares for us and watches over us day and night. He alone can solve our problems, guide our paths, shape our futures, and accomplish His decrees by His invincible power. "He reveals deep and secret things; He knows what is in the darkness, and light dwells with Him" (Daniel 2:22).

3. Since the whole world is in God's hands, your world is in God's hands. "Who has measured the waters in the hollow of His hand, measured heaven with a span and calculated the dust of the earth in a measure? Weighed the mountains in scales and the hills in a balance?" (Isaiah 40:12). If Almighty God can hold the entire world in His hands, He can also control all that is going on in the governments of the world, as the book of Daniel shows us. Is it not reasonable, then, to trust Him with your world? When you feel overwhelmed with your problems and daily pressures, remember that God can handle those, too. You can leave them in His mighty and gracious hands.

Chapter 3

THE COLOSSUS

Daniel 2:31-49

DANIEL DIDN'T HESITATE as he made his way up the steps of Nebuchadnezzar's palace. Arioch, waiting anxiously, greeted him at the door. "Daniel, I see that you have come, as promised. Where would you like to go? To the throne or to the dungeon?"

"Let me put it this way," Daniel replied with a smile. "You will not need to destroy the king's astrologers."

Relief washed over the captain's face. He escorted Daniel to the doors of the throne hall. "I wish you well," he said, ushering Daniel into the opulent room.

Nebuchadnezzar sat on his throne. Surrounding the dais before him stood a circle of finely dressed men whom Daniel recognized as provincial governors and other high-ranking officials.

When the king saw Daniel, he immediately waved a hand at the others, saying, "Leave me for now. All of you. I will call for you shortly."

The governors backed their way toward the great doors. When the throne room was empty, Daniel approached the king.

"Belteshazzar, you have returned," said Nebuchadnezzar. "I am in the midst of important business, so if you've come with excuses like the rest of my so-called sages, I'll have you thrown out before you finish a sentence. But if you can describe and interpret my vision, you'll have my full attention."

"Your majesty," Daniel said, "your counselors were correct: no man can tell you what you dreamed." The king's jaw clenched. Before he could reply, Daniel continued. "But the Lord of heaven and earth is able to accomplish what no mere mortal can. In His grace, He has revealed to me the vision He gave you—a vision that opens the curtain to the future, revealing far-reaching secrets about the ages to come—secrets that have never been revealed to any human being."

The king, still skeptical, leaned back in his throne. "Very well," he said, with a sigh of exaggerated patience. "I will hear you. But you know what will happen if you try to deceive me. You may begin."

Daniel stood erect before the king. "This is the dream that came to you in the deepest hours of the night as you lay on your royal bed. You thought you had awakened from a deep sleep. You were in absolute darkness; not even your own hand was visible in front of your face. You could sense that something was about to happen, but you had no idea what. As you peered into the blackness, you began to detect dim swirls of movement, which you soon recognized as masses of thick, churning clouds."

As Daniel spoke, the air in the room seemed to grow heavy. The king's spine tingled as he was transported back into the world of his dream.

"As you looked on, O king," Daniel continued, "the clouds and fog began to dissipate, revealing the vast expanse of the plain of Dura. You could see distant foothills of a mighty mountain range. As the fog lifted, you could barely make out what appeared to be two enormous feet resting on an expansive plateau in the hills. They were sculpted from a mottled, grayish material veined with strips of reflective metal. You could see the ankles and the lower parts of the legs rising up through the fog."

Nebuchadnezzar gripped the arms of his throne. He stared into the distance beyond Daniel, as if witnessing the vision all over again.

"Then the curtain of fog and clouds swirled away. You lifted your head toward the heavens, gaping at the colossal figure that loomed above you. It was a statue of a man, towering far above the hills and the lofty peaks in the distance. The top of the head was so high it seemed to graze the sky. The image was perfectly proportioned and powerfully built, its face noble and godlike. You trembled violently as you gazed at it, fearing it was alive."

Daniel looked at the king and saw that he was trembling now, too.

"Then, O king, you began to notice the uncanny construction of the image. Its head, beautifully formed and bearded in the Babylonian style, was of the purest gold, glimmering with dazzling shafts of light.

"The shoulders, chest, and arms were formed in godlike perfection and made of highly polished silver, bright and shimmering as lightning. The muscled belly and thighs were made of richly hued bronze. The knees and calves consisted of forged iron, and the mottled substance that formed the feet was a mixture of iron and clay."

The king hadn't moved a muscle. He sat rigid as he stared trancelike into the otherworldly realm of the dream.

"As you stared at the statue, an ominous rumbling resounded from the distant mountains and echoed across the plains. You looked up to see a rift forming in the craggy surface of the highest peak as if some great, invisible hand were cutting away the summit. The rift widened, sending rubble and boulders cascading down the slopes. You stood by in horror as an enormous stone broke free and tumbled down the mountain. As the stone neared the colossus, you braced yourself and raised your arms to guard against debris from the inevitable impact."

The king pressed his back against the back of his throne.

"In the next instant," Daniel continued, "the monstrous stone crashed into the feet of the image, scattering iron and clay across the plain. The image began to collapse, plunging downward and sinking into clouds of metallic dust that billowed hundreds of feet into the air. At that moment, a strong wind arose from the east. It increased in force until the clouds were swept away like chaff from a summer threshing floor. When the wind ceased, no trace of the image was left. The plain was as empty as if the statue had never existed.

"You continued to watch, my king, and in the space of twenty heartbeats, nothing happened. Then you detected movement near the stone, which still lay where the image had fallen. At first you thought the stone was dissolving, because it seemed to be spreading over the plain like candle wax. But you soon realized that the opposite was true. The stone was not diminishing; it was expanding. In a matter of moments, it had increased both in height and in width until it spread completely across the plateau. It continued to grow, surpassing the height of the image it had destroyed and covering the entire plain of Dura.

"You quaked with terror at the unearthly sight, unable to tear your eyes away as the swelling mountain penetrated the clouds and spread across nations and seas. Soon it covered the entire earth, engulfing even you in the process. That's when you woke up screaming."

Nebuchadnezzar emerged from his trance, his eyes darting around the throne room in confusion. "Yes, that was my vision." His voice was subdued and filled with awe. "You described every detail exactly as I dreamed it. That was a supernatural feat—one I didn't think any man could accomplish."

"I accomplished nothing," Daniel replied. "The revelation of your dream was given to me by the God of heaven and earth."

"Having given you the dream, surely your God has also given you the interpretation of it."

"He has, my king. I will now reveal that to you. What you saw was a succession of kingdoms that will reach far into the future. The golden head represents the first of these kingdoms, which is yours, O king. You reign in immense power and glory—the likes of which the world has never seen. You are the head of gold.

"But mighty as your kingdom is, no earthly kingdom lasts forever. After your time, Babylon will fall, and another kingdom—the shoulders, chest, and arms of silver—will arise to replace it. That kingdom will be rich and mighty but inferior to yours, as silver is to gold. In time, a third kingdom will rise to replace the second—a kingdom of bronze, like the lower torso and thighs of the image. It, too, will be a strong kingdom, ruling the world of the previous kingdoms, yet inferior to them.

"The fourth kingdom—the legs of iron—will be powerful but brutal. Just as iron shatters everything it strikes, so will this kingdom crush everything in its path, including the previous kingdoms. Eventually that kingdom will be divided, because its subjects will be an unstable mix of peoples. Just as the feet of the image were an unstable mix of iron and clay, this kingdom will be partly strong as iron and partly fragile as clay."

Daniel paused as a servant brought him a goblet of water.

"Surely you're not finished," the king said. "What about the stone that became a mountain? That symbol certainly must have some great meaning."

"It does!" Daniel replied. "In fact, not only is the stone the climax of the dream, it is the climax of the history of this world." Daniel returned the goblet to the servant and continued. "That stone represents the final kingdom of the earth—one that will demolish and replace every kingdom ruled by humankind. It will be the ultimate kingdom, which will fill the entire earth and never be destroyed. It will endure forever, for the eternal God of heaven and earth will be its king. And He will reign over the earth forever and ever.

"That, O king, is what the God of heaven has chosen to reveal to you."

"But Belteshazzar, why did He reveal these things to me? Is it a warning that I should take steps to prevent this coming cycle of destruction?"

"No, what the dream revealed is not merely a possible future; it is a certain and unalterable future. Everything foretold in your dream will come to pass exactly as prophesied. The Lord of heaven has honored you with this revelation so the world will know that human governments will fall, but His Kingdom will endure in a glorious triumph of eternal perfection, joy, and peace."

When Daniel finished talking, Nebuchadnezzar II, the conqueror and ruler of nations, and king over the most magnificent city ever constructed, did something unheard of—something that shocked Daniel. He arose from his throne, stepped down from the dais, and bowed before this junior sage.

"No! You must not bow to me," Daniel cried. "I am not God."

Nebuchadnezzar stood, placed his hands on Daniel's shoulders, and looked into his eyes with the warmth of a friend. "My dear Belteshazzar, I must honor you in some way. I will have my servant bring an offering of incense before you. Then I will—"

"No, my king, you must not do such a thing. I am merely a man, a servant of the most high God, who is the true Giver and Interpreter of your vision. All the honor and worship goes to Him, not to me or to anyone on earth."

"No doubt you are right." Nebuchadnezzar returned to his throne. "Your God is truly the God of all gods, the King of all kings, the keeper and revealer of the deepest secrets of the universe. But Belteshazzar, you are not like any man I have ever known. Your demeanor is confident but not arrogant or rude. Yesterday, when you came before me, you were under the sentence of death. Yet you didn't grovel or beg. You addressed me directly, with deep respect, and without a trace of fear. How could you give your conqueror that kind of honor and respect?"

"You are a son of Adam, created in God's image, and He has ordained you to be the king of nations," Daniel replied, "both of which are reasons for respect and honor."

"None of my other ministers understand that. They think their groveling will make me feel greater, but the opposite is true. Do they think there is greatness in ruling a nation of cowards? I long for a nation of strong, confident, truthful citizens. To rule a kingdom of such individuals would be the mark of true greatness."

Daniel opened his mouth, but Nebuchadnezzar held up his hand. "Allow me to continue, Belteshazzar. You are that kind of man. You are young, and you are a Jewish captive. Yet you possess all the qualities of a great ruler—vast knowledge, deep wisdom, integrity, dedication, and loyalty.

"The conference you interrupted this morning was to resolve an issue I'm having with the governor of the Babylonian province. I must replace him, and I was consulting with those officials to determine a successor. But now I don't need to call them back—I've found the solution. Belteshazzar, it is my pleasure to name you the new governor of the central province of my empire: Babylon itself. Your authority in Babylon will be second only to mine."

Daniel couldn't speak for a moment. Finally he managed to exclaim, "My king!"

"Hold your tongue," the king interrupted. "I haven't finished. Not only am I elevating you to this high position, but I am also giving you a palatial residence and robes befitting your office. You will have manservants, maidservants, and gold to meet your every want. Is there anything else you desire?"

"Yes, if it pleases my king, there is one thing more."

"Ask, and it is yours." The king waved his hand expansively. "Anything up to half of my kingdom."

"I have three close companions who impressed you greatly when we were presented at the completion of our training. Their Babylonian names are Shadrach, Meshach, and Abed-Nego. As you will remember, they are wise, discerning, and knowledgeable beyond their years. But their abilities have not been put to use. I request that you promote these men to positions that suit their talents. I assure you that in doing so, you will be blessed."

"I will give the order," Nebuchadnezzar said. "These men will be your aides and subordinates, reporting only to you. They, too, will be given gifts and residences appropriate to their offices."

The king dismissed Daniel with a smile. The young captive left the throne room praising God for His mighty hand at work.

* * *

Malik crouched in the prison cell with the other astrologers. His stomach convulsed as he thought of his imminent death. Though he came from a people who taught that Sheol is not the end, he had doubts. He could picture nothing beyond the impenetrable darkness of the grave that yawned before him.

Suddenly the lock to the cell clicked and the door creaked open. Malik looked up to see the imposing figure of Arioch, silhouetted against the torch-lit wall behind him.

"He's here! The demon of death!" Malik shrieked. "He has come for us!" Malik collapsed to the floor in a dead faint.

Moments later, he awoke, sputtering from the water Arioch had splashed onto his face. "Pull yourself together, young man," the captain said sternly. "You have no more need to fear; you're free to go."

"Free?" Malik said. "Has the king pardoned us?"

"It's not the king you have to thank; it's Daniel. He has interpreted the king's dream, and in return, Nebuchadnezzar has released all the astrologers and promoted Daniel to the governorship of Babylon."

Malik's elation at his reprieve was swallowed instantly by jealousy.

There was no way he could be grateful for Daniel! Not only had he succeeded where Malik and his fellow astrologers had not, but he had also been elevated to heights Malik could only dream of. Malik got up and followed his companions out of the prison, his insides churning.

This cannot go on, Malik thought. *Daniel's day of reckoning is coming. I vow it by the stars of heaven.*

* * *

THE SCRIPTURE BEHIND THE STORY

The second chapter of Daniel has been called "the alphabet of prophecy." Anyone who wants to understand what the Bible teaches about the future must study this chapter. It's centered on King Nebuchadnezzar's dream of a huge statue made of various substances that decrease in value from the head to the chest to the legs and down to the feet. God communicated this vivid prophecy to a Gentile king because it concerned the beginning and ending of Gentile rule.

Some scholars struggle with the idea of a divine message being communicated to a wicked man. But there's a twist of irony in Nebuchadnezzar's honor: the dream Nebuchadnezzar received was the foretelling of his own kingdom's destruction. Preserved in the prophetic Word of God, this dream is also a message to every earthly king: no human kingdom is permanent; every kingdom will fall before the coming of the Kingdom of God.

This message was also intended to encourage God's chosen people while they were captives in Babylon. God wanted to show them that there was much more to their future than they could see. It was God, not Nebuchadnezzar, who held the key to their future and the future of all humankind.

The Revelation

> Daniel answered . . . "You, O king, were watching; and
> behold, a great image! This great image, whose splendor was
> excellent, stood before you; and its form was awesome. This
> image's head was of fine gold, its chest and arms of silver, its
> belly and thighs of bronze, its legs of iron, its feet partly of
> iron and partly of clay."
>
> DANIEL 2:27, 31-33

In his dream, Nebuchadnezzar saw a colossal image of a man. Its
gargantuan size and dreadful appearance reduced the king to a state
of utter terror.

The image was that of a man because it represented the history
of human civilization. God wanted to show Nebuchadnezzar the
inevitable fate of all the nations of the world. The image wasn't a
complete history of human kingdoms—other powers that had radically affected Israel, such as Egypt and Assyria, were omitted. Rather,
the image portrayed the kingdoms that would play a critical role
in Israel's existence prior to the inauguration of God's Kingdom in
Jesus Christ.

The enormity of this image represented humanity's inflated sense
of its own accomplishments. People see their achievements as something great and splendid—a brilliant, colossal construction. The
image was meant to convey this world power's outward greatness—
from a human perspective, at least.

In addition, the colossus portrays the transfer of world authority
from the hands of God's people, the Jews, into the hands of Gentile
rulers. Babylon, represented by the image's head of gold, is the nation
that ended the era of Jewish power. Until Christ comes in glory, the
city of Jerusalem will be continually trodden down or under surveillance by Gentile nations (Luke 21:24).

The great statue was made up of five parts: the head of gold, the breast and arms of silver, the belly and thighs of copper or bronze, the legs of iron, and the feet that were part iron and part clay. According to verses 38-40, these five sections symbolize five empires of the world, four of which were yet to come into power at the time of the dream. These kingdoms had the authority to rule the whole world, and as we look back at history, we discover that they did just that.

Nebuchadnezzar reigned over the vast Babylonian kingdom, which comprised much of the known civilized world. The Medes and Persians conquered Babylon and, as the book of Esther describes, ruled the world from Persia. Greece, in turn, conquered Persia under the leadership of Alexander the Great, who became the next ruler of the world's kingdoms.

Sixty years before the birth of Christ, Rome followed Greece as the world's dominant power. Scripture says that the Roman leader Caesar Augustus sent out word that the whole world was to be taxed, indicating the all-encompassing extent of his rule (Luke 2:1). At the end of time, the revived Roman Empire will attempt to rule the world again through a newly constituted, ten-king confederacy.

These are the five world dominions that the king saw represented in his dream. As Nebuchadnezzar heard Daniel unfold the content of the dream, it was as if he were reliving his dream all over again. There was no doubt about it: Daniel was telling the truth.

The Interpretation

After Daniel told the king what he'd dreamed, Daniel began to explain the meaning of the dream. The dream was a prophecy delivered in visual form, and it outlined the sequence and nature of the coming world kingdoms. The word *kingdom* is used ten times between verses 37 and 44. The overriding message to Nebuchadnezzar was that God was carefully watching over the Gentile kingdoms as they came and went—and He will continue to do so until the eternal Kingdom of the Lord Jesus Christ.

BABYLON: THE HEAD OF GOLD

> You, O king, are a king of kings. For the God of heaven has given you a kingdom, power, strength, and glory; and wherever the children of men dwell, or the beasts of the field and the birds of the heaven, He has given them into your hand, and has made you ruler over them all—you are this head of gold.
>
> DANIEL 2:37-38

In revealing the meaning of the colossus, Daniel began at the top. He explained that the head of gold represented the kingdom of Babylon, a major power in the ancient world that lasted until 539 BC.

It's fitting that Babylon would be represented by gold in Nebuchadnezzar's dream, for it was saturated with gold. When the Greek historian Herodotus described Babylon about one hundred years after Nebuchadnezzar's reign, he noted the extravagant amount of gold in the temple.[1] Perhaps that's why Isaiah wrote, "You will take up this proverb against the king of Babylon, and say: 'How the oppressor has ceased, the golden city ceased!'" (Isaiah 14:4). It also explains why Jeremiah said, "Babylon was a golden cup in the LORD's hand" (Jeremiah 51:7).

MEDO-PERSIA: THE CHEST AND ARMS OF SILVER

> After you shall arise another kingdom inferior to yours.
>
> DANIEL 2:39

The second kingdom was inferior to Nebuchadnezzar's. Babylon's section was made of gold, this one of silver. The chest and arms of silver represented the Medo-Persian Empire, which endured for more than two hundred years, from approximately 539 to 331 BC. The two arms depicted on the image represented the divided nature of the second empire, which consisted of two branches: the Medes and the Persians.

GREECE: THE BELLY AND THIGHS OF BRONZE

> Another, a third kingdom of bronze . . . shall rule over all
> the earth.
>
> DANIEL 2:39

The belly and thighs of bronze represented the kingdom of Greece under Philip II of Macedon and his famous son Alexander the Great. Alexander was the ruler who, when he had completed his quest for world dominion, is said to have sat down in his tent and wept because there were no more worlds for him to conquer.[2]

Bronze was used to symbolize this kingdom partly because Alexander had begun to equip his soldiers with helmets, breastplates, shields, and swords made of bronze.

ROME: THE LEGS OF IRON

> The fourth kingdom shall be as strong as iron, inasmuch as
> iron breaks in pieces and shatters everything; and like iron
> that crushes, that kingdom will break in pieces and crush
> all the others.
>
> DANIEL 2:40

While Scripture doesn't specifically identify Rome as the fourth empire, history indicates that it must be so. The Romans conquered Alexander's empire through what became known as the "iron legions" of Rome. The word *iron* is used fourteen times in Daniel 2.

According to H. C. Leupold, "The Roman legions were noted for their ability to crush all resistance with an iron heel. There is apparently little that is constructive in the program of this empire in spite of Roman law and Roman roads and civilization because the destructive work outweighed all else, for we have the double verb 'crush and demolish.'"[3]

In a dream of his own, Daniel saw the four parts of Nebuchadnezzar's image as four beasts. The fourth beast, representing Rome, was terrible to behold: "After this I saw in the night visions, and behold, a fourth beast, dreadful and terrible, exceedingly strong. It had huge iron teeth; it was devouring, breaking in pieces, and trampling the residue with its feet. . . . The fourth beast shall be a fourth kingdom on earth, which shall be different from all other kingdoms, and shall devour the whole earth, trample it and break it in pieces" (Daniel 7:7, 23).

It was the Roman Empire that put our Lord on the cross, and it was the imperialistic Romans who ruled so ruthlessly in New Testament days. But they, too, would be defeated by another kingdom.

THE TEN-KINGDOM ROMAN CONFEDERACY: THE FEET OF IRON AND CLAY

As the toes of the feet were partly of iron and partly of clay, so the kingdom shall be partly strong and partly fragile. As you saw iron mixed with ceramic clay, they will mingle with the seed of men; but they will not adhere to one another, just as iron does not mix with clay.

DANIEL 2:42-43

Many prophetic scholars see the two iron legs of the image as representing the division of the Roman Empire in AD 395, which resulted in the Eastern Roman (Byzantine) Empire, with its capital in Constantinople, and the Western Roman Empire, with its capital in Rome. The feet of the image represent yet another division of the empire, not of two, as indicated by the two legs, but of ten, as symbolized by its ten toes.

Daniel foretells a time when the Roman Empire will consist of ten kingdoms or leaders. This is made much clearer in the seventh chapter, where Daniel expands on the ten-king coalition. Since the chronology of events is marked by a downward movement from one section of the statue to the next, the "feet and toes" stage must follow the "legs" stage. But when we look back at the history that followed Daniel's prediction, we find nothing that even remotely corresponds to a tenfold Roman coalition. That shows us that this final stage of Daniel's prophecy is yet to come—and yet to perform its prescribed role in human history.

Daniel gives us one other piece of information that helps us understand the timing of the events conveyed in Nebuchadnezzar's dream. Daniel says that the final form of the Roman Empire will be on the earth when God sets up His earthly Kingdom: "In the days of these kings [the rulers of the ten segments of the Roman kingdom], the God of heaven will set up a kingdom which shall never be destroyed; . . . it shall break in pieces and consume all these kingdoms, and it shall stand forever" (Daniel 2:44).

The old Roman Empire deteriorated by stages, but no other world empire has ever taken its place as a single ruler of its former territories. Daniel's prophecy, however, makes it clear that in the last days, the Roman Empire, or some version of it, will be revived.

As we look back at Nebuchadnezzar's dream and view the Gentile kingdoms as he saw them, we can't help but observe the *decreasing stability* in the governments of the world. As we see with Nebuchadnezzar's colossus, this world is standing on a delicate foundation. The huge, top-heavy statue is resting on a brittle base of clay and iron. This depicts the unstable nature of the tottering governments of the earth.

As we study the image, we also see the *deteriorating morality* in human government. The course of Gentile dominion and civilization is one of continuous degeneration and decay.

THE DETERIORATION OF HUMAN GOVERNMENT

KINGDOM	METAL	SPECIFIC GRAVITY (density of metal)	GOVERNMENT
Babylon (605 - 539 B.C.)	Gold	19	Monarchy
Medo-Persia 539–331 BC	Silver	11	Oligarchy
Greece 331 BC–146 BC	Bronze	8.5	Aristocracy
Rome 146 BC–395 AD	Iron	7.8	Imperialism
Restored Rome Unknown	Clay	1.6	Democracy

In his book on Daniel, John F. Walvoord makes this observation: "The descending scale of value of the four metals suggests the degeneration of the human race through the ages. . . . This concept contradicts the evolutionist's interpretation of human history. Instead of man beginning in the dust and consummating in fine gold, God reveals man in the times of the Gentiles to begin with fine gold and end in dust."[4]

Although the value of the metals decreases from the top to the bottom of the statue, their strength increases (from gold to iron). In other words, as the kingdoms degenerate in morality, they increase in force. The result is a devastating combination of continually stronger power yoked with continually weaker character.

Finally, we observe in the image the *disintegrating unity* of human government: "As the toes of the feet were partly of iron and partly of clay, so the kingdom shall be partly strong and partly fragile" (Daniel 2:42). In the stream of human affairs, we see two conflicting elements: the iron will of authority and the clay-like voice of the people.

As we near the end of this age, the tension between these forces will increase until nations are torn apart by strife, both internal and external. All attempts at unification with other governments will fail. This will prepare the way for the Antichrist's world rule.

As John F. Walvoord describes it, "The final form of the [Roman] kingdom will include diverse elements whether this refers to race, political idealism, or sectional interests; and this will prevent the final form of the kingdom from having a real unity. This is, of course, borne out by the fact that the world empire at the end of the age breaks up into a gigantic civil war in which forces from the south, east, and north contend with the ruler of the Mediterranean for supremacy, as Daniel himself portrays in Daniel 11:36-45."[5]

THE FINAL KINGDOM OF CHRIST: THE STONE CUT FROM THE MOUNTAIN THAT FILLS THE WHOLE EARTH

In the days of these kings the God of heaven will set up a kingdom which shall never be destroyed; and the kingdom shall not be left to other people; it shall break in pieces and consume all these kingdoms, and it shall stand forever.

DANIEL 2:44

In this verse, Daniel describes the eternal Kingdom of Christ. Though it is yet to be realized in the physical realm, this Kingdom is already at work in the hearts of God's people. Someday Christ will rule over all the earth just as surely as Nebuchadnezzar, Cyrus, Alexander, and the Roman emperors did.

Nebuchadnezzar's dream depicts the coming of Christ and His Kingdom in two graphic images: the stone and the mountain.

The Stone: The Coming King

> You watched while a stone was cut out without hands, which struck the image on its feet of iron and clay, and broke them in pieces. Then the iron, the clay, the bronze, the silver, and the gold were crushed together, and became like chaff from the summer threshing floors; the wind carried them away so that no trace of them was found.
>
> DANIEL 2:34-35

Without a doubt, this is the climax of the vision. After the stone strikes the image, the image is annihilated and the stone expands into a mountain, which soon fills the entire earth.

The question is, who or what is the stone? We need not wonder, for the Word of God clearly identifies it as the Messiah, the Lord Jesus Christ. Author and pastor William G. Heslop explains,

> Seven times in the sacred scriptures our Lord is called a stone. It is the symbol of strength, durability, and firmness. . . . Christ is the Stone (Acts 4:10-11). Christ came in the form of a servant and thus became a stone of stumbling to the nation of Israel. Israel fell on this stone and was broken (Matthew 21:44). Christ is the Rock upon which the Church is built and other foundation must no man lay. Christ is the

THE GREAT IMAGE

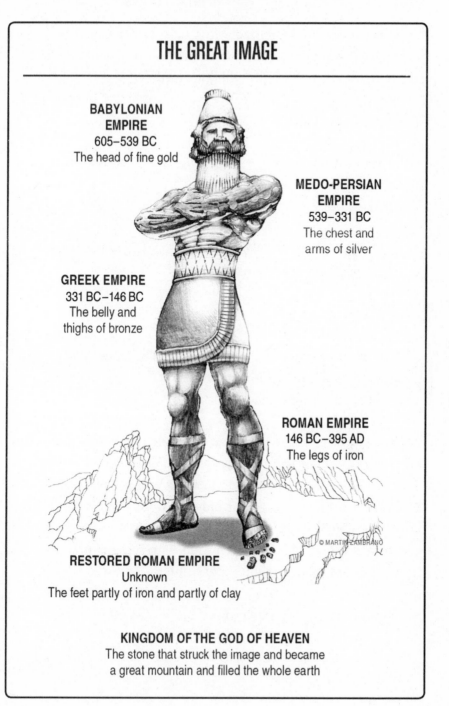

**BABYLONIAN
EMPIRE**
605–539 BC
The head of fine gold

**MEDO-PERSIAN
EMPIRE**
539–331 BC
The chest and
arms of silver

GREEK EMPIRE
331 BC–146 BC
The belly and
thighs of bronze

ROMAN EMPIRE
146 BC–395 AD
The legs of iron

© MARTIN ZAMBRANO

RESTORED ROMAN EMPIRE
Unknown
The feet partly of iron and partly of clay

KINGDOM OF THE GOD OF HEAVEN
The stone that struck the image and became
a great mountain and filled the whole earth

Stone who is to fall on the stately Colossus of man and grind it to powder (Matthew 21:44; Daniel 2:34-35). Christ is the Stone who shall descend and fill the earth."[6]

The Mountain: The Coming Kingdom

The stone that struck the image became a great mountain and filled the whole earth.

DANIEL 2:35

Daniel's prophecy highlights five overarching features that characterize the Kingdom of Christ.

1. IT'S A SUPERNATURAL KINGDOM

A stone was cut out without hands. . . . The stone was cut out of the mountain without hands.

DANIEL 2:34, 45

Twice in Daniel 2, we read that the stone that becomes a mountain is cut "without hands." That means the Kingdom of Christ is not man-made; it is divinely originated. William Heslop has said that man can make bricks, but only God can make a stone.[7] The image of Nebuchadnezzar's dream is man's creation; the Kingdom of Christ that displaces it is God's creation. This supernatural stone is a "symbol of strength, durability, and firmness."[8]

2. IT'S A SUDDEN KINGDOM

A stone . . . struck the image on its feet of iron and clay, and broken them in pieces.

DANIEL 2:34

The Kingdom of Christ will come suddenly, not gradually. It will happen overnight, in a moment. All the earthly kingdoms emerge from the ruins of another—Medo-Persia from Babylon, Greece from Medo-Persia, Rome from Greece. But Christ's Kingdom won't emerge from any other. It will arrive from a heavenly source with a sudden, decisive blow. Every passage that addresses the second coming of Christ speaks of it as arriving without warning (Zechariah 14:4-5; Matthew 24:29-30; Revelation 1:7).

In my study of this part of Daniel's prophetic interpretation, I came across this study note that summarizes what will happen when Christ's Kingdom arrives:

> The Striking Stone . . . destroys the Gentile world system (in its final form) by a sudden and irremediable blow, not by the gradual processes of conversion and assimilation; and then and not before, does the Stone become a mountain which fills "the whole earth." . . . Such a destruction of the Gentile monarchy system did not occur at the first advent of Christ. On the contrary, He was put to death by the sentence of an officer of the fourth empire, which was then at the zenith of its power. . . .
>
> . . . The deadly wound suffered by the fourth empire will not be healed by the restoration of the empire until the Church Age has been completed. . . .
>
> Thus Gentile world power still continues, and the crushing blow is still suspended.
>
> The detail of the end-time is given in Dan. 7:1-28 and Rev. 13–19. It is important to see (1) that Gentile world power is to end in a sudden catastrophic judgment (Revelation 16:14; 19:21); (2) that it is immediately to be followed by the kingdom of heaven, and that the God

of the heavens will not set up His kingdom till after the destruction of the Gentile world system. It is noteworthy that Gentile world dominion begins and ends with a great statue, or image (Dan. 2:31; Rev. 13:14-15).[9]

3. IT'S A SEVERE KINGDOM

The iron, the clay, the bronze, the silver, and the gold were crushed together, and became like chaff from the summer threshing floors; the wind carried them away so that no trace of them was found.

DANIEL 2:35

When the text says that the nations will become like chaff, it brings to mind the process of threshing grain as practiced in that day. After the grain was flailed on a threshing floor, it was tossed into the air so the worthless chaff, which was lighter than the grain, would be blown away by the wind. The various metals of the colossus are thus symbolized as worthless, and they are scattered without a trace.

The message is one of severe judgment. All the previous kingdoms that make up the image are destroyed by the final kingdom. The toxic elements of each succeeding kingdom seem to have been duplicated in each successor. So when the final kingdom is destroyed, so are the fatal flaws of its predecessors.

4. IT'S A SOVEREIGN KINGDOM

The stone that struck the image became a great mountain and filled the whole earth.

DANIEL 2:35

When the stone that came from the mountain has done its work, it will expand into a mountain once again and create a sovereign rule that will fill the entire universe. The stone comes from heaven and ultimately brings heaven to earth.

> The LORD shall be King over all the earth.
> In that day it shall be—
> "The LORD is one,"
> And His name one.
> ZECHARIAH 14:9

Christ will seize the reins of earthly government, placing authority rightfully in His own sovereign hands. He will fill the earth with His presence, power, and glory. The familiar prayer "Your kingdom come. Your will be done on earth as it is in heaven" (Matthew 6:10) will at last be answered.

5. IT'S A SUCCESSFUL KINGDOM

> In the days of these kings the God of heaven will set up
> a kingdom which shall never be destroyed; . . . it shall
> stand forever.
> DANIEL 2:44

In the dream, the world empires keep changing hands; each has its day, but not one has permanence. But Christ's Kingdom will never be destroyed. It will never decay. It will never be in danger of revolution. Christ will be a King unconquerable and unconquered, a monarch without a successor. His Kingdom will endure forever. His sovereignty will never be relinquished.

The question that remains is this: Has anything like what Daniel describes in the ultimate scene of the dream happened yet? Can we find, anywhere in history, a supernatural, sudden, severe, sovereign, and successful kingdom?

It was certainly not achieved by the kingdoms depicted by the image. Not the Babylonian head, not the Medo-Persian torso, not the Grecian belly and thighs, and certainly not the Roman legs. History makes it clear that such a kingdom has never existed. Stalin, Mussolini, and Hitler all tried to acquire absolute power, but they were never able to establish universal dominion.

The Appreciation

Daniel finished explaining the meaning of Nebuchadnezzar's dream with these final words of tribute to the God of Heaven: "The great God has made known to the king what will come to pass after this. The dream is certain, and its interpretation is sure" (Daniel 2:45).

What Nebuchadnezzar does next is nothing short of astounding.

NEBUCHADNEZZAR PRAISES DANIEL

King Nebuchadnezzar fell on his face, prostrate before Daniel, and commanded that they should present an offering and incense to him.

DANIEL 2:46

Nebuchadnezzar, the greatest king on earth, was so awed by Daniel's ability to reveal the secrets of his dream that he fell on his knees and tried to worship this teenage Jewish boy. He even commanded that offerings be given to Daniel as one would give to a god.

Josephus records a similar instance in which Alexander the Great bowed before the high priest of the Jews. One of his generals asked him why he would lower himself to bow before a mere Jewish priest when even kings would prostrate themselves before Alexander the

Great. The world conqueror replied, "It was not before him that I prostrated myself, but the God of whom he has the honor to be high priest."[10]

The next verse in Daniel's narrative indicates that Nebuchadnezzar may have bowed to Daniel for the same reason.

NEBUCHADNEZZAR PRAISES DANIEL'S GOD

> The king answered Daniel, and said, "Truly your God is the God of gods, the Lord of kings, and a revealer of secrets, since you could reveal this secret."
>
> DANIEL 2:47

When Nebuchadnezzar referred to Daniel's God as the God of gods, he was essentially saying that even the Babylonian gods he had worshiped all his life couldn't measure up to Daniel's God. Notice that the focus of his worship is not Daniel but the God of Daniel. This is because, in every situation, Daniel had given the praise and glory to his God and refused to receive any credit for his interpretive powers.

NEBUCHADNEZZAR PROMOTES DANIEL

> The king promoted Daniel and gave him many great gifts; and he made him ruler over the whole province of Babylon, and chief administrator over all the wise men of Babylon.
>
> DANIEL 2:48

King Nebuchadnezzar promoted Daniel to second-in-command in all of Babylon, with special authority over his wise men. He also enriched Daniel with "many great gifts." The words used to describe these gifts tell us that they were numerous and valuable. What makes

Daniel's promotion all the more amazing is that he had not yet turned twenty years of age.

NEBUCHADNEZZAR PROMOTES DANIEL'S FRIENDS

> Daniel petitioned the king, and he set Shadrach, Meshach, and Abed-Nego over the affairs of the province of Babylon, but Daniel sat in the gate of the king.
>
> DANIEL 2:49

As soon as Daniel was honored by the king, he remembered the three friends who had been with him through this whole Babylonian journey, and he sought to honor them. Without hesitation, King Nebuchadnezzar granted Daniel's wish, and his friends were promoted to positions of responsibility and honor under Daniel.

When the text says that Daniel "sat in the gate of the king," it simply means that Daniel's position, above that of his friends, was in the actual court of Nebuchadnezzar.

Years after Nebuchadnezzar's dream, Daniel had a similar vision that is recorded in Daniel 7. In one of my other books, I discuss the relationship between the two:

> Daniel had a vision of his own that confirms and expands our understanding of Nebuchadnezzar's dream. In Daniel's vision, a powerful wind stirred the ocean, and "four great beasts came up from the sea, each different from the other" (Daniel 7:3). These beasts represented the same gentile kingdoms as those depicted in the king's dream of the image of the man, but this time the character of those kingdoms was revealed. The first vision (Daniel 2) characterized the kingdoms of the world *as man assessed them*—majestic, massive, impressive, gigantic, and overwhelming. Man is

impressed with his accomplishments. In the second vision (Daniel 7), the kingdoms were shown as savage beasts of the jungle, slashing and attacking one another and fighting to the death.

This second vision gives us *God's appraisal* of these gentile kingdoms—destructive, divisive, angry, and cruel."[11]

As we come to the end of this chapter and look back over the rise and fall of human kingdoms, we must affirm the observation of biblical scholar H. C. Leupold, who writes, "Each new combination of forces or nations that has tried to achieve the result of a lasting kingdom invariably meets with the same overthrow. So history is a succession of defeats. But for the one who knows Almighty God there is hope. . . . He has a kingdom that will never be overthrown, and that will finally stand out as eternal and entirely successful."[12]

Today we are living on the threshold of that age to come. The days of human rule on earth are nearly over. It's almost time for the arrival of the stone that has been "cut out without hands." We should not be discouraged or depressed that the end of earthly kingdoms will soon come; rather, we should be elated that the glorious Kingdom of Christ will soon begin.

* * *

DANIEL FOR TODAY

Confidence! What a wonderful way to live—undaunted, unshaken! Does that sound like you? When we look at the culture around us, it's easy to fall into despair. But when we keep an eye peeled above, we don't have to spend our time griping or grappling with hopelessness.

Daniel didn't lose heart. He evaluated everything with the end in mind, and he stayed calm and confident under stress. Confidence is a uniquely biblical attitude that affects all we do in the public arena.

So when facing tomorrow, be confident!

1. When surveying the political landscape, be confident. Remember that you have a way to influence things through prayer. At a moment of crisis, Daniel and his companions sought mercies from the God of heaven, and the rest of the chapter unfolds in answer to their prayer (Daniel 3:18).

2. When casting your vote, be confident. If elections don't go your way or judicial decisions disappoint you, remind yourself that God is unaffected. He removes kings and raises up kings according to His plan (Daniel 2:21).

3. When hearing news of catastrophes and instability on earth, be confident. Remember: "There is a God in heaven" (Daniel 2:28). When you feel discouraged about the course of world affairs, don't lose heart. One day the God of heaven will set up a Kingdom that will never be destroyed (Daniel 2:44).

4. When you think all is lost, think again! "The dream is certain, and its interpretation is sure" (Daniel 2:45). We know the script in advance, and we're clued in to the ending.

Having studied this chapter of Daniel, we now know a divine secret: the framework of all of history, including its conclusion. So good-bye, insecurity! Good-bye, fearfulness! These are days that call for boldness. This is the time to be confident in Him who has begun a good work in us (Philippians 1:6). This is the time to pray, "Thy Kingdom come!"

Chapter 4

THE FIRE MEN

Daniel 3:1-30

THE ROYAL CHAMBERLAIN ushered Shadrach, Meshach, and Abed-Nego into King Nebuchadnezzar's private chambers.

"We have come as you commanded, O king," Shadrach said.

The king invited them to sit before him, a privilege granted to only a select few. Daniel, his premier and closest adviser, had been sent to the outlying provinces of the empire on a diplomatic mission. In his absence, the king called in these three high-ranking members of Daniel's cabinet for consultation.

After completing his agenda, the king said, "Let me draw on your wisdom for one more matter. Trouble is brewing in several of my provinces, particularly Carchemish, Phoenicia, and Arabia. The root of the conflict is religious in nature. These conquered nations retain their own gods—the Phoenicians have Ba'al and Ashtoreth, the people of Carchemish worship their Hittite deities, and the Arabians have more gods than all the others combined."

As Nebuchadnezzar spoke, his eyes began to dart around the

room. "These religious differences stir up dissension. Some nations have even destroyed the temples of their weaker neighbors. You men are deeply religious, just as Daniel is. So tell me, how would you resolve these conflicts?"

Without a moment's hesitation, Meshach spoke up. "Dissension would end if the people of all lands worshiped the one true God of heaven and earth, the all-powerful God."

"By 'the one true God' you mean your Yahweh, of course. How can you call Him all powerful when He couldn't even save His own nation?"

"He allowed you to destroy Israel because we had been disobedient to Him. Our people had become idol worshipers like the nations around us, and He chose you, my king, to be His avenging agent. But He has preserved His people, and in time He will restore us to our land."

"You are right that my people need a god everyone can worship." The king shook his head. "But your God won't do. He's invisible. He can't be seen or heard. Marduk won't do either, because the provinces see him as Babylon's god, not theirs. The only god that would work is one not identified with a particular nation or culture. And it has to be a god they can see—one that will dazzle their senses and remain imprinted on their memories. If I were to offer my empire such a god, how would your people respond?"

"Your majesty," Abed-Nego said, "your army taught Israel that the living God of the universe cannot be ignored or disobeyed. We would never again bow to any other god."

"Ha! I assure you that under penalty of death, all convictions crumble and all knees bend. Everyone has a price."

Nebuchadnezzar dismissed the three men. As they left his chambers, they passed the king's astrologers, led by Nimatar and followed closely by his protégé, Malik. Malik thrust his chin forward and shot the three Jews a look of disdain.

Shadrach turned to his two companions. "I'm afraid something is amiss."

"I agree," Abed-Nego said. "When the king spoke of religious conflict, he wouldn't look us in the eye. He's hiding something."

"That became clear months ago when we asked the purpose of the huge ziggurat being constructed just outside the city. He didn't want us to press the subject further," Meshach agreed.

"Nebuchadnezzar's entire attitude has changed," Abed-Nego said. "In the years since Daniel became his premier—even his friend—the king's pride has abated, and he has at least shown respect to our God. But now that Daniel is gone, that old arrogance has crept back in, and the king's respect for Yahweh has shrunk to mere tolerance."

"It's not just Daniel's absence," Meshach said. "The king has been leaning more heavily on the astrologers lately. They've been called into his presence almost daily since Daniel left."

"I sense a crisis looming," Shadrach said. "Do we stand together on this? Are we ready to face whatever comes and remain firm despite the threats and danger?"

"We are," Meshach replied. "We must remain diligent in our prayers that God will uphold us in our faith and resolve."

* * *

One week later, the three men received invitations sealed with the imprint of the king's signet ring. Their presence was requested at a three-day celebration that would include every governor and the highest officials throughout the Babylonian Empire. The event would be held in thirty days.

In the days leading up to the celebration, gilded chariots and plush carriages disrupted trade and snarled the streets of Babylon as governors, administrators, and their entourages arrived from every province in Nebuchadnezzar's empire. Men and women in rich linens and silks paraded into the palace to pay homage to their sovereign.

Shadrach, Meshach, and Abed-Nego were well known to these officials. They were men of power who had the ear of the king and were often sought for advice on matters of governance and diplomacy.

That evening Nebuchadnezzar hosted a sumptuous feast. The enormous dining hall filled and emptied three times so the thousands of guests could be served. At each sitting, the king welcomed the diners and encouraged them to eat and drink their fill. He invited them to assemble at the tenth hour the next day at the newly constructed ziggurat on the plain of Dura, just outside the city.

Though no one said so explicitly, it was understood that the invitation was compulsory. No one would dare to be absent.

At the tenth hour the following day, several thousand prominent men and women stood on the plain facing the temple. Atop the twelve-tiered tower sat a granite pedestal, and soaring above the pedestal to a height of ninety feet was a towering object shrouded in linen.

Shadrach, Meshach, and Abed-Nego stood toward the rear of the crowd, some two hundred feet from the pedestal. Though they were filled with foreboding, they were as ignorant as the other guests as to the purpose of the assembly.

When the bell chimed the tenth hour, King Nebuchadnezzar appeared, sitting high in a gilded ivory chair. His chair was mounted on two parallel poles and supported by eight robust slaves. They carried him up the stairway of the ziggurat and set him in his chair at the base of the pedestal.

Nimatar then mounted the steps and faced the people, dwarfed by the towering structure behind him. A hush came over the crowd. "Noble guests!" His voice rang out over the plain. "Listen as I explain to you the purpose of this assembly. It's no secret that there is turmoil among the provinces of the empire over religious differences. Each province has its local deities, which the people have worshiped for centuries: Moloch, Ba'al, Ashtoreth, Dagon, Isis, Ra, Ishtar, and a host of others. Such fragmentation breeds strife and threatens the unity of the empire.

"What the empire needs is a single god all people can bow down to in harmony and unity. Therefore, King Nebuchadnezzar wishes to add a new god—one the entire kingdom can worship together. This will bind us all together under his benevolent headship."

Shadrach leaned toward his companions and spoke in a low voice. "I think we can now guess what's coming. When Nebuchadnezzar asked us about religious unity, he wasn't really seeking advice; he was testing us. Obviously, this event has been planned for some time. Whatever is at the top of that tower wasn't constructed overnight."

Nimatar continued. "In a moment you will have the great honor of witnessing the birth of this new god. After the veil is removed, you will have several moments to gaze on his glorious face. Then the orchestra will play a hymn devoted exclusively to him. When you hear the first chords struck, you will have the privilege of bowing on your faces as the first to give him worship and honor."

The chief astrologer paused briefly, and then his tone grew more severe. "As sub-rulers of this empire, every one of you must bow—both today and every day this ritual is repeated. Anyone who fails to do so will suffer the penalty inflicted on all who dare to defy the royal edicts. He will be cast into the furnace of fire."

Nimatar stepped down, and the veil above him slid away, revealing a towering image of a man made of pure gold.

The guests gaped at the magnificent statue, its golden surface gleaming in the morning sun. "Look at the face," someone said. "It's Nebuchadnezzar himself. He is our new god."

At that moment, the first notes of the hymn sounded, and the crowd fell to their knees as one. Their robes covered the plain like a patchwork carpet.

The astrologers had appointed themselves monitors for the occasion and were stationed around the perimeter to survey the worshipers. Malik was stunned to see three men in his section standing tall, their backs turned to the golden image. He was outraged. Who would dare defy the king's edict so blatantly? But as he moved closer and realized who the violators were, his anger gave way to elation. He was about to bring down three of the four men he hated most in the kingdom.

When the ceremony ended, Malik fought his way through the crowd to reach Nimatar and report what he had seen.

"The king must hear this immediately," the chief astrologer responded. They hurried along the procession route and caught up with Nebuchadnezzar just as he was approaching the Ishtar gate.

"O King Nebuchadnezzar," Nimatar cried, panting from the exertion.

The king ordered his bearers to stop. "What is it? Be quick."

"Three of your highest officials have refused to bow to your image."

The king's brow darkened. "Surely not! No man would dare."

"We thought the same, my king," Malik said. "But I saw them clearly, standing proud, with their backs to your image. They were flaunting their defiance for all to see."

"This is not to be borne!" the king shouted. "Summon Arioch. Have him bring these traitors to my throne immediately. By nightfall their ashes will blow across these plains. I will see to it."

Before an hour had passed, the door to the throne hall opened, and the king sat glaring as Arioch marched the three prisoners toward him. Nimatar and Malik followed. When they stood before the throne, Nebuchadnezzar's anger melted into dismay. "Shadrach . . . Meshach . . . Abed-Nego . . . tell me it isn't true."

"It's true, O king," Malik said. "I saw them clearly when—"

"Enough!" The king faced the accused men. "You three have served me long and well. You've sat with me as friends and eaten at my table. I've given you wealth and position. Surely there's some mistake. You couldn't have defied me as your accusers claim you have."

"We had no desire to defy you," Shadrach answered. "But we must be loyal to our God. We can't bow to any other god."

"Why waste such loyalty on a God you cannot see or hear or touch—one who has no form and won't even show His face?"

"My king," Meshach said, "in what way is the idol you have erected superior? Though it's outwardly striking, it's nothing but earthly materials fashioned by the hands of man. It has a mouth that cannot speak, eyes that cannot see, and ears that cannot hear. Why should anyone worship a mass of molded metal that is obviously inferior even to the artisans who made it?"

"You know why. You are politicians, just as I am. You know I'm not demanding that you believe in the god of the image; all I require is an outward display of belief to accomplish my goal of unity. I can't allow prominent leaders to express disobedience to the king. If your God is all you say He is, surely He understands that."

"It's a matter of our integrity," Shadrach said. "We must live according to the truth we know in our minds and hold in our hearts."

"Oh, you Yahweh worshipers are too rigid for your own good! I should cast you into the furnace immediately. But because you have served me well, and for the sake of Daniel, I will do what I wouldn't do for anyone else in the empire. I'll give you another chance."

"My great king," Nimatar said, "should you bend your will that far? They have already—"

"Quiet!" the king snapped. "Listen to me, Shadrach, Meshach, and Abed-Nego. I will overlook today's affront and spare your lives if you swear that you will bow down to my image tomorrow. If I am willing to go that far, surely you can do this small thing. What do you say?"

Abed-Nego stepped forward. "O Nebuchadnezzar, we can answer you only one way. If you sentence us to death by the furnace, our

God whom we serve can deliver us from the flame. But even if He does not, know that we will stand firm and never serve your gods. Nor will we worship your golden image, tomorrow or any other day."

The king's face reddened. "You fools!" he bellowed. "How dare you continue to defy me? You trample my mercy as if it were dirt under your feet. I will endure it no longer."

Nebuchadnezzar turned his back on the three friends. "Arioch!" he called. "Get these ungrateful traitors out of my sight. Have the execution furnace heated to seven times its normal temperature. Nimatar, send messengers to all the guests, inviting them to the square in three hours. I want all of them to witness the fate of those who defy me. Go on! Do it now!"

* * *

The square was a flagstone-paved court set before the open-fronted execution furnace. Large as the plaza was, it could accommodate only a fraction of Nebuchadnezzar's guests. An hour before the appointed time, it was already filled with curious officials watching as workers coaxed the glowing coals into billowing flames.

The furnace itself was a stone structure some thirty feet square with walls four feet thick to contain the intense heat. It was vented by an opening that measured six feet in diameter in the center of its low, domed roof. The opening also served as a portal where victims were dropped into a chute and sent into the scorching furnace. Steps made of stone ascended the left side of the dome, providing guards with access to the opening.

Soon the fire roared, and black smoke belched from the hole in the roof. King Nebuchadnezzar arrived and took his seat on the elevated platform opposite the furnace, flanked by his chief advisers and astrologers. When the king was satisfied with the heat of the flame, he nodded to Nimatar, who rose and addressed the crowd.

"Esteemed governors and officials of the empire, it is with deep regret that we announce the traitorous action of three of your peers, Shadrach, Meshach, and Abed-Nego of the Babylonian province. They have refused to worship the king's image."

A murmur of surprise rippled through the spectators.

"Today these men will be cast into the furnace of fire. The same will be done to all who defy the king's edict." He turned toward the holding cell at the left of the square. "Bring out the prisoners!" he called. "Let the execution begin."

The cell door opened and the three prisoners stepped out, escorted by six guards. The condemned men held their heads high. Their expressions were serene, and they showed no trace of fear.

After binding the prisoners' hands and feet, the soldiers carried them up the steps of the dome in pairs, one gripping the shoulders and another the feet. The overheated blaze now shot upward through the vent. Even before they reached the top, the guards flinched from the blistering heat. Their only chance of surviving was to swing their victims into the opening quickly and dart away before the heat overcame them.

Their attempts were futile. As they heaved their burdens into the flame, screams of agony pierced the air—not from the prisoners, but from the guards. The spectators watched in horror as the soldiers' clothing burst into flame and the skin of their faces burned away. They tumbled, writhing and shrieking, down the sloping dome and fell to the pavement below, dead.

Nebuchadnezzar ignored the guards and peered into the flames, searching for the three convicted men. He spotted them struggling to rise from the glowing embers. But something wasn't right—their clothing and skin seemed intact. Surely he wasn't seeing things clearly. In the next instant, all three men stood erect, their hands and feet now free.

The king squinted and looked again. Now the men, still seemingly unharmed, were walking around inside the furnace and speaking calmly, as if meeting in the hallways of the palace. The king looked again and was startled by what he saw. Could that be another figure in the fire with them? Impossible! He rose and stepped closer for a better look. Yes, there was surely a fourth man in the fire.

"Nimatar," he croaked, "didn't we cast just three men into the furnace?"

"That's correct, my king," the adviser stammered.

"Then tell me why I see a fourth man with them—if you can call such a magnificent being a man."

King Nebuchadnezzar didn't wait for a reply. Forgetting all dignity, he leaped down the steps and ran toward the furnace. "Shadrach! Meshach! Abed-Nego! Come out! Come out from the flames."

Moments later, the three Jews stood on the plaza facing the king as the fire continued to rage behind them.

He could only stare at them, not believing his eyes.

"Look at you!" the king finally said. "The fire hasn't harmed you in any way. Not a hair or an eyebrow is even singed. And your clothes—they aren't charred in the least. The smell of smoke doesn't even linger about you. How is such a thing possible?"

"Our God was with us," Meshach said simply.

"Yes, I know." The king placed his hand over his mouth. "I saw Him myself."

Nebuchadnezzar turned and addressed the crowd. "Listen, all of you. I wish to announce a change in plans. The three-day celebration that brought you here is now ended. All remaining events are canceled. Tomorrow you may return to your own provinces. These three courageous men standing before you have shown the futility of worshiping a dead image made of metal. They have trusted their God with their very lives, and He has delivered them. No one has ever seen another god with such power.

"Therefore, as you return to your homes, I charge you to deliver this decree: anyone within my empire who speaks any word against Yahweh, the God of Shadrach, Meshach, and Abed-Nego, will be cut into pieces, and their houses will be burned to the ground. You are dismissed."

The three vindicated heroes turned to walk back to their own homes.

"Stop," Nebuchadnezzar called. The three men turned to face the king. "My dismissal did not include you. There is only one other man in my entire empire who has shown the kind of unbending courage you three demonstrated today—and I don't have to tell you who that is. Such integrity is sorely lacking in my kingdom. Therefore, it's my desire to promote the three of you to even higher positions." He extended his arm toward them. "Come with me to the palace. We will discuss the details as we dine together."

* * *

THE SCRIPTURE BEHIND THE STORY

Most British commoners in the sixteenth century probably envied the royal and titled classes from a distance—their money, their ease, their power. But one thing they certainly didn't envy was their likelihood of short life spans. King Henry VIII had two of his six wives beheaded, and two others were discarded. Henry's first lord chancellor, Cardinal Wolsey, was stripped of his office and accused of treason, and the second, Thomas More, was beheaded. Henry's lawyer and most trusted confidant, Thomas Cromwell, after years of favor, was also beheaded. When Henry's staunch Catholic daughter, Mary, gained the throne for five years, she had more than three hundred Protestant leaders and clerics executed—many burned at the stake—earning her the moniker "Bloody Mary."

In the royal court in that day, a person's life hung by a thread—and that thread was tied to the throne of the reigning king or queen. Nebuchadnezzar II, king of Babylon, attempted to kill three of his most valuable advisers simply because they defied his edict. They were faced with a choice—to please God or to please the king—and they chose God.

As hard as it is to believe, similar edicts are still being issued today. When the so-called Islamic State (ISIS or ISIL) began marauding through northern Iraq in 2014, its members began giving Christians an ultimatum: convert to Islam, leave, or die. While most Western Christians today will not face such a harsh reality, there are plenty of other difficult choices to be made. Will we stand for Christ in the marketplace? Will we remain strong against ungodly peer pressure? Will we trust God's Word above the pundits of the day?

One of the first things we notice as we begin Daniel 3 is that Daniel doesn't appear anywhere in the chapter. There is a great deal of conjecture among biblical scholars as to where he might have been. Most believe it's likely he was representing King Nebuchadnezzar in some foreign court.

This third chapter tells the familiar story of Shadrach, Meshach, and Abed-Nego. In the first two chapters of the book, they appear only as Daniel's friends, and in the remaining chapters, they don't appear at all. But here they occupy center stage.

Scholars believe there's at least a twenty-year gap between the events of the second and third chapters of Daniel. At the end of chapter 2, King Nebuchadnezzar makes a glorious tribute to Daniel and to Daniel's God: "Truly your God is the God of gods, the Lord of kings, and a revealer of secrets, since you could reveal this secret" (verse 47).

In chapter 3, we see that something has drastically changed in the heart of this powerful king. The God of Daniel is no longer elevated in the king's mind. He has decided to compel his kingdom to worship a common idol—a massive image on the Babylonian plain of Dura: "Nebuchadnezzar the king made an image of gold, whose height was sixty cubits and its width six cubits" (Daniel 3:1).

To demonstrate the extent of his wealth and glory, Nebuchadnezzar had the entire image made of gold. Though he was wealthy enough to have built it out of solid gold, it was probably constructed of wood and only plated with gold. Isaiah and Jeremiah both describe contemporary idols that were made of wood and overlaid with gold (Isaiah 40:19; 41:7; Jeremiah 10:3-9).

The word *image* here refers to a statue in human form. In this particular image, that form was grotesque and oddly proportioned. Scripture says it was sixty cubits high (ninety feet) and six cubits wide (nine feet). That's a ratio of 10 to 1. The average ratio of an actual person is 5 to 1. That means the image was extremely elongated—tall and thin.

Nebuchadnezzar decreed that all the leaders in Babylon would bow before his image. This was clearly intended to be a religious act, for the word *worship* appears eleven times in this passage.

Why was there such a paradigm shift in Nebuchadnezzar's heart away from honoring the God of Daniel and his friends? If we read carefully, we can identify at least three reasons.

First, in the last account about this king, he had experienced a traumatic encounter with another image, which God had conveyed to him through a dream. The head of that image represented Nebuchadnezzar himself, thus lifting him up as a great king of a great nation.

However, that dream also told the king that the duration of his kingdom was limited. Another kingdom, inferior to his, would soon take its place. I believe that as Nebuchadnezzar grew older, that prophecy weighed heavily on his heart.

Perhaps Nebuchadnezzar's threat to kill those who refused to bow before his likeness was a way for him to trample any potential rebellion within his kingdom that might lead to his downfall. It may be that this statue completely plated in gold was created to stand in contrast to the statue in his dream, where only the head of Babylon was made of gold: *My physical statue, made entirely of gold, means there will be no kingdoms to come of silver, bronze, or iron.*

Second, over the first twenty-two years of Nebuchadnezzar's reign, Babylon had grown rapidly. Many people groups with diverse religions had become part of the kingdom, and all worshiped their own gods. Nebuchadnezzar decided he could unify his disparate empire by bringing them together under a single religion.

William Heslop observes that "Nimrod was the first person to attempt to unify the religions of man by self deification. Nebuchadnezzar here attempts exactly the same thing and both were types of the coming 'Beast' the last head of the Gentile world who will insist on being worshipped (Revelation 13:11-15; 19-20)."[1]

John F. Walvoord writes, "Nebuchadnezzar may have regarded the image as representing himself as the embodiment of divine power, and the worship of the image would then be a recognition of his personal power. In view of his pride as dealt with in chapter 4, this becomes a plausible explanation."[2]

Third, Nebuchadnezzar had some diplomats on his staff who hated Daniel and his three Jewish friends. They hatched a plot to rid themselves of these Jews (Daniel 3:12) and may well have incited the king to erect the statue, knowing the three men wouldn't bow down to it.

The third chapter of Daniel begins with a detailed description of the dedication ceremony for Nebuchadnezzar's golden image.

The Dedication

Nebuchadnezzar the king sent to gather together the princes, the governors, and the captains, the judges, the treasurers, the counsellors, the sheriffs, and all the rulers of the provinces, to come to the dedication of the image which Nebuchadnezzar the king had set up.

DANIEL 3:2, KJV

To appropriately dedicate his image, Nebuchadnezzar sent out an invitation to the entire Babylonian official family. Here's one Bible commentary's explanation of the dignitaries who were invited to the event:

> The princes are administrators, guardians or watchers, and the chief representatives of the king, corresponding to the Greek expression satrap. The governors were commanders or military chiefs. The captains seemed to refer to presidents or governors of civil government. The judges were counsellors of the government or chief arbitrators. The treasurers were superintendents of the public treasury. The counsellors were lawyers or guardians of the law. The sheriffs were judges in a stricter sense of the term, that is, magistrates who gave a just sentence. The rulers were lesser officials who were governors of the provinces subordinate to the chief governor.[3]

Verse 2 (invitees) and verse 3 (attendees) are the same list. In Babylon, there was no RSVP. If you were invited, you attended.

The Demand

> A herald cried aloud: "To you it is commanded, O peoples, nations, and languages, that at the time you hear the sound of the horn, flute, harp, lyre, and psaltery, in symphony with all kinds of music, you shall fall down and worship the gold image that King Nebuchadnezzar has set up; and whoever does not fall down and worship shall be cast immediately into the midst of a burning fiery furnace."
>
> DANIEL 3:4-6

Since the mid-eighteenth century, audiences have stood for the "Hallelujah Chorus" in George Frideric Handel's *Messiah*. Though it isn't documented, tradition holds that the practice originated at the London premiere of *Messiah* in 1743. King George II was supposedly in attendance and stood when the "Hallelujah Chorus" began. Accordingly, everyone else in the venue stood as well. When the king stands, everyone stands.

Just the opposite was planned on the plain of Dura. Instead of having people stand in honor of the image, Nebuchadnezzar wanted everyone to bow down and worship his image at the same time, and he employed his royal orchestra to signal their response. Leon Wood says, "In keeping with the grandeur of the occasion, the members likely were dressed in colorful costume and seated on a raised decorated stage."[4]

The types of instruments in the orchestra are listed four times in this chapter (verses 5, 7, 10, 15). From our modern-day perspective, this was indeed a strange collection. First there was a horn, a wind instrument. Next there was a flute, which is translated from a Hebrew word meaning "to hiss or to whistle." Then there was a harp and a lyre, called in some versions a trigon—a triangular stringed instrument that played high notes. There was also a psaltery, an instrument with strings positioned beneath a sounding board. Bible translators have had a heyday with this list, identifying some of the obscure instruments by other names, such as zither, dulcimer, lute, sackbut, trumpet, sambuca, and even bagpipe.

Someone has estimated that the head count at this assembly may have been as many as three hundred thousand, with people coming from all over the vast Babylonian empire. When the orchestra began to play, all three hundred thousand attendees bowed down.

All but three.

The Defiance

At that time certain Chaldeans came forward and accused the Jews. "There are certain Jews whom you have set over the affairs of the province of Babylon: Shadrach, Meshach, and Abed-Nego; these men, O king, have not paid due regard to you. They do not serve your gods or worship the gold image which you have set up."

DANIEL 3:8, 12

The same Chaldean officials who had been spared from death twenty years earlier by Daniel's discernment of the king's dream and its meaning now turned on the Hebrew men. They stood shamelessly before the king and brought three accusations against them. First, they accused them of disrespecting King Nebuchadnezzar: "they have not paid due regard to you." Their second accusation was that "they do not serve your gods." It is their final accusation, however, that infuriated the king: "they do not worship your image."

The Dialogue

THE CHANCE

Nebuchadnezzar spoke, saying to them, . . . "Now if you are ready at the time you hear the sound of the horn, flute, harp, lyre, and psaltery, in symphony with all kinds of music, and you fall down and worship the image which I have made, good! But if you do not worship, you shall be cast immediately into the midst of a burning fiery furnace. And who is the god who will deliver you from my hands?"

DANIEL 3:14-15

Before the men could answer the charges, Nebuchadnezzar offered them a second chance to comply with his demand. This singular offer demonstrated the loyalty King Nebuchadnezzar felt toward Shadrach, Meshach, and Abed-Nego. Any but these three, who had been in his service for more than twenty years, would have immediately been executed. Nebuchadnezzar was showing his magnanimous spirit in offering these men a second chance.

According to John F. Walvoord, "The repetition of the entire edict no doubt was done with a flourish; and, although he was probably well aware of the jealousy of the Chaldeans and took this into account, he makes it clear that there is no alternative but to worship the image."[5]

The king warned them that if they failed to fall down and worship the image a second time, they would certainly be cast into the fiery furnace. And then, I believe with a sneer on his lips, Nebuchadnezzar asked, "Who is the god who will deliver you from my hands?" (verse 15).

THE COMMANDMENT

In response to the king's demand, Shadrach, Meshach, and Abed-Nego uttered one of the greatest statements of faith in the entire Bible. But before we get to that, we need to understand what's behind their conviction. They knew the Old Testament law, and they knew what it says about idolatry: "You shall not make for yourself a carved image—any likeness of anything that is in heaven above, or that is in the earth beneath, or that is in the water under the earth. You shall not bow down to them" (Exodus 20:4-5).

At the base of Mount Sinai, the newly redeemed Hebrews created an image of a gold calf (Exodus 32:4). On the plain of Dura, Nebuchadnezzar created an image of a golden man. In both cases, the commandment was violated.

Theologian John Calvin writes, "A true image of God is not to be found in all the world; and hence . . . His glory is defiled, and His truth corrupted by the lie, whenever He is set before our eyes in a visible form. . . . . Therefore, to devise any image of God, is in itself impious; because by this corruption His Majesty is adulterated, and He is figured to be other than He is."[6]

These men knew that to worship an idol, an image made by human hands, would be to defy and defile the almighty God.

THE COURAGE

The great reformer Martin Luther was called before the Diet of Worms in Germany in 1521 to answer for breaking from the doctrine of the Roman church. He closed his testimony by saying, "I cannot and will not recant anything, since it is neither safe nor right to go against conscience. Here I stand. I can do no other. May God help me."

Some believe that the words "Here I stand. I can do no other" were inserted later—that Luther didn't say those words in his speech. But he could have; that was certainly what he'd demonstrated since 1517, when he nailed his Ninety-Five Theses on the door of the church in Wittenberg. His was the same attitude expressed by Shadrach, Meshach, and Abed-Nego: *Here we stand, in the same place we have stood for the last twenty years, bowing our knee to none other but the God of Abraham, Isaac, and Jacob. We will not bow to the king's image.*

Without being disrespectful, these heroic men, Shadrach, Meshach, and Abed-Nego, gave the world's most powerful king their answer. There was no need for them to consider Nebuchadnezzar's second-chance offer. They'd already made up their minds. They would never bow down to a false image. Here are their inspiring words: "O Nebuchadnezzar, we have no need to answer you in this matter. If that is the case, our God whom we serve is able to deliver us from the burning fiery furnace, and He will deliver us from your hand, O king. But if not, let it be known to you, O king, that we do not serve your gods, nor will we worship the gold image which you have set up" (Daniel 3:16-18).

When they said, "But if not," they were not questioning God's ability to deliver them; they were placing themselves in submission to His will. Theirs was the same attitude expressed by Jesus in the garden of Gethsemane a few centuries later: "Father, if it is Your will, take this cup away from Me; nevertheless not My will, but Yours, be done" (Luke 22:42). If it wasn't His will to deliver them, they would accept that and glorify their God anyway.

The twentieth-century Old Testament scholar H. C. Leupold writes, "The quiet, modest, yet . . . positive attitude of faith that these three men display is one of the noblest examples in the Scriptures of faith fully resigned to the will of God. These men ask for no miracle; they expect none. Theirs is the faith that says, 'Though He slay me, yet will I trust in Him' (Job 13:15, KJV)."[7]

Studdert Kennedy was a chaplain during World War I. His role often thrust him into danger on the front lines of battle. One day while traveling through war-ravaged France, he wrote this letter to his young son:

> The first prayer I want my son to learn to say for me is not "God keep daddy safe," but "God make daddy brave, and if he has hard things to do make him strong to do them." Life and death don't matter . . . right and wrong do. Daddy dead is daddy still, but daddy dishonoured before God is something awful, too bad for words. I suppose you'd like to put in a bit about the safety too, old chap, and mother would. Well, put it in, but afterwards, always afterwards, because it does not really matter near so much.[8]

The Deliverance

THE ANGER OF THE KING

Nebuchadnezzar was full of fury, and the expression on his face changed toward Shadrach, Meshach, and Abed-Nego.

> He spoke and commanded that they heat the furnace seven
> times more than it was usually heated.
>
> DANIEL 3:19

After hearing their refusal to bow down before the statue, Nebuchadnezzar was furious. No one, not even three loyal and trusted aides, could so blatantly defy him, the ruler of the world's greatest empire, and live to tell about it. He ordered that the furnace be heated seven times hotter than usual.

Geoffrey R. King writes, "He lost his temper! That is always the mark of a little man. His furnace was hot, but he himself got hotter! And when a man gets full of fury, he gets full of folly. There is no fool on earth like a man who has lost his temper. And Nebuchadnezzar did a stupid thing. He ought to have cooled the furnace seven times *less* if he had wanted to hurt them; but instead of that in his fury he heated it seven times *more*."[9]

THE ACTIVITY OF THE KING

> He commanded certain mighty men of valor who were in
> his army to bind Shadrach, Meshach, and Abed-Nego, and
> cast them into the burning fiery furnace. Then these men
> were bound in their coats, their trousers, their turbans,
> and their other garments, and were cast into the midst of
> the burning fiery furnace. Therefore, because the king's
> command was urgent, and the furnace exceedingly hot, the
> flame of the fire killed those men who took up Shadrach,
> Meshach, and Abed-Nego. And these three men, Shadrach,
> Meshach, and Abed-Nego, fell down bound into the midst
> of the burning fiery furnace.
>
> DANIEL 3:20-23

Nebuchadnezzar summoned the strongest men in his army to bind Shadrach, Meshach, and Abed-Nego with ropes and cast them into the fire. Strangely enough, they were bound fully dressed—a fact that soon became significant: "The Scriptures relate that they are bound in their coats, hose, and hats as well as other garments. Normally criminals are stripped before execution; but in view of the form of the execution and the haste of the whole operation, there was no particular point in stripping off their clothes. This later becomes a further testimony to the delivering power of God."[10]

The furnace was so hot that the only way the soldiers could get close enough to carry out their orders was to swing the three men toward the opening at the top of the furnace. But even then, the searing heat of the flames fried the skin from their bodies, and they fell down dead. The three Jews, bound hand and foot, plummeted into the blazing furnace.

THE AMAZEMENT OF THE KING

> King Nebuchadnezzar was astonished; and he rose in haste and spoke, saying to his counselors, "Did we not cast three men bound into the midst of the fire?" They answered and said to the king, "True, O king." "Look!" he answered, "I see four men loose, walking in the midst of the fire; and they are not hurt, and the form of the fourth is like the Son of God."
>
> DANIEL 3:24-25

Although we have no data on how the furnace was constructed, we can safely assume that in addition to being open at the top, it was also open in front, allowing witnesses to view the executions. We do know that Nebuchadnezzar could see inside the furnace—and that what he saw astonished him.

The king called his associates and asked, in essence, "Didn't we cast three men into this fire? Look! I see four men strolling about in the midst of the furnace, making no attempt to escape. The flames have not hurt them, and one of them is like the Son of God."

He wasn't merely *like* the Son of God; He *was* the Son of God. He wasn't *a* god; He was *the* God. When the fourth figure showed up in the flames, the event was what we call a theophany—a manifestation of the Lord in the Old Testament. Amazing as it may be, some 580 years before the virgin birth, Nebuchadnezzar saw Christ in the fiery furnace.

THE ACKNOWLEDGMENT OF THE KING

Shadrach, Meshach, and Abed-Nego came from the midst of the fire. And the satraps, administrators, governors, and the king's counselors gathered together, and they saw these men on whose bodies the fire had no power; the hair of their head was not singed nor were their garments affected, and the smell of fire was not on them. Nebuchadnezzar spoke, saying, "Blessed be the God of Shadrach, Meshach, and Abed-Nego, who sent His Angel and delivered His servants who trusted in Him."
DANIEL 3:26-28

Nebuchadnezzar called for Shadrach, Meshach, and Abed-Nego to come out of the furnace. When they approached, the king and his men were astounded that the hair of their heads hadn't been singed and their clothing hadn't been scorched. They didn't even have the smell of smoke lingering around them. Only the cords that had bound them were consumed by the fire—the one item in the flames that had belonged to the Babylonian Empire.

The Decree

> Nebuchadnezzar spoke, saying, ". . . I make a decree that
> any people, nation, or language which speaks anything amiss
> against the God of Shadrach, Meshach, and Abed-Nego shall
> be cut in pieces, and their houses shall be made an ash heap;
> because there is no other God who can deliver like this."
> Then the king promoted Shadrach, Meshach, and Abed-
> Nego in the province of Babylon.
>
> DANIEL 3:28-30

Remember Nebuchadnezzar's effusive acknowledgment of Daniel's God at the end of chapter 2? He does the same thing here at the end of chapter 3. In chapter 4 we will find that the king makes yet one more statement of faith.

Because of the courage of these three young men, a loud-mouthed, proud, vain king was led to praise the God of heaven. He himself had asked the question, "What god is able to deliver you from my hand?" and at last he answered his own question: the God of Shadrach, Meschach, and Abed-Nego!

* * *

DANIEL FOR TODAY

In these early stories from the book of Daniel, there are past, present, and future lessons for us.

1. The lesson from the past is one of an inspiring example. This book shows that in Daniel's day, there were faithful individuals who stood up for what they believed, even when the penalty was death.

There are no finer examples of courage under fire in the entire Bible than those we find in the early chapters of this book.

2. The lesson for the present is that we must determine in advance how we will respond to trials. Before our time on earth is finished, we may well be called on to take a stand for our God. I believe the days of surface faith and cowardly Christianity are quickly coming to an end. Being a Christian—a real Christian—will soon cost more than many are willing to pay. Will you stand for your faith? Do you have the courage to say, as these men did, that you will honor God no matter what?

3. The lesson for the future is that we look forward to a prophetic promise. Arno C. Gaebelein explains:

> When Antichrist terrorizes Jerusalem and the image is set up we read that all who do not worship the image of the beast shall be killed. And in that time of fiery trial, the great tribulation, there will be a faithful Jewish remnant. They will refuse to worship the image and many of them will suffer martyrdom while others will be miraculously kept by the Lord's mighty power and pass through the great tribulation without being harmed by it. . . . But blessed be God. . . . In all our trials and sorrows the Son of God is with us. And the fire but burns off our bands and sets us free.[11]

The three heroes of this chapter experienced firsthand a promise God had given through Isaiah some 130 years earlier. That promise is one we can hold on to as we face what may come in the future:

Fear not, for I have redeemed you;
I have called you by your name;

You are Mine.
When you pass through the waters, I will be with you;
And through the rivers, they shall not overflow you.
When you walk through the fire, you shall not be burned,
Nor shall the flame scorch you.
For I am the LORD your God,
The Holy One of Israel, your Savior.

ISAIAH 43:1-3

Chapter 5

THE WOLF-MAN

Daniel 4:1-37

Twelve-year-old Aniku sat in the moonlit meadow, looking out over the sleeping sheep. Tonight was a milestone for him: it was the first time his father had trusted him with a nighttime watch. There was little danger, as their village wasn't far from the mighty walls of Babylon and predators seldom ventured into their pastures.

Aniku's watch was almost over, and his father would soon replace him. But he wasn't in a hurry. He loved the chirping of the crickets and the croaks of frogs in the nearby creek. He gazed at the outlines of Babylon against the starlit sky. He'd heard tales of its magnificence, and maybe someday . . . *Wait, what was that noise?* Something splashed in the creek some fifty paces away. Aniku stood, nocked an arrow into his bowstring, and crept toward the brushy growth along the stream.

The splashing continued as Aniku approached, crouching low. He reached the brush and peered in, his heart beating wildly. A large, hairy creature hunched in the stream, grappling with something in the water. Suddenly the creature stood, clutching a flapping fish in its claws.

Aniku stepped back, his breath catching in his throat. The creature turned toward the noise, his wild eyes staring through a tangle of hair and his beard hanging like tree moss over his face and shoulders. His hands were humanlike except for the inch-long claws protruding at their tips.

The creature's mouth opened, emitting a guttural roar. Aniku froze in terror. But suddenly the creature turned and loped away on all fours, disappearing into the woods.

Aniku ran back to the sheep as fast as his trembling legs could carry him. When his father arrived, the boy told him in a quavering voice about the monster. "I've never seen anything like it, Father. It was like a wolf, but also a little like a man. I know it sounds crazy, but—"

"I believe you, son. I heard the roar. And the neighbors have reported a similar tale. They believe it's some kind of demon or jinn from the desert. They won't report it to the village magistrate, thinking they'll look like fools. But it's time. I'll make the report in the morning."

* * *

Arioch, now chief minister over Babylon's armies, stepped into Daniel's chambers in Nebuchadnezzar's palace. The two men had been friends for years, and the general needed no invitation to sit in his customary chair facing the prime minister of the empire.

"We've found the wild man you asked us to search for," he said. "My men followed up on the report of a shepherd whose son saw the creature in their pasture."

Daniel laid aside his quill. "What have you done with him?"

"The soldiers followed your instructions. They captured him without harm, using nets. He is now locked inside a room in the garrison. We're treating him well, as you insisted, but he has gone mad with the confinement. He howls and paces continuously. He won't wear clothes or touch the food we give him."

"He won't survive in captivity," Daniel said. "I have secured a place for him, and you can take him there tomorrow."

"Something strange is going on here." Arioch gazed sternly at his friend. "Just who is this insane man you insist on treating like a king?"

"He *is* the king," Daniel replied.

The general stared at the prime minister in disbelief. "You mean I have Nebuchadnezzar himself locked in my prison?"

"Yes. I'll explain everything to you," Daniel said. "I need your help." Daniel called for a servant to bring bread, fruit, and water. He canceled his appointments and began to recount the entire story to Arioch.

He began with an incident that had occurred three years earlier, when King Nebuchadnezzar called all his governors and top administrators to Babylon for a conference. His real purpose, however, was to impress them with the glories of the city he'd made into one of the wonders of the world. Few meetings on policy or administration were held, and those were brief. The rest of the time was filled with opulent feasts and tours of Babylon.

Nebuchadnezzar conducted the tours himself, leading a grand procession of gilded carriages. He showed off the fifty temples to Babylon's gods that he'd restored. Then they crossed his great bridge, which spanned the Euphrates River, and returned through a paved tunnel beneath it. They drove along the top of Babylon's towering city walls and paraded through the arched Ishtar Gate, which was adorned with bas-relief dragons and aurochs made of plated gold.

At the climax of the tour, Nebuchadnezzar told the story of his wife Amytis, daughter of the Median king Cyaxares. Not long after their wedding, his bride had become homesick for the forested mountains of Media. "As a remedy," Nebuchadnezzar said, "I built for her a mountain of gardens. Come and see them."

His guests stood speechless before the multilayered floral terraces, verandas, stairways, and marble-columned porticos. One awestruck governor said, "It looks as if the gardens are hanging from the heavens."

When his guests had departed, Nebuchadnezzar invited Daniel to dine with him privately. He was aglow with the adulation that had been showered on him during the conference.

"Belteshazzar," he said, "you are my one true friend. All the others simply flatter me. But you have always been forthright with me, even when you disagree—something no one else dares to do. I know I can always trust you to tell the truth."

"Thank you, my king."

"So tell me, how do you think my guests reacted to my accomplishments?"

"They seemed highly impressed."

"And what about you, Belteshazzar? You were noticeably quiet during the tours. What do you think of my accomplishments?"

"Babylon is indeed a beautiful and majestic city, my king. But I must remind you of the vision God gave you almost two decades ago. The head of gold will fall. Babylon will not last long past your own lifetime."

"Oh, Belteshazzar, why do you seek to restrain my happiness? Why not rejoice in my glory?"

"Because I fear for you. Your pride has risen so far that it could topple you under its own weight. All your power and glory came from the God of heaven. When you proclaim yourself the author of it, your fall is virtually assured."

Throughout the rest of the meal, Nebuchadnezzar said little. He dismissed Daniel early, and it wasn't long before the kings's once-frequent summons for Daniel's conversation and advice ceased altogether.

* * *

"Malik! Malik! Wake up." The chamberlain to the new chief astrologer shook his master's shoulder.

"What do you want?" Malik snapped, squinting in the glare of the lamp.

"The king has summoned you. He wants the entire college of astrologers, advisers, and magicians immediately."

Malik bounded from his bed, and within the hour, he and his colleagues stood at the door of the throne room, waiting to be ushered in. He looked around him and, not seeing Daniel, gloated inwardly. *Ha! He hasn't been invited. At last, my star rises as his falls.*

Malik and the others entered the hall, and after bowing low, Malik addressed the king. "My glorious sovereign, we are deeply honored that you have given us yet another opportunity to—"

"Stop your babbling," the king interrupted. "I had a dream of such clarity that I know it to be from the gods. I want you to tell me its meaning."

Malik's heart lodged in his throat. He remembered the near disaster the last time he was called to interpret the king's dream. "We are eager to serve our king if it pleases him to tell us the dream."

"I was standing on the plain of Dura," Nebuchadnezzar said, "when a live sprig emerged from the earth before me. It grew and sprouted branches until it became a thriving bush. It shot upward, growing new branches and the brightest green leaves I've ever seen. Soon it penetrated the clouds and touched the roof of the heavens. It was laden with rich fruit—enough to feed the world. Birds flocked to its branches, and beasts rested in its shade.

"Then I saw a holy being descend from heaven, crying, 'Fell the tree, saw off its branches, strip away its leaves, and scatter its fruit. But leave the stump to be soaked with dew, and bind it with iron and bronze.'

"From that point on, the angel spoke of the tree as a person who will change from man to beast and for seven years will graze like an ox in the field. In the end, he will know the Most High God who rules the kingdom of humankind.

"There you have the dream; now tell me what it means."

The astrologers bowed and withdrew to consult. A half hour later they returned, and Malik announced that the gods had imparted to them the meaning of the dream.

"The tree with many branches, O great king, represents all the nations of our world, with riches as abundant as the fruit on that tree. Yet none is as rich and strong as you, O mighty one, for it is you who subdued them. That is the meaning of the felling of the tree. The stump bound with iron means you have bound these nations under your rule. The being from the heavens is our god Marduk telling you that the man becoming a beast represents the people of these lands, who are now like cattle to you, subject to your will and power."

The king glared at Malik, his face darkening in fury. "You witless brood of grovelers! My chambermaid could make up a better lie. I've already learned enough about the future of nations to know that you are spewing nonsense. Out! All of you! Chamberlain, call in Belteshazzar."

The hall emptied quickly, and within minutes, Daniel stood alone before the king. Nebuchadnezzar recounted to him the dream and the astrologers' false interpretation. "I'm relying on you, Belteshazzar. You have the Spirit of your God, and I know He will give you the meaning of the dream."

Daniel stood quietly, looking at the floor.

After a moment, the king said, "I perceive by your silence that the interpretation may not please me. If I wanted to be pleased, I would have swallowed Malik's lie. I want the truth, and I know you will tell it regardless of how distasteful it may be."

Tears filled Daniel's eyes. "My king, I wish the interpretation of your dream applied to your enemies instead of you. But I must tell you what my God has revealed. The tree is you. You have grown until your greatness has reached the heavens and your dominion has extended to the ends of the earth. But pride has eaten away the core of your being, and you must be cut down like a diseased tree, beautiful on the outside but hollow within. For seven years, you will become less than a man—a beast without speech or reason, eating grass in the fields. The stump bound with iron and bronze means you will be preserved and your kingdom will remain intact until your return. Afterward you will realize that the Most High God rules over the kingdoms of humankind, ordaining and deposing rulers at will."

Nebuchadnezzar took a deep breath. "What will be done will be done. There's nothing I can do about it."

"Perhaps there is," Daniel replied. "This dream may be God's merciful warning. Put away your pride now. It may be that He will relent and remove this humiliation from you."

Nebuchadnezzar nodded slowly. "I will consider what you say."

* * *

In the year that followed, all seemed to go well with Nebuchadnezzar and the kingdom. But a day came when Daniel needed to consult the king. He searched throughout the palace, asking servants if they'd seen the monarch. One finally said, "Look in the hall of the scribes. Lately he has been spending hours there every day."

Daniel entered the hall and stood speechless at the scene before him. Nebuchadnezzar sat on an elevated chair overlooking some fifty scribes, all facing him with quills in hand and scrolls unrolled in front of them. They were writing diligently as the king dictated.

"And in the twelfth year of my reign, after I made my capital city the first Wonder of the World, I built for myself a palace such as no king on earth has ever imagined. The walls, rooms, floors, and ceilings are made of cedar, bronze, gold, silver, and rare and precious stones. It is the envy of—"

"My king!" Daniel interrupted. "What are you doing?"

Nebuchadnezzar turned in surprise. "Oh, Belteshazzar . . . I was just, well . . . since, as you have told me, my kingdom will be replaced by lesser kingdoms, I am dictating the chronicles of my reign so future generations will know of its wonders."

Daniel shook his head sadly. "My dear king, you have failed to heed God's warning. Your doom is upon you."

"Surely my accomplishments have earned me the right to do this," Nebuchadnezzar retorted. He led Daniel from the room, through the halls, and onto a rooftop terrace, where he waved his arm expansively over the city. "Is this not great Babylon, which I have built for a royal dwelling by my mighty power and for the honor of my majesty?"

As he spoke, a great voice came from heaven, reverberating off the palace walls. "King Nebuchadnezzar, the kingdom has now departed from you!"

Instantly the king's words became nothing more than a series of inarticulate grunts and snarls. He stared wild eyed at Daniel and fell to the floor, writhing and howling as he clawed at his robes. Once he was naked, he rose to a crouch and leaped over the balcony railing.

Daniel gaped in horror as Nebuchadnezzar plunged into the fountain two stories below. He clambered over the edge and dropped into the canal that would eventually sweep him into the Euphrates River.

* * *

"That's where you came into the story, Arioch." Daniel looked across the table at the general. "I wanted to tell you immediately, but you've been on the Egyptian front for almost a year. I didn't trust anyone else, so I kept all this to myself. The moment you returned, I sent you to find him."

"What an astounding story!" Arioch said. "What do you propose to do now?"

"You know the abandoned field a mile outside the city, where the priests once kept their sacrificial bulls?"

"The one that is enclosed with an iron fence on three sides and faces a sheer vertical wall on the fourth side? It has been used to graze a few oxen and donkeys since Nebuchadnezzar built the new Marduk temple."

"That's the one," Daniel replied. "Turn the king loose in that field. Set a guard to ensure no one enters. See to it that daily food from the king's kitchen is placed within the fence. He may choose not to eat it, but we'll make sure it's available. And place warm blankets in the cave you'll find along the cliff wall."

"How have you dealt with the king's absence?" Arioch asked. "Surely people have wondered where he is. Ambitious nobles and enemy kings could easily take advantage."

"I've been telling supplicants and administrators truthfully that the king is temporarily indisposed and in isolation. I have his signet ring and the authority to use it, which is why the provinces have seen no interruption in the government. But people are beginning to ask questions, so I'm glad you've returned. Together we must preserve the throne for the king."

"I'll increase the palace guard to prevent attempted coups, and I'll fortify the army's presence in the capitals of the empire," Arioch said.

Daniel himself went daily to the field where Nebuchadnezzar was kept. He seldom saw the king, but when he did, he called for him to approach. Each time, the wild man merely scampered away into the brush.

* * *

Daniel was in a conference with Arioch when a servant announced that Malik sought an audience with him. "Go into the room next door and wait," Daniel told Arioch. "But leave the door slightly ajar, and listen carefully."

He then received Malik and asked the purpose of his visit.

The chief astrologer pointed an accusing finger at the premier. "Daniel, you've been hiding something from the kingdom. I learned from palace informers that no one has entered King Nebuchadnezzar's bedchamber in more than two years. It's clear that he isn't in the palace."

"Just where do you think he is?" Daniel feared that Malik had learned where the king was being kept.

"We both know where Nebuchadnezzar is," Malik said. "About two years ago, a servant heard screaming from a rooftop balcony and a loud splash in the fountain below. Nebuchadnezzar hasn't been seen since. Clearly you murdered him, cast his body into the fountain to be swept into the Euphrates, and assumed rule of the empire yourself."

"If you believe this, what do you propose to do about it?"

"Why, as a loyal subject of the king, I must expose your crime."

"Is there no way to prevent this?"

Malik rose from his chair and stepped toward Daniel, his eyes glinting. "Share the kingdom with me, and no one ever needs to know what you've done. The Babylonian Empire is enormous. We can split it between us and both be great kings."

"I'm sure I could trust you to never use your dark secret to steal my half of the empire."

"Of course!" Malik spread his hands in a gesture of magnanimity. "Why should I be greedy? Half an empire is enough for anyone."

"Since you desire a kingdom, I shall give you one," Daniel said. "Arioch, please come in." Arioch entered through the side door. "Arrest this man for high treason against the king of Babylon. He wants a kingdom. Give him a prison cell to rule until the king returns."

* * *

Nebuchadnezzar opened his eyes to the morning light and called for a servant. When none came, he sat up and looked around him.

"Where am I?" he muttered. His bed was a dirt-caked blanket spread over the earthen ground. He appeared to be inside a cave. At first he thought he was looking through a ragged curtain but soon realized it was his own matted hair. He reached up to brush it away and winced as his clawlike nails scraped his forehead.

Bewildered, he stood and peered out of the cave. Suddenly, everything came back to him. Daniel's God had struck him down, just as He said He would. "But He didn't kill me," he said in wonder. "He must care about me, or He wouldn't have bothered with such elaborate discipline."

Nebuchadnezzar draped the blanket around his naked body and walked out into the field. He saw a figure standing just outside the fence, looking toward him.

"Daniel!" he cried, running toward him. "My friend, I'm back! I'm myself again. Praise be to your God!"

Daniel, overjoyed at the king's restoration, took him discreetly to his own home. Throughout the day, the servants provided him with baths, groomed his hair and nails, dressed him in fine clothing, and fed him nourishing food.

The next morning, Daniel took him to the palace, where he and Arioch recounted to the king all the significant events that had occurred over the past seven years.

"I'm amazed that my kingdom is still intact," Nebuchadnezzar responded. "The two of you are to be greatly commended. I've never seen such loyalty and integrity, and I thank you both from the depths of my heart."

King Nebuchadnezzar resumed the reins of government. On the basis of Daniel's testimony, he sent Malik into exile among the Scythians near the Black Sea. Daniel met with the king as needed to offer advice and counsel.

Some weeks later, Daniel needed to consult the king, but he was nowhere to be found. Again, a servant directed him to the hall of scribes. *No, no!* he thought. *Has the king learned nothing?* He approached the room with deep foreboding.

Upon entering, he saw that his fear was confirmed. Nebuchadnezzar sat in the elevated chair, dictating to the fifty scribes facing him.

"My king!" Daniel cried. "How can you do this?"

"I couldn't leave my chronicles unfinished, could I? A good leader should always complete what he begins. But I had to discard all I had written and begin again. It wasn't grand enough."

Daniel couldn't speak. He merely shook his head in dismay.

"Wouldn't you like to hear what I've written so far?" the king asked. He took a scroll from the nearest scribe and read, "Nebuchadnezzar the king, to all peoples, nations, and languages that dwell in all the earth: peace be multiplied to you. I thought it good to declare the signs and wonders that the Most High God has worked for me. How great are His signs, and how mighty His wonders! His kingdom is an everlasting Kingdom, and His dominion is from generation to generation."[1]

* * *

THE SCRIPTURE BEHIND THE STORY

In *Mere Christianity*, C. S. Lewis calls it the "great sin": "There is one vice of which no man in the world is free; which every one in the world loathes when he sees it in someone else; and of which hardly any people, except Christians, ever imagine that they are guilty themselves. . . . There is no fault which makes a man more unpopular, and no fault which we are more unconscious of in ourselves. And the more we have it ourselves, the more we dislike it in others."[2]

Lewis is talking about pride. Pride is the sin at the top of God's hate list: "These six things the Lord hates, yes, seven are an abomination to Him: a *proud look*, a lying tongue, hands that shed innocent blood, a heart that devises wicked plans, feet that are swift in running to evil, a false witness who speaks lies, and one who sows discord among brethren" (Proverbs 6:16-19, emphasis added).

Pride is an exaggerated and dishonest self-evaluation. It's when we want people to believe something about us even though we know it isn't true or is, at best, a gross inflation of some self-perceived virtue. Pride seeks value, honor, importance, reputation, and significance that isn't deserved. Pride is an ego-motivated maneuver to hide from ourselves and others the truth about our inner reality. According to Mark 7:20-23, pride is a sin that "comes from within and defiles a man."

Nebuchadnezzar's sin wasn't that he knew he was talented. His problem was that he considered himself the source of his talent. He wanted the whole world to acknowledge his abilities, and he didn't give credit to the thousands of talented laborers and craftsmen who actually *built* the city of Babylon, much less to God. It's possible to be talented and gifted yet humble at the same time (as Jesus was). The sin of pride rears its head when we refuse to acknowledge that all good gifts come from God alone. The sin of pride leads us to brag, flaunt, and self-promote to such a degree that there's nowhere left to go but down.

In the wisdom literature of the Bible, pride is a frequent topic. Consider these proverbs:

- "Pride and arrogance and the evil way and the perverse mouth I hate" (Proverbs 8:13).
- "When pride comes, then comes shame; but with the humble is wisdom" (Proverbs 11:2).
- "Everyone proud in heart is an abomination to the LORD; though they join forces, none will go unpunished" (Proverbs 16:5).
- "Pride goes before destruction, and a haughty spirit before a fall" (Proverbs 16:18).

- "A haughty look, a proud heart, and the plowing of the wicked are sin" (Proverbs 21:4).
- "A man's pride will bring him low, but the humble in spirit will retain honor" (Proverbs 29:23).

In his New Testament book, James summarizes God's evaluation of pride: "God resists the proud, but gives grace to the humble" (James 4:6).

Throughout the Bible, there isn't a better example of the disaster of pride in a person's life than that of Babylon's King Nebuchadnezzar II in Daniel 4.

When God was finished with him, Nebuchadnezzar filed this report: "Now I, Nebuchadnezzar, praise and extol and honor the King of heaven, all of whose works are truth, and His ways justice. And those who walk in pride He is able to put down" (Daniel 4:37).

This chapter is unlike any other found in the Bible for at least two reasons:

1. It's a Babylonian state document written in large measure by King Nebuchadnezzar himself.
2. It's a "personal testimony" that gives a first-person account of Nebuchadnezzar's own experience with God.

This chapter tells us of King Nebuchadnezzar's second dream. At least two or three decades have passed since the first one recorded in Daniel 2. One scholar places this dream "between the thirtieth and thirty-fifth year of Nebuchadnezzar's reign, when Daniel was between forty-five and fifty years old, and when twenty-five to thirty years had elapsed since the deliverance of the three friends from the fiery furnace."[3]

It's apparent from our study of the first chapters of Daniel that God has been dealing with Nebuchadnezzar's heart. This is the third time the Babylonian king has been confronted by his Maker.

The Reason for the Story

> Nebuchadnezzar the king, to all peoples, nations, and
> languages that dwell in all the earth: Peace be multiplied
> to you. I thought it good to declare the signs and wonders
> that the Most High God has worked for me. How great are
> His signs, and how mighty His wonders! His kingdom is an
> everlasting kingdom, and His dominion is from generation
> to generation.
>
> DANIEL 4:1-3

The first three verses of Daniel 4 form a preamble, telling us
that the account we are about to read is Nebuchadnezzar's own. The
use of the personal pronoun *I* certifies his authorship and indicates
that Daniel incorporated the king's words into the inspired record of
this book.

The king declares that his testimony is universal in scope. It is
to "all peoples, nations, and languages that dwell in all the earth"
(Daniel 4:1). This is the same formula used in Daniel 3:29, and it
was commonly used among the Near Eastern cultures of that day.

The king's statement is also personal. This isn't someone else's
story; this is Nebuchadnezzar's story: "I thought it good to declare
the signs and wonders that the Most High God has worked for me"
(Daniel 4:2). It's apparent that Nebuchadnezzar wanted to take this
opportunity to explain his mysterious absence from the throne for a
period of seven years. This document does the job quite effectively.

In verse 3, the king summarizes the attitude of his heart toward
God. This is his attitude *after* the events of chapter 4 have transpired.
Logically, these first three verses belong at the end of the chapter.
But he announces his heart change up front because he now sees the
transitory nature of the kingdom of Babylon in light of the eternal
Kingdom of God. He had just lost his kingdom for a period of seven

years, but God will never lose His Kingdom. That's because God's Kingdom is everlasting.

Nebuchadnezzar's words echo those of David in Psalm 145:13: "Your kingdom is an everlasting kingdom, and Your dominion endures throughout all generations."

The Reception of the Dream

I, Nebuchadnezzar, was at rest in my house, and flourishing in my palace. I saw a dream which made me afraid, and the thoughts on my bed and the visions of my head troubled me. Therefore I issued a decree to bring in all the wise men of Babylon before me, that they might make known to me the interpretation of the dream. . . . I told them the dream; but they did not make known to me its interpretation. But at last Daniel came before me.

DANIEL 4:4-8

While Nebuchadnezzar was at rest in his private life and prosperous in his royal life, he discovered that security in his kingdom did not bring peace, and personal prosperity did not enable him to sleep. His dream troubled him deeply, and he responded by summoning the same wise men who had consistently failed him in the past.

This time, instead of requiring that the counselors describe his dream, the king gave them the content of his dream and simply asked for their interpretation of it. But the wise men failed to give Nebuchadnezzar a message he was happy with. Even if they'd known the correct interpretation, they likely would have been unwilling to deliver it to the king. No one wants to deliver a message of doom to someone who has the power to condemn them to death. Daniel was the only one of the king's wise men who didn't live in fear of him.

Finally Nebuchadnezzar summoned Daniel. The king's reason for doing so is mentioned no less than three times in this text. Daniel was a man in whom was "the Spirit of the Holy God" (Daniel 4:8-9, 18).

During the thirty-some years of their association, Nebuchadnezzar had come to see in Daniel the difference that is always apparent in someone who is filled with the Spirit. So he asked Daniel to "explain to me the visions of my dream that I have seen, and its interpretation" (Daniel 4:9).

The Repetition of the Dream

Nebuchadnezzar described his dream to Daniel in two sections.

THE MAGNIFICENT TREE

> I was looking, and behold, a tree in the midst of the earth, and its height was great. The tree grew and became strong; its height reached to the heavens, and it could be seen to the ends of all the earth. Its leaves were lovely, its fruit abundant, and in it was food for all. The beasts of the field found shade under it, the birds of the heavens dwelt in its branches, and all flesh was fed from it.
>
> DANIEL 4:10-12

As we can see, Nebuchadnezzar's dream depicts the tree in specific detail. Each characteristic is superlative and carries hints of prophetic significance. According to the details given to Daniel, the tree had the following characteristics:

- strategically located: "in the midst of the earth"
- strong: "the tree grew and became strong"
- stretched to heaven: "its height reached to the heavens"
- seen by the entire world: "it could be seen to the ends of all the earth"

- superbly productive: "its leaves were lovely, its fruit abundant"
- supplied nourishment for everyone: "in it was food for all"
- sheltered the animals: "the beasts of the field found shade under it"
- sustained the birds: "the birds of the heavens dwelt in its branches"

It isn't uncommon in the Bible for a tree to be used for symbolic purposes (2 Kings 14:9; Psalm 1:3; 37:35; 52:8, 92:12; Ezekiel 17). And as we will see, in Daniel 4, this tree carries significant meaning.

THE MESSAGE FROM HEAVEN

He cried aloud and said thus: "Chop down the tree and cut off its branches, strip off its leaves and scatter its fruit. Let the beasts get out from under it, and the birds from its branches. Nevertheless leave the stump and roots in the earth, bound with a band of iron and bronze, in the tender grass of the field. Let it be wet with the dew of heaven, and let him graze with the beasts on the grass of the earth. Let his heart be changed from that of a man, let him be given the heart of a beast, and let seven times pass over him."

DANIEL 4:14-16

The next thing Nebuchadnezzar saw in his dream was a messenger descending from heaven. He identified the messenger as a watcher, a holy one. Nebuchadnezzar saw this angel in tangible form as he delivered a decree from the Most High: the tree was to be cut down, leaving only the stump, which would be surrounded by a band of iron and bronze. The stump would be wet with dew every morning. And then, with a shift in imagery signified by the use of the personal pronoun *he*, the stump is personified as a sentient being that would lose his reasoning capacity and graze in the field like an animal for seven years.

Even when a tree has been cut down, the stump provides the possibility of restoration and new life. So when Daniel painted a picture for Nebuchadnezzar of his life as a cut-down tree but with a stump protected by iron and bronze, he was painting a harsh but hopeful picture. The cut-down tree in the ancient world was a sign of judgment, but the protected stump heralded a future for that tree (Daniel 4:26). It was a message of judgment and restoration all in one.

In Daniel 4:17, the angel gives the reason for the pronouncement: "This decision is by the decree of the watchers, and the sentence by the word of the holy ones, in order that the living may know that the Most High rules in the kingdom of men, gives it to whomever He will, and sets over it the lowest of men."

The Revelation of the Dream

Before the interpretation of the dream is revealed, we are told that Daniel was astonished "for a time" (Daniel 4:19). He wasn't astonished in the sense of not knowing the meaning of the dream; he was astonished because of the ominous nature of the dream and what it meant to Nebuchadnezzar, who was his friend.

The nineteenth-century scholar C. F. Keil wrote, "As Daniel at once understood the interpretation of the dream, he was for a moment so astonished that he could not speak for terror at the thoughts which moved his soul. The amazement seized him because he wished well to the king, and yet he must now announce to him a weighty judgment from God."[4]

When Daniel hesitated, Nebuchadnezzar encouraged him to speak. Daniel answered that he wished the dream were meant for those who hated Nebuchadnezzar instead of for Nebuchadnezzar himself (Daniel 4:19).

In his compassion for the recipient of this grim message, Daniel showed the way for preachers of the gospel everywhere. The message of judgment should always be delivered with a broken heart.

Finally, it was time for Daniel to drive home what must be said: "It is you, O king, who have grown and become strong; for your greatness has grown and reaches to the heavens, and your dominion to the end of the earth" (Daniel 4:22).

These sound like the words spoken by Nathan when he confronted David with his sin. He said to David, "You are the man!" (2 Samuel 12:7). From this point on, there was no doubt in King Nebuchadnezzar's mind as to the meaning of his dream. He was the tree of his night vision.

Daniel went on to explain to the king that he would be deposed from his throne and suffer a seven-year period of insanity until he realized that God rules over every human kingdom.

While this prophecy of judgment was severe, it was interwoven with evidences of God's mercy:

- God promised to preserve Nebuchadnezzar's life and kingdom during his seven years of insanity. As Daniel told him, "Inasmuch as they gave the command to leave the stump and roots of the tree, your kingdom shall be assured to you, after you come to know that Heaven rules" (Daniel 4:26).
- This judgment was preceded by a warning: God sent His angel to warn the king. God always warns before He judges (Daniel 4:13).
- The judgment was presented with a condition. God gave the king twelve months to repent (Daniel 4:29).
- The judgment was proposed with a remedy. "Break off your sins by being righteous, and your iniquities by showing mercy to the poor. Perhaps there may be a lengthening of your prosperity" (Daniel 4:27).

But as so often is the case, God gives people space and grace, and people often use those mercies to harden their hearts against God.

The Realization of the Dream

THE KING'S PRIDE

> All this came upon King Nebuchadnezzar. At the end of the twelve months he was walking about the royal palace of Babylon.
> DANIEL 4:28-29

The king's story reopens one year later in the Babylonian palace. He was surveying his city—and what a city it was! The New King James Version says that he was walking "about" his royal palace, but the word is better translated by the word *upon*, suggesting that he was walking on the roof of his palace. From this vantage point, he could see the entire city.

Babylon was probably the most famous city in the ancient world. Its huge walls may have been forty feet high and eighty feet wide—so wide that several chariots could be driven side by side along the top of them. The city boasted wide streets, more than fifty temples, and countless public buildings. The mighty Euphrates River flowed through it, and gardens, palm groves, orchards, and farmland dotted the countryside, providing enough food to feed the entire city. Gigantic shrines to Babylonian deities were set up everywhere. The pinnacle of the city's beauty, however, must have been the naturally air-conditioned hanging gardens Nebuchadnezzar had built for his homesick wife.

Remembered as one of the Seven Wonders of the World, these gardens were planted in layered terraces at a considerable height. Water was pumped from the Euphrates River to irrigate the lush vegetation.

As Nebuchadnezzar walked along the palace terrace and viewed the magnificent cityscape, he was overcome with pride, and his heart erupted with these vain words: "Is not this great Babylon, that *I* have built for a royal dwelling by *my* mighty power and for the honor of *my* majesty?" (Daniel 4:30, emphasis added).

Note the personal pronouns in Nebuchadnezzar's words. Every syllable drips with glory, pride, arrogance, and self-glorification. Nebuchadnezzar, like Lucifer (Isaiah 14:12-14), was about to learn that "God resists the proud" (James 4:6).

THE KING'S PUNISHMENT

> That very hour the word was fulfilled concerning Nebuchadnezzar; he was driven from men and ate grass like oxen; his body was wet with the dew of heaven till his hair had grown like eagles' feathers and his nails like birds' claws.
>
> DANIEL 4:33

While the arrogant words were still in the king's mouth, a voice came from heaven pronouncing his doom. Immediately Nebuchadnezzar was struck with insanity. His mental disease is known as lycanthropy, from the Greek word *lykos*, meaning "wolf," and the word *anthropos*, meaning "man."

Lycanthropy stems from a centuries-old belief that some humans can transform into wolves—and revert back to human form. But clinical lycanthropy is a psychiatric diagnosis of a person who believes he or she has become a nonhuman animal (not necessarily a wolf). There's no indication in Daniel 4 that Nebuchadnezzar became a certain type of animal, only that he became *like* a wild animal in appearance and actions. In any event, the cause for his mental condition was the judgment of God, and the result was the humbling of a prideful king for seven long years.

The one who had tempted Daniel and his three friends to eat forbidden food from the royal table now ate grass like an ox.

The Restoration of the King

> At the end of the time I, Nebuchadnezzar, lifted my eyes
> to heaven, and my understanding returned to me; and I
> blessed the Most High and praised and honored Him who
> lives forever. . . . At the same time my reason returned to me,
> and for the glory of my kingdom, my honor and splendor
> returned to me. My counselors and nobles resorted to me,
> I was restored to my kingdom, and excellent majesty was
> added to me. Now I, Nebuchadnezzar, praise and extol and
> honor the King of heaven, all of whose works are truth,
> and His ways justice. And those who walk in pride He is
> able to put down.
> DANIEL 4:34-37

The first thirty-three verses of Daniel 4 illustrate that God resists the proud, but these last four verses demonstrate that He also gives grace to the humble. When the king had lived out his seven-year sentence of insanity, he lifted his eyes to heaven, and his reason returned. He couldn't wait to praise God as the King of all kings and the absolute monarch of the universe. He told of the great things God had done for him, and once again, God's mercy and grace are on display:

- He restored the king's reason.
- He restored the king to his throne.
- He restored the king's officials and administrators to him.

- He protected the kingdom from usurpers during his seven-year absence.
- He added to the king majesty and honor.

For many years, God had warned Nebuchadnezzar. He had allowed him the privilege of witnessing Daniel's personal life and testimony for more than three decades. There came a time, however, when the era of God's patience came to an end, and He sent judgment to the king. God's judgment taught Nebuchadnezzar the lesson he sorely needed, as we see in his final recorded words: "Those who walk in pride He is able to put down" (Daniel 4:37).

The sovereignty of God over the affairs of human beings is one of the great lessons we draw from this chapter. Five times in our text that message is plainly declared:

- "The Most High rules in the kingdom of men, gives it to whomever He will, and sets over it the lowest of men" (Daniel 4:17).
- "The Most High rules in the kingdom of men, and gives it to whomever He chooses" (Daniel 4:25).
- "Your kingdom shall be assured to you, after you come to know that Heaven rules" (Daniel 4:26).
- "The Most High rules in the kingdom of men, and gives it to whomever He chooses" (Daniel 4:32).
- "I blessed the Most High and praised and honored Him who lives forever: For His dominion is an everlasting dominion, and His kingdom is from generation to generation" (Daniel 4:34).

Charles W. Colson was a close political aide to President Richard Nixon. At the time, he was a godless, prideful man who wielded enormous power as Nixon's hatchet man. It was said that "Colson would walk over his own grandmother if necessary."[5] He once insti-gated a plan to arm two hundred union workers with steel construc-tion bars to attack student demonstrators. He proposed bombing the Brookings Institution to steal politically damaging documents in the resulting confusion.

In the wake of the Watergate scandal that destroyed Nixon's presi-dency, Colson was sentenced to prison as one of the conspirators in the cover-up.

While Colson was in prison, a friend gave him a copy of C. S. Lewis's *Mere Christianity*. After reading the book, Colson was con-verted to Christ, and his life changed radically. On his release from prison, he became one of the most dedicated, dynamic, and effective Christian leaders in the United States. He founded several evangelis-tic and service organizations, such as Prison Fellowship Ministries, the Chuck Colson Center for Christian Worldview, and the daily radio program *BreakPoint*. He was a frequent public speaker on the Christian worldview and wrote thirty books and uncountable articles on the subject before his death in 2012.

Charles Colson learned the same lessons as King Nebuchadnezzar: pride goes before a fall; God rules every earthly kingdom; and He is merciful and generous with grace to the fallen.

As we say good-bye to the Bible's most prominent pagan king, we do so with this summary from Dr. Graham Scroggie: "Here we take leave of Nebuchadnezzar. How does he bid us farewell? Not only as a sane man but as a converted man. The last thing related of him is the humble public confession which he made, and the noble testimony to the true God. . . . With the restoration of his reason and kingdom came the regeneration of his soul. There is nothing in this Book more sublime than this testimony of Nebuchadnezzar's. To him light came at eventide, and he turned his throne into a pulpit, and his State papers into sermons."[6]

* * *

DANIEL FOR TODAY

No illness spreads faster than the "disease of me"! In Daniel 4, we saw two men with contrasting values. King Nebuchadnezzar was obsessed with one person—himself. Daniel, on the other hand, was more concerned for his king than for himself. By the end of the chapter, the proud man had been humbled, and the humble man had been exalted. We can't miss the lessons.

1. Be humble in heart. Acknowledge Christ as Lord of your affections. When He's enthroned in the center of your heart, He'll help you keep yourself in check. Humility isn't thinking less of yourself; it's thinking of yourself less. Romans 12:3 tells us not to think of ourselves more highly than we ought, but to think of ourselves "soberly." We all have strengths to be grateful for, weaknesses to be contrite over, and gifts designed to make us useful. Let Christ be first, and don't think of yourself much at all. Keep the focus on Him.

2. Be humble in deed. Make a habit of serving others. The best way to develop humility is to put others first and go out of your way to quietly meet their needs. The Bible says, "Let nothing be done through selfish ambition or conceit, but in lowliness of mind let each esteem others better than himself. Let each of you look out not only for his own interests, but also for the interests of others" (Philippians 2:3-4). Find a quiet way to help someone today.

3. Be humble in word. In conversation, shift the subject to the other person. Instead of talking so much about your trip, your illness, your job, or your family, ask about the other person. Learn to listen. Commit to pray over what others tell you.

If only Nebuchadnezzar had been humble in heart, deed, and word, he wouldn't have contracted the "disease of me." It took seven long years for him to recover. Let's humble ourselves before the Lord today and be like Daniel. Anything else is insanity.

Chapter 6

THE FINGERS OF GOD

Daniel 5:1-31

THE IMPOSING FIGURE OF CYRUS rode slowly across the battlefield, his horse picking its way through the bodies strewn across the ground like broken dolls. Seven of his generals clustered around him. He turned to Gobryas, his second in command. "Has Nabonidus been found?"

"No, my lord. He fled the field with the few troops that were left."

"It's just as well," the great commander replied. "He's forever disgraced, not only for his poor generalship but also for his inattention to his rule. He has been away from Babylon more than he's been present."

"And now he has lost most of Babylon's army," Gobryas said. "I'll command our troops to begin the siege."

"We must make it a short siege," Cyrus replied.

"But how? With Babylon's vast stores of food and a river running through the heart of the city, they could hold out for years."

"I have a plan. Come, I'll show you." Cyrus led his generals along the banks of the Euphrates until they came to a sharp bend in the river that was hidden from the city walls by a low hill. "Look to your right," he said. "What do you see?"

"Nothing but a putrid swamp," Gobryas replied.

"Mobilize our men to dig a channel from the river to the swamp. The swamp will overflow into the plain of Dura, which will leave the river little more than a trickle from here to Babylon."

"A brilliant strategy!" Gobryas said. "Dry up their water supply, and they'll surrender within a month."

"We'll do even better than that." A cryptic smile crept across Cyrus's face. He wheeled his horse about and rode back to his army.

* * *

The Queen Mother stood on a palace balcony overlooking the Persian army camped just outside the city walls. Deep in thought, she hardly noticed when Naram, the high priest of Bel, walked up to her and bowed.

"It is truly a disconcerting sight, my queen," the priest said. "Your late husband never would have allowed the great city of Babylon to be so humiliated."

"Certainly not," she replied. "Nebuchadnezzar would have met Cyrus's army on some strategically chosen battlefield long before he reached the city gates. What brings you here, Naram?"

"I had an appointment with the king at the tenth hour. While waiting for him, I've been wandering through the hallway."

"Do you mean he's not up yet? It's an hour past noon. I'll never understand why Nabonidus named his drunken sluggard of a son ruler in his place. Wait here. I'll speak to his chamberlain." Queen Alittum strode away, her jaw set and her eyes flashing fire.

The chamberlain refused to wake the king. "I woke him once," he said, "and it earned me ten lashes. He vowed that next time I'd be thrown over the wall."

Without hesitating, Alittum took from his table a silver pitcher, dumped the wine onto the floor, and banged the vessel repeatedly against the king's door.

"You dog of a chamberlain!" a voice bellowed from inside. "You know better than to—"

"I'm not your chamberlain; I am Queen Alittum. You get out of that bed and come down to the throne room. The high priest of Bel has been waiting for three hours. It's a bad omen to insult the servants of the gods."

Several minutes later, Belshazzar staggered out, his face puffy and his eyes bloodshot. Alittum was a woman with a strong personality, and he had feared her since childhood—a fear he couldn't shake even now that he was king. She was a widow of Nebuchadnezzar, while his own mother had been one of the wives of King Nabonidus.

Belshazzar bellowed for a cup of wine. Servants arrived and groomed his hair and beard as he emptied the cup and demanded another. After eating an elaborate meal, he plodded off to the throne room.

His prime minister, Urak, was already in the room when Belshazzar entered and took the throne. Naram was ushered in and stood before him.

"O great king, I have come to hear your desires for the upcoming annual feast of Bel."

"My desire is to skip it altogether," Belshazzar replied. "I detest religious feasts. Women are prohibited from attending, and the king is prohibited from drinking. Go plan your feast any way you wish. I will not be there."

The priest gave him a cold look. "If the king missed the feast, it would be a grave affront to Bel. Must I remind you that your own name means 'Bel protect the king'? Surely you don't want to risk the withdrawal of his protection."

Belshazzar's jaw clenched. "If that is a threat—"

"My lord, hear me." Urak stood quickly. "May I propose a compromise that could meet both your needs? Attend Bel's feast, my king, as the priest desires. And Naram, all you need to do is make a slight adjustment to protocol. Invite the women, and allow the king to drink his wine."

"A fine solution!" Belshazzar exclaimed. "Do as Urak suggests, and I'll come to your party."

"Impossible! Such sacrilege would affront Bel and defy tradition."

"Tradition!" Belshazzar snorted. "That's merely another word for ruts that force wagons to go where other wagons have gone. It's time for new roads, new ways, new ideas."

"Perhaps we can persuade Bel to be less resistant to new ideas," Urak said. "What if the king were to demonstrate to the celebrants Bel's superiority over all other gods?"

"What are you proposing?"

"In his treasury the king has the golden bowls, goblets, furnishings, lampstand, and other precious items that King Nebuchadnezzar took from Jehovah's Temple in Jerusalem. What if we displayed those items at the feast and drank to Bel from the defeated God's sacred golden containers?"

A small smile tugged at the corners of the priest's mouth. "That would indeed be a grand gesture, my lord. And it would go a long way toward cooling Bel's wrath. But for him to be completely appeased, you would need to offer these treasures to his temple."

"I'll give Bel one tenth of them," Belshazzar said.

"Half," the priest countered.

Belshazzar stood firm at one fourth, and the priest left the hall eager to prepare a feast for one thousand nobles—plus government officials and women—where wine would flow freely at the king's table.

That evening Belshazzar dined with his usual circle of nobility. After glutting himself with pork and wine, he began to brag about the bargain he'd struck with Naram. "Not only will women attend the feast, but at the height of the celebration, I will drink from the golden bowl taken from the Temple in Jerusalem."

The color drained from Alittum's face. "Don't do it, Belshazzar." Her voice was urgent. "The Hebrews' God has power you know nothing of. King Nebuchadnezzar defied Him several times before finally acknowledging Him as the true and only God. Don't repeat his mistake. Leave Jehovah's treasures safe in your vault."

"Oh, Alittum, you take religion too seriously. Nebuchadnezzar became enamored with Jehovah, my sister is a priestess of the moon god, and you serve Bel but fear Jehovah. Surely you don't think these gods have any real power."

"Don't you believe in any god?"

"I certainly do!" Belshazzar turned up his goblet and drank deeply, wiped his dribbling mouth, and idly caressed the servant girl who refilled his cup. "I believe in the god of pleasure. Think about it: everyone must die, and who knows what lies beyond the grave? So the only thing that makes sense is to pack into each day and night every ounce of pleasure they can hold. Why bother about anything besides whether your desires are met? Pleasure, wealth, and power are the only realities. Wealth has meaning only because it can buy pleasure, and power only because it can coerce it."

A shiver of fear chilled Alittum to the bone. She finished her meal in silence and returned to her own chambers. Once there, she made a solemn vow to herself: she would not attend the feast.

* * *

The week of the annual rite of Bel arrived. It was a time of celebration for all echelons of Babylonian society. The days were marked by holy rituals in the temples of the gods; the nights were filled with reveling in the streets. The palace was packed with guests who were arriving for the great feast.

As guests began to fill the vast dining hall, it quickly became clear that there would be many more women than men—not only wives and favorite concubines, but also consorts and mistresses. Every table was filled long before the feast began.

At the appointed time, Belshazzar made his grand entrance, followed by his wives, select concubines, Prime Minister Urak, and his six closest counselors. When they sat down at the high tables on the multitiered dais, the gong sounded to begin the feast.

The priestesses of Bel escorted the high priest Naram down the aisle to the center of the hall, where he lit the fire of incense in the holy brazier and uttered sacred ritual words honoring the Babylonian god.

Once the priest took his seat, the festivities began in earnest. Servants streamed into the hall, bearing trays full of meats, cheeses, fruits, and other delicacies, as well as pitchers of wine . . . and more wine.

Soon the hall rang with laughter, drunken shouting, and the clash of goblets. It wasn't long before a number of guests collapsed onto the table or floor in a drunken stupor. King Belshazzar drained one goblet after another and dallied with wives, concubines, and servant girls without distinction.

Naram waited as long as he dared. If he didn't act now, Belshazzar's drunkenness would render him unable to fulfill his promise. He stepped over to the king's table and whispered in his ear. Belshazzar nodded and instructed the servants to bring in the treasures from the Temple in Jerusalem.

The enormous golden lampstand was carried in first and set high against the wall to the king's left. All seven candles were lit. Hundreds of golden goblets were distributed among the nobility, and an elaborate filigreed golden bowl was set before the king and filled with wine. He stood unsteadily, and the chamberlain sounded the gong. The din subsided, and the guests who were still able to turned toward the king.

He spoke in a slurred voice: "Honorable guests and officials of Babylon. Of all the gods that have infiltrated our lands, none is more odious than the God of the Hebrews. False tales of His miraculous deeds contaminate the literature of every land, yet the Jews think He is the only God." The king's sneer ended in a rumbling belch.

"But tonight," he continued, "we will demonstrate to you that Bel, not Jehovah, is the god above all gods. His foot now presses hard into the neck of Jehovah, for Bel has destroyed Jehovah's Temple and His holy city and plucked His sacred golden treasures from His weak hand. Tonight we will drink an oblation to Bel from those very vessels."

The crowd burst into a raucous cheer as Belshazzar lifted the bowl to his lips and drank deeply.

Suddenly the king's eyes went wide. The bowl fell from his hands and clattered to the table. Wine dribbled down his beard, and he collapsed into his chair, staring in horror at the wall above the Temple lampstand.

All eyes in the room followed his stare. Suddenly women shrieked and men gaped, petrified. A gigantic hand, human in form but the size of an ox, was writing with an extended forefinger on the plaster wall. The hand floated across the wall, unconnected to a body. After writing four enormous words, it withdrew toward the high ceiling and disappeared.

"Naram, what do those words say?" Belshazzar demanded. "Tell me! What do they say?"

"I—I don't know, my king. I can't make sense of them."

"Urak, you must tell me what those words say."

"The words are cryptic. It is certainly a message from the stars."

"Then call in the astrologers," the king cried. "Bring them now!"

The chamberlain sent for the astrologers. But when they arrived, they had no more insights than Urak or the priest. Belshazzar was beside himself. He ranted, berated, and threatened. He hurled wine cups and even heaved the golden bowl across the table. His counselors were unable to calm him. A servant offered him a goblet of wine, but he slapped it away. At Urak's urging, a girl, smiling with promise, went to Belshazzar and whispered in his ear. But he shoved her away with an obscene oath.

Then Urak took the chamberlain aside and said, "Go quickly and bring Queen Alittum. She knows how to speak to him."

A few moments later, the chamberlain escorted Alittum into the hall. He pointed to the writing and explained to her what had happened. She nodded, stepped up the dais, and gazed at Belshazzar with disgust. "O king, may you live forever." Every word dripped with sarcasm. "The answer to your dilemma resides in this city not far from the palace. Your father, Nabonidus, foolishly dismissed the wisest of his counselors. His name is Daniel—a man of great wisdom and judgment who interpreted dreams and mysteries by the Spirit of the holy God. I assure you that if any man on earth can tell you the meaning of these words, he is the one."

The king sent for Daniel. As the guests awaited his arrival, they began to forget the ominous words looming above them, and the debauchery resumed. The party was regaining its momentum when a hush abruptly descended over the hall. All eyes turned toward the door, where an aged man stood tall, his eyes flashing fire. With resolute steps, he strode down the aisle, ignoring the drunken, half-naked bodies and spilled wine strewn around him.

He ascended the dais and stood before the king. Belshazzar pointed a trembling finger toward the wall. "See the words etched up there above the Hebrews' lampstand? None of these fools can read them. If you can do it, I will make you third ruler in my kingdom and adorn you with robes and golden chains."

"Keep your rewards for yourself," Daniel said. "Even so, I will read the inscription and give you its interpretation. But first, I have other words that you need to hear. You know the stories told of your predecessor Nebuchadnezzar. God gave him the kingdoms of the world and made him a great ruler. But instead of honoring God, he swelled with pride over his accomplishments. Therefore the Lord brought him down to the level of a beast in the field, eating grass and waking in the mornings wet with dew.

"King Nebuchadnezzar learned the lesson the Lord graciously gave to him. He realized that the God of heaven rules all the kings and kingdoms of the earth, and he humbled himself before Him."

Daniel stepped toward the king and thrust his finger in his face. "But you, Belshazzar, have refused to humble yourself. You have bowed to dead images of stone, wood, and silver, which you stupidly call gods. And tonight you have presumed to set yourself above the true God of heaven, insulting Him by putting your drunken lips to His holy vessels and proclaiming Him to be nothing before your gods. Therefore, He has pronounced your judgment. The hand you saw tonight was His messenger, and the words it wrote bear His message."

Daniel turned toward the inscription. "The words you see are *Mene, Mene, Tekel, Upharsin.* This is what they mean: the number of days allotted to your kingdom is over. You have been weighed on the scale and found inadequate. And your kingdom has been divided between the Medes and the Persians."

Without a bow or another word, Daniel turned and stepped down from the dais.

"Wait," Belshazzar called. As Daniel paused, the king beckoned for Urak to approach and spoke low in his ear. "I must at least appear to fulfill my promise before this crowd. Give this man your outer robe and your chain of office. I will get them back for you tomorrow."

Urak removed his robe and chain and placed them on Daniel. The prophet neither acknowledged the gesture nor turned toward the king. Instead, he walked away as every eye in the room watched. Without breaking stride, he removed the robe and dropped it to the floor, and a few steps later the chain fell clattering after it.

* * *

As the drama inside the palace was playing itself out, General Gobryas stood in darkness on the bank of the Euphrates River just outside the walls of Babylon. A battalion of Persian soldiers stood behind him, armed with swords hidden beneath civilian robes. The din of revelry reverberated through the wide tunnel in the wall that ushered the river into the city.

The portal was well protected by a heavy iron portcullis that usually descended deep into the river. But tonight its lower bars hovered some four feet above the water, which now flowed into the city at a depth of no more than two feet. Cyrus gave the signal, and General Gobryas led his troops into the river and through the tunnel.

None of the drunken Babylonians filling the streets noticed as the invaders climbed out of the river and mixed among them, covering their mission by whooping and shouting like the celebrants. They began striking down the men and women in their path, making their way toward the palace and leaving behind a trail of blood and bodies.

Soon the sounds of revelry turned into screams as people realized what was happening and tried to run away from the invaders. But the massive crowds clogged the streets, and almost as many people were trampled as were slaughtered by Persian swords.

Gobryas reached the gates of the palace and found the guards drunk. His men dispatched them easily.

By then the rising tumult reached the ears of the celebrants at the feast. Belshazzar sent the captain of his guard to determine its cause. When the captain reached the gate, he stared through the bars in shock. All the guards but one lay dead, and the only survivor lay on the ground, groaning and bleeding.

The captain unlocked the gate and rushed out to ask the dying man what had happened. At that moment, Gobryas and his men emerged from hiding. They killed the captain, rushed through the open gate, and found their way to the banquet hall. They burst through the doors and entered the hall, their bloody swords drawn.

Pandemonium erupted. The panicked guests screamed and tried to run for their lives, tripping over bodies, chairs, and tables in a futile attempt to escape the slaughter.

Belshazzar could only stand in terror as Gobryas led a contingent of his men to the dais. His soldiers attacked the defenseless nobles as Belshazzar drew his scimitar, holding it in quaking hands. In an instant, Gobryas knocked the weapon from the king's hand and thrust his sword though the king's belly.

By sunrise Babylon was in Gobryas's hands. He ordered the Ishtar Gate to be opened, and Cyrus the Great, the emperor of the combined empires of the Medes and Persians, marched triumphantly into the city.

* * *

THE SCRIPTURE BEHIND THE STORY

As we explore the events in chapter 5 of the book of Daniel, it's helpful to get some perspective on the timeline. At this point, about seventy years have passed since Daniel was taken captive as a teenager. And more than a quarter of a century has elapsed since the end of chapter 4. King Nebuchadnezzar is now dead after a reign of forty-four years, and Daniel is in his early eighties.

"There was a succession of kings in Babylon after Nebuchadnezzar died. Most of them experienced untimely deaths. One was assassinated by his brother, another was killed in battle, and another was captured by the Medes and the Persians and lived the life of a prisoner of war. Onto the scene comes Belshazzar, a fellow who was addicted to wine, women, and song."[1]

KINGS OF BABYLON

Nebuchadnezzar
(605–562 BC)

Amel-Marduk
(562–560 BC)

Neriglissar
(560–556 BC)

Labashi-Marduk
(556 BC)

Nabonidus
(556–539 BC)

Belshazzar
(553–539 BC)

Belshazzar was co-regent with his father, Nabonidus, until Nabonidus was captured by the Persian king Cyrus. At that point, Belshazzar became the sole ruler of Babylon.

With Belshazzar identified and in place, it's time to see how God used Daniel to foretell the immediate takeover of Babylon by Cyrus the Persian. Daniel's prophecy was fulfilled the same night it was spoken.

The story begins in the massive banquet hall of Belshazzar's palace as the king hosted a feast for more than one thousand attendees. Meanwhile, outside the walls of Babylon, the Persian armies had laid siege to the city, and Cyrus was about to execute his plans for an invasion.

The Feast of Belshazzar

> Belshazzar the king made a great feast for a thousand of his
> lords, and drank wine in the presence of the thousand.
>
> DANIEL 5:1

The feast Belshazzar hosted was great in more ways than one.
First, there were one thousand of Belshazzar's lords in attendance.
That meant the actual numbers would have far exceeded that count
when attendants, servers, guards, wives, concubines, and lower-level
officials were included. Twentieth-century Old Testament scholar
H. C. Leupold cites the ancient historian Ktesias, who indicated
that ancient monarchs were frequently known to dine daily with
fifteen thousand people.[2]

Second, the hall the feast was held in was massive. It has been
unearthed by archaeologists and measures roughly 52 feet wide
by 170 feet long. The entire main section of the White House in
Washington, DC, is approximately that size. This was a huge party.

THE SENSUALITY OF THE FEAST

> Belshazzar the king . . . drank wine in the presence of
> the thousand.
>
> DANIEL 5:1

Belshazzar was not hosting a dignified, royal state dinner; this was
a drunken party. King Belshazzar violated royal protocol by drinking with his lords and inviting women to the feast. In most ancient
Near Eastern cultures, men and women had very little public interaction with each other and were customarily separated on social occasions. When the Persian king Xerxes gave a banquet for his officials,

Scripture says that "Queen Vashti also made a [separate] feast for the women" (Esther 1:2-3, 9).

When this protocol was violated, it usually meant that sensuality was involved. We see this in the Bible's explanation for why Xerxes violated custom and demanded that Queen Vashti leave the women's banquet to come to the men's party: "He wanted the nobles and all the other men to gaze on her beauty, for she was a very beautiful woman" (Esther 1:11, NLT).

Ancient kings abstained from wine at banquets in order to maintain an aura of authority and self-control in the presence of their subjects. The Old Testament, consistent with ancient Near Eastern standards, warned kings against becoming intoxicated: "It is not for kings, O Lemuel, it is not for kings to drink wine, nor for princes intoxicating drink; lest they drink and forget the law, and pervert the justice of all the afflicted" (Proverbs 31:4-5).

It is for good reason that "wine, women, and song" has been a catchphrase for trouble. All three were present at Belshazzar's feast, a sensual sinkhole of indulgence.

THE SACRILEGE OF THE FEAST

> While he tasted the wine, Belshazzar gave the command
> to bring the gold and silver vessels which his father
> Nebuchadnezzar had taken from the temple which had been
> in Jerusalem, that the king and his lords, his wives, and his
> concubines might drink from them. Then they brought
> the gold vessels that had been taken from the temple of the
> house of God which had been in Jerusalem; and the king
> and his lords, his wives, and his concubines drank from
> them. They drank wine, and praised the gods of gold and
> silver, bronze and iron, wood and stone.
>
> DANIEL 5:2-4

While Belshazzar was drinking his wine, he ordered the vessels Nebuchadnezzar had taken from the Temple in Jerusalem to be brought to the party. From these holy vessels, Belshazzar and his guests guzzled down drink after drink as they "praised the gods of gold and silver, bronze and iron, wood and stone" (verse 4).

In his book *Voices from Babylon,* Joseph Seiss writes, "Not only their ill-timed merriment, their trampling on the customary proprieties, and their drunkenness, but even their foolhardy and blasphemous insult to the most high God, is veiled over and cloaked up with a pretence of devotion! This was as far as it was possible for human daring and infatuation to go. It was more than the powers of Heaven could quietly endure. The divine resentment broke forth on the spot."[3]

THE STUPIDITY OF THE FEAST

Belshazzar didn't know it, but he was celebrating at his own funeral. The prophet Jeremiah gave specific details about Babylon's fall more than fifty years before it happened:

- A northern nation would conquer the city (Jeremiah 50:1-3, 9).
- This nation would be associated with the Medes (Jeremiah 51:11, 28).
- Babylon was described as a greatly fortified city (Jeremiah 51:53).
- Babylon would be taken by a trick or a snare (Jeremiah 50:24).
- The city's demise would involve the drying up of water (Jeremiah 51:36).
- This would be accomplished while a great feast was in progress (Jeremiah 51:39).
- This would be accomplished when Nebuchadnezzar's grandson was in power (Jeremiah 27:6-7).

When Belshazzar held this licentious feast, he was well aware that the armies of Cyrus had amassed around Babylon's walls. How could he and the Babylonians have been so naive to utterly ignore this threat to their city and their safety? John F. Walvoord helps us answer that question: "In many respects, Babylon was the most fabulous city of the ancient world both for the beauty of its architecture and for the safety of its huge walls and fortifications. It was hard for the Babylonians to believe that even the Medes and the Persians who had surrounded their beloved city could possibly breach the fortifications or exhaust their supplies which were intended to be ample for a siege of many years. Their confidence in their gods was bolstered by their confidence in their city."[4]

But it was misplaced confidence. Herodotus, famed as the father of history, gave a detailed report of Babylon's destruction, which I will include at the end of this chapter.

The Finger of God

THE SUPERNATURAL SIGN

> In the same hour the fingers of a man's hand appeared and wrote opposite the lampstand on the plaster of the wall of the king's palace; and the king saw the part of the hand that wrote.
> DANIEL 5:5

No doubt you recognize the following phrases commonly heard in everyday English: "a cross to bear," "a house divided against itself," "a labor of love," "sign of the times," "a two-edged sword," "reap what you sow," "go the extra mile," and "the twinkling of an eye." Do you know what they have in common? Along with many others, they are all taken from the Bible, most of them originating in the Authorized Version of 1611. For hundreds of years, English speakers have borrowed well-turned phrases from Scripture to express every-day realities. One of the best known of all—"the handwriting on the wall"—comes from Daniel 5, where God's prophetic message is written by supernatural fingers for all to see.

This is not the only time we see divine handwriting in Scripture. The finger of God wrote the Law on stone tablets for Moses (Exodus 31:18), and the finger of God wrote in the Judean sand in defense of a fallen but penitent woman (John 8:6). In this instance, the finger of God wrote a prophecy on the wall of Belshazzar's banquet hall that spelled the end of Babylon.

THE SOBERING SIGNIFICANCE

> The king's countenance changed, and his thoughts troubled him, so that the joints of his hips were loosened and his knees knocked against each other.
> DANIEL 5:6

It wasn't what was written on the wall that terrified Belshazzar. The king had no idea what the writing meant. Rather, it was the extraordinary sight of the fingers of a disembodied hand hovering in the air and writing words in giant letters—probably inscribing them over illustrated accounts of Babylon's conquests and achievements.

Imagine yourself in Belshazzar's situation: in a drunken crowd of thousands, surrounded by a decibel level off the charts, with your head swimming and your body out of control. Suddenly, shrieks and pointed fingers cause the drunken horde to fall silent as a giant hand moves across the illuminated wall.

The following phrases describe Belshazzar's reaction as he gaped at the eerie movements of the phantom fingers:

- "His countenance changed." Literally, "his color changed." We might say, "He turned white as a sheet."

- "His thoughts troubled him." An understatement, no doubt. Maybe he wondered if he'd aroused the anger of the Judean God he'd just mocked. Maybe it occurred to him that Babylon might not be as secure against the Persian army as he'd assumed.
- "The joints of his hips were loosened." Literally, the "knots of his loins" loosened. He had knots in his stomach, and his legs could no longer support him.
- "His knees knocked against each other." To this day, knocking knees remains a symbol of extreme fear.

This was certainly one of the fastest examples of sobering up in human history.

THE SIMULTANEOUS SUMMONS

The king cried aloud . . . , saying to the wise men of Babylon, "Whoever reads this writing, and tells me its interpretation, shall be clothed with purple and have a chain of gold around his neck; and he shall be the third ruler in the kingdom." Now all the king's wise men came, but they could not read the writing, or make known to the king its interpretation. Then King Belshazzar was greatly troubled, his countenance was changed, and his lords were astonished.
DANIEL 5:7-9

Belshazzar, along with everyone else in attendance, could read the letters that formed the writing on the wall, as it was Aramaic, the common language of the day. But they couldn't make sense of the words or their message. So Belshazzar cried out for his wise men to tell him what the words said and what they meant.

In the previous verse, we're told that when Belshazzar saw the writing on the wall, his "thoughts troubled him" (Daniel 5:6). But when his counselors couldn't tell him what the writing meant, we are told that he was "greatly troubled" (verse 9). Apparently, as he waited for his wise men to arrive, Belshazzar recovered some of the color in his face. But when they failed to give him the answer he sought, it all drained out again (verse 9).

The Fame of Daniel

Belshazzar had heard of Daniel's ability to interpret dreams and visions (Daniel 5:14-16). Even though it had last happened five kings ago, in Nebuchadnezzar's reign, Daniel's amazing prophetic gift was still the stuff of legend in the royal courts.

THE RECOLLECTION OF THE QUEEN

> The queen, because of the words of the king and his lords, came to the banquet hall. The queen spoke, saying, "O king, live forever! Do not let your thoughts trouble you, nor let your countenance change. There is a man in your kingdom in whom is the Spirit of the Holy God. And in the days of your father, light and understanding and wisdom, like the wisdom of the gods, were found in him; and King Nebuchadnezzar your father—your father the king—made him chief of the magicians, astrologers, Chaldeans, and soothsayers."
>
> DANIEL 5:10-11

When the king's wise men admitted that they couldn't interpret the handwriting on the wall, the queen entered the room. This is not Belshazzar's wife. His wives were already accounted for; they were right there in the banquet hall drinking with the king (Daniel 5:2).

Most scholars believe that the queen was the wife of the late

Nebuchadnezzar. She was literally the Queen Mother. She knew of Daniel's reputation and how her husband, Nebuchadnezzar, had honored him. Without hesitation, she stepped forward to make her recommendation.

THE RECOMMENDATION OF THE QUEEN

> Inasmuch as an excellent spirit, knowledge, understanding, interpreting dreams, solving riddles, and explaining enigmas were found in this Daniel, whom the king named Belteshazzar, now let Daniel be called, and he will give the interpretation.
>
> DANIEL 5:12

The queen could not say enough about Daniel. By her account, he was significant, spiritual, superior, and skillful. She had good reason for her glowing report, as she knew this man had not only interpreted Nebuchadnezzar's dream but also told the king what he'd dreamed—a feat unheard of among the king's royal counselors (Daniel 2). He had then interpreted the king's second dream, which was complex and prophetic, and his interpretation was fulfilled to the letter (Daniel 4).

The queen described Daniel the same way Nebuchadnezzar had: as a man filled with "the Spirit of the Holy God" (Daniel 4:8-9, 18).

THE REQUEST OF THE KING

> Daniel was brought in before the king. The king spoke, and said to Daniel, "Are you that Daniel who is one of the captives from Judah, whom my father the king brought from Judah? I have heard of you, that the Spirit of God is in you, and that light and understanding and excellent

wisdom are found in you. . . . And I have heard of you,
that you can give interpretations and explain enigmas.
Now if you can read the writing and make known to me its
interpretation, you shall be clothed with purple and have a
chain of gold around your neck, and shall be the third ruler
in the kingdom."

DANIEL 5:13-16

The king referred to Daniel in a way that makes it obvious he
no longer held a position among the wise men of Babylon. But he
seemed to have arrived at the palace promptly, which indicates that
even though he wasn't involved in Belshazzar's government, he still
lived in the vicinity.

I find it interesting that Daniel, now in his eighties, wasn't
invited to Belshazzar's banquet, but when a crisis hit, he was the one
summoned to save the day. Imagine the scene: Daniel arrives, and
Belshazzar wants to be sure this is the same Daniel who was brought
by Nebuchadnezzar as a captive from Jerusalem. Even as he spoke,
the holy vessels from the Temple of Daniel's God were scattered all
around them, some sloshing with wine, others lying on the floor or
overturned on the king's banquet table. Seeing these vessels—which
had been sanctified for the worship of God—desecrated by an inebri-
ated, pagan king must have broken Daniel's heart.

It's possible that Belshazzar felt a bit sheepish for asking a favor
of a man Babylon had wronged deeply in making him a captive.
Perhaps it was to make amends that Belshazzar offered Daniel gold,
a purple robe, and a position of prominence if he could interpret the
handwriting on the wall. Had Daniel glanced at the wall? Did he
already know the interpretation of the words? If so, he knew that this
was Babylon's last night. He could have laughed and said, "A position
in what kingdom?" But he held his tongue.

The Faithfulness of Daniel

Daniel knew his role. It wasn't to belittle the king of Babylon or to get rich and powerful at the king's expense, but to speak the truth of God.

HE REFUSED THE KING'S GIFTS

> Daniel answered, and said before the king, "Let your gifts be for yourself, and give your rewards to another; yet I will read the writing to the king, and make known to him the interpretation."
>
> DANIEL 5:17

Today we're familiar with the Latin term *quid pro quo*, especially in the realm of political deal making. It means "something for something"—you give me this, and I'll give you that in return. Similar expressions include "tit for tat" and "you scratch my back, and I'll scratch yours." They all mean the same thing: for a favor, I'll do what you want.

To avoid any semblance of a quid pro quo, Daniel refused the king's offer of gold, royal symbols, and a position of authority. Daniel worked for God, not for gold.

HE REVIEWED THE KING'S HERITAGE

> O king, the Most High God gave Nebuchadnezzar your father a kingdom and majesty, glory and honor. . . . But when his heart was lifted up, and his spirit was hardened in pride, he was deposed from his kingly throne, and they took his glory from him. Then he was driven from the sons of men, his heart was made like the beasts, and his dwelling was with the wild donkeys. They fed him with grass like

oxen, and his body was wet with the dew of heaven, till he knew that the Most High God rules in the kingdom of men, and appoints over it whomever He chooses.

DANIEL 5:18-21

After refusing the king's reward, Daniel recited for Belshazzar the history of Nebuchadnezzar's fall into temporary insanity. It was God's judgment against the king's pride. Daniel recounted this history to make it clear to the king that God is the supreme power above all earthly rulers. This account was a preamble for what Daniel said next: Belshazzar had fallen into the same prideful self-importance that had caused Nebuchadnezzar's undoing. This set up Belshazzar for the logical conclusion: if God had judged his predecessor, Nebuchadnezzar, why would He allow his own sin to go unpunished?

HE REBUKED THE KING'S SIN

Daniel detailed three sins God was holding Belshazzar accountable for.

1. The Charge of Premeditated Sin

You . . . Belshazzar, have not humbled your heart, although you knew all this.

DANIEL 5:22

History is a superb teacher, but Belshazzar failed as a student. He knew the history of Nebuchadnezzar's pride and God's subsequent judgment, but he failed to learn from it. He had witnessed in person Nebuchadnezzar's humiliation, and he still refused to humble himself under the hand of the almighty God. This was not a case of ignorance; it was arrogant defiance. It matters what we know, and it matters how we respond.

"Of how much worse punishment, do you suppose, will he be thought worthy who has trampled the Son of God underfoot, counted the blood of the covenant by which he was sanctified a common thing, and insulted the Spirit of grace?" (Hebrews 10:29).

2. The Charge of Profane Sacrilege

You have lifted yourself up against the Lord of heaven. They have brought the vessels of His house before you, and you and your lords, your wives and your concubines, have drunk wine from them.

DANIEL 5:23

The charges against Belshazzar became more serious: now Daniel moved on to blasphemy. Belshazzar had dishonored and demeaned the God of heaven by taking precious implements created for His worship and desecrating them with the worst kinds of sinful indulgence. It was a brazen display of impiety and contempt.

3. The Charge of Pagan Sacrifice

You have praised the gods of silver and gold, bronze and iron, wood and stone, which do not see or hear or know; and the God who holds your breath in His hand and owns all your ways, you have not glorified.

DANIEL 5:23

Not only did Belshazzar dishonor the living God by desecrating His vessels of gold and silver, but he also worshiped lifeless idols made of gold and silver.

Everything Belshazzar owned came from God (1 Chronicles 29:14). Instead of worshiping the living God out of gratitude for His gifts,

Belshazzar worshiped inanimate idols made of silver, gold, bronze, iron, wood, and stone, which do not hear or see or know (Deuteronomy 4:28; Psalm 115:5-7; 135:16-17).

Belshazzar chose to worship dead images instead of the true God of heaven "in whose hand is the life of every living thing, and the breath of all mankind" (Job 12:10).

HE REVEALED THE KING'S MESSAGE

The handwriting on the wall was brief: "MENE, MENE, TEKEL, UPHARSIN" (Daniel 5:25). Three words in Aramaic, the first word repeated for emphasis. These words were terms for measuring quantities, weighing goods on a scale for purchase or trade, and apportioning items. Generally, here's what they mean:

- *Mene* ("numbered"): Belshazzar had been measured, counted, and scrutinized.
- *Tekel* ("weighed"): Belshazzar had been weighed according to God's standards of righteousness and found to come short.
- *Upharsin* ("and divided" or "halved"): This is a reference to Babylon being divided between the Medes and Persians.

String the words together, and the message is essentially, "Numbered, weighed, and divided." It's little wonder that the Babylonian wise men could find no meaning in this sparse phrase. It was a cryptic code, impossible to make sense of unless one already knew its meaning. Daniel could read it because God had revealed the meaning to him.

Leon Wood wraps up the meaning of this scene for us: "In summary, Daniel's interpretation set forth that Belshazzar's kingdom would be destroyed, for the reason that he had been found lacking in moral and spiritual value, and that the encroaching enemy, the Medes and Persians, would absorb the kingdom into their larger domain."[5]

The Fall of Babylon

> That very night Belshazzar, king of the Chaldeans, was slain. And Darius the Mede received the kingdom, being about sixty-two years old.
>
> DANIEL 5:30-31

The most famous military tactic in history may be the Greeks' use of a giant wooden horse to sneak soldiers into the city of Troy. But ranking right up there with the Trojan horse is the story of how the Medo-Persian armies captured Babylon. Scholars debate whether the Trojan horse is fact or legend, but Cyrus's conquest of Babylon is certified fact. The highly regarded Greek historian Herodotus wrote a full account of the event:

> Cyrus . . . having thus stationed the bulk of his army near the passage of the river where it enters Babylon, and again having stationed another division beyond the city, where the river makes its exit, . . . gave orders to his forces to enter the city as soon as they should see the stream fordable. Having thus stationed his forces and given these directions, he himself marched away with the ineffective part of his army; and having come to the lake, Cyrus . . . diverted the river, by means of a canal, into the lake, which was before a swamp, he made the ancient channel fordable by the sinking of the river. When this took place, the Persians who were appointed to that purpose close to the stream of the river, which had now subsided to about the middle of a man's thigh, entered Babylon by this passage. . . . It is related by the people who inhabited this city, that . . . the Babylonians who inhabited the centre knew nothing of the capture (for it happened to be a festival); but they were dancing at the

time, and enjoying themselves. . . . And thus Babylon was taken for the first time.[6]

On the night of October 11, 539 BC, the Medo-Persian army slipped beneath the wall of Babylon and put Belshazzar to death. The prophecies of Jeremiah were fulfilled; Babylon had fallen to its enemies.

Daniel 4 marks the end of Nebuchadnezzar, the builder of Babylon. Chapter 5 marks the end of Belshazzar and of Babylon. The head of gold on the colossus was now defeated by the chest and arms of silver. Babylon was absorbed into the inferior empire of the Medes and Persians.

As we close this chapter, we do well to heed the words of John F. Walvoord:

The downfall of Babylon is in type the downfall of the unbelieving world. In many respects, modern civilization is much like ancient Babylon, resplendent with its monuments of architectural triumph, as secure as human hands and ingenuity could make it, and yet defenseless against the judgment of God at the proper hour. Contemporary civilization is similar to ancient Babylon in that it has much to foster human pride but little to provide human security. Much as Babylon fell on that sixteenth day of Tishri (Oc. 11 or 12) 539 B.C., as indicated in the Nabonidus Chronicle, so the world will be overtaken by disaster when the day of the Lord comes (1 Th 5:1-3). The disaster of the world, however, does not overtake the child of God; Daniel survives the purge and emerges triumphant as one of the presidents of the new kingdom in chapter 6.[7]

[God] brings the princes to nothing;
He makes the judges of the earth useless.

Scarcely shall they be planted,
Scarcely shall they be sown,
Scarcely shall their stock take root in the earth,
When He will also blow on them,
And they will wither,
And the whirlwind will take them away like stubble.

ISAIAH 40:23-24

* * *

DANIEL FOR TODAY

The scenes of Belshazzar's banquet are painted so vividly that we can close our eyes and imagine we're there. Opening our eyes, we find ourselves in a similar world—a culture awash with the sensual, gluttonous, provocative, and unholy. Since we are today's Daniels standing in the banquet halls of modern Belshazzars, I want to leave you with three things to remember.

1. Don't ever think God is finished with you. Daniel, now in his eighties, was no longer serving Babylon in an official capacity, and as far as we can tell, the younger generation had forgotten him. But God kept him alive for this moment, and when the time came, only Daniel could deliver the message. Whatever your stage in life, stay spiritually healthy and ready to serve at a moment's notice.

2. Don't worry too much about fame and fortune in a perishing world. Daniel had undoubtedly been a wise steward of his possessions and made provisions for his later years, but he had no interest in the king's offer of robes and a high position. He knew those were merely temporary trinkets. Daniel was awaiting an eternal reward.

3. Don't neglect passages about God's wrath and judgment. We consume lots of information on positive topics, which is needed. But we hear little of the kind of prophetic and apostolic warnings issued in the Bible. When the apostle Paul met privately with Governor Felix, he spoke to him about "righteousness, self-control, and the judgment to come" (Acts 24:25). The writer to the Hebrews warned of "a certain fearful expectation of judgment, and fiery indignation" falling on the unrepentant world (Hebrews 10:27). It's hard to find a revival movement in history that didn't contain prophetic preaching about the reality of the judgment of God. This message is mission critical for our times.

These days aren't for the faint at heart! Like Daniel, we need strength to stay useful, wisdom to focus on the unseen, and courage to warn our world of the judgment to come.

Chapter 7

THE LION KING

Daniel 6:1-28

KING DARIUS SAT in his palace chambers poring over yet another letter from one of his provinces. As he rubbed his forehead with his thumb and fingers, his chamberlain entered the room. "My king, may I bring you a drink to ease your pain?"

"It will take more than that," Darius replied. "And I'm afraid things are about to get worse. Call in Belok and Kamur."

While the king waited for two of his three governors to arrive, he thought back over the year that had passed since Cyrus the Persian conquered Babylon and placed him on the throne as deputy ruler. Most of the transitional chaos in the 120 provinces had now been brought under control. But recently he'd been receiving a number of complaints of government corruption and financial fraud. The people were starting to strain against the firm rule of the military units that occupied the territories. The only provinces free of such complaints were the forty ruled by his third governor, Daniel. In fact, Daniel had been known to *reduce* the military presence in his provinces. In spite of these reductions, Darius was unable to trim the size of his expensive army, because these units had to be deployed to other provinces to put down rebellions.

Belok and Kamur entered and took the seats offered to them at the king's table. Darius summarized the complaints he'd received and demanded explanations from the two governors.

"O great king," Belok said, "we are most happy to answer you. Resentment and resistance are to be expected among conquered peoples. Your Babylonian predecessors, Nabonidus and Belshazzar, gave little attention to ruling the empire, which allowed these resentments to simmer and boil over. The only way to deal with them is the tried and true Persian way—by force. It's all these people understand."

"Why haven't I received any complaints from Daniel's provinces?"

"I'm glad you brought up his name," Kamur replied. "He isn't as honest and loyal as you think. We've learned that he has discharged more than half the satraps you appointed for his provinces."

"Well, then, let's bring in Daniel to answer the charge for himself."

In a matter of moments, Daniel was ushered in, still tall and clear eyed despite his eighty-plus years.

"Daniel," Darius said, "you have been charged with dismissing half of your provincial satraps. What do you have to say for yourself?"

"I didn't dismiss them, my king; they chose to resign rather than accept my conditions. I demanded strict independent accounting of all their expenditures, and I required that they move to the provinces they would govern instead of administrating from here in Babylon. No satrap can be effective in absentia. Most of them chose to remain here among their peers."

"That's an outrageous demand!" Belok said. "No statesman wants to leave the center of power and exile himself in the backcountry."

"The kind of leaders we need will do exactly that," Daniel replied. "They'll want to know and understand their people, and that means living among them."

"Daniel," Darius said, "why don't you use force to deal with unrest in your provinces, as your fellow governors do?"

"Unrest always has an underlying—and often legitimate—cause," Daniel replied. "It serves us well as leaders to listen and learn. In most cases, a simple compromise can appease the people and protect our interests while costing us nothing. And when we work for an agreeable resolution, the people begin to trust us and become cooperative, which eliminates the need for force."

Darius turned to Belok and Kamur. "That, my dear governors, is exactly how I want my empire to be run. To ensure that it happens, I have chosen to restore Daniel to the position he held under Nebuchadnezzar. He will be appointed the new prime minister of the empire."

The king ended the meeting, and the three governors bowed and left.

Belok, seething with anger, pulled Kamur aside. "This won't do! I've been Darius's counselor for two decades. I should have been the one promoted."

"I can't stand the thought of reporting my every move to a Jew," Kamur said.

"We can't allow this appointment to stand. We must find a way to discredit Daniel before the king."

"But how? From everything I've heard about Daniel, he's blameless in all his actions."

"Trust me, there's not a man alive who doesn't hide some vile habit, corruption, or depravity. We must find that corner in Daniel's life and expose it."

The two conspirators met for the next several days in the king's park just outside the city and worked out an elaborate investigation of Daniel. They bribed a house servant to report his every activity. They hired spies to follow him every time he left his house. They paid off servants in the palace to eavesdrop on all his conversations, open his scrolls and letters at night, and report their contents.

Yet after three months of intense surveillance, they found nothing. Just as they were ready to scrap their plan and devise another, one of the servants reported seeing a young woman enter Daniel's house shortly after sundown. Belok summoned Haban, the informer in Daniel's home. "It appears that Daniel has formed an illicit liaison with a young woman who visits him after dark."

"No, my lord," Haban replied. "She's a recently widowed Jew. Daniel gave her money to stave off poverty. He often does things like that for people in need."

"But surely she gave him something in return."

"No, she did nothing of the sort."

"Did you see them the entire time she was there?"

"No, my lord."

"Then how can you possibly know that they did nothing immoral?"

"Because Daniel is a eunuch, my lord."

The two frustrated conspirators met in the park again. "I've never seen anything like it," Kamur said.

"Apparently this Daniel has no stain on his past and no vice in his present. His only unusual behavior is what Haban reported to us—that he faces Jerusalem and prays to his God three times every day, no matter what."

"If that's all we have, then we must find a way to use it," Belok replied.

* * *

The two men began proposing and rejecting one scheme after another until suddenly a deep roar thundered from the direction of the king's stables.

Kamur froze. "What was that?"

"It's a lion. They're brought from the mountains for the king's hunting parties. The holding den is filled with them."

"That's the most terrifying sound I've ever heard."

Belok stopped suddenly. "I have an idea. You know that Darius has been sending all the idols Nebuchadnezzar took during his conquests back to the provinces. It's a boon to the provinces, but their removal from Babylon sometimes frustrates those who worshiped them. Perhaps we can convince the king that it's a problem needing to be addressed."

"What does that have to do with Daniel?"

"Just hear me out. We convince Darius that he could solve this problem by providing a new god that everyone must worship. We provide this god by appealing to his vanity. Then we convince him to issue an edict that no one can pray to anyone but him for thirty days."

A grin lit up Kamur's face. "Yes, I see now. Daniel will keep praying to his God, and we'll arrest him for violating the law. The king will be forced to depose him."

"No—not depose him. Feed him to those lions. That will be the punishment for violating the edict."

"But can we convince the king that such a law is needed? I've heard only a handful of minor complaints over the removal of the images."

"But there were complaints," Belok replied. "We'll have our satraps stand before the king and amplify those complaints. They hate Daniel just as much as we do."

"I like it," Kamur said. "I really think this could work."

Belok set up a meeting with the king. He picked a time seven days away, knowing the appointment would be wedged between the negotiation of a trade agreement and an evening banquet. The king would be exhausted and easy to manipulate. Kamur, meanwhile, bribed the king's huntsman to withhold food from the lions until further notice.

On the appointed day, the two governors and their satraps gathered in the great hall before the king and presented their petition. The satraps gave an exaggerated report of religious unrest, according to Belok's script. Then Kamur proposed a solution to cool things down: for thirty days, no resident of Babylon would be allowed to pray to or petition anyone other than the king. Those who violated the edict would be cast into the den of lions.

"Your proposal has two problems," Darius responded. "First, I am not a god, nor do I have any interest in becoming one."

"Of course not, my king," Belok replied. "You are the very model of kingly modesty. That's why we limited the decree to thirty days."

"After which you'll allow me to revert to mere humanity," the king said wryly. "The second problem is your penalty. Being devoured by lions is a severe punishment for a mere religious infraction."

"True, O king," Belok replied. "But the severity will deter the rioting."

"Is the problem really so bad? I've heard nothing of it until this meeting."

"That's because of your diligence in performing the higher duties of your office. We, your governors and satraps, take seriously our duty to insulate you from mundane issues. We would not be unified in our request if it were not truly urgent."

After several more minutes of discussion, King Darius, tired to the bone and strangely attracted to the idea of being viewed as a deity, signed the edict. It was entered into the records of the kingdom, which according to the laws of the Medes and Persians could not be altered or rescinded, even by the king.

* * *

Daniel was working in his wing of the palace when news of the edict reached him. Fully understanding the implications, he dismissed his staff for the day and went home. Belok, along with two of his most trusted satraps, followed at a discreet distance. The informer, Haban, let them into Daniel's house through the servants' door and led them stealthily up the stairway.

Daniel entered his private chambers, opened his window toward Jerusalem, and dropped to his knees in prayer to God. Belok and the two satraps listened silently from behind the door and then crept away.

The following morning, the conspirators were waiting at the entrance of the throne room when King Darius arrived. They bowed low, and Belok spoke in a voice dripping with false sorrow.

"O my king, how deeply I regret that I must be the bearer of disturbing news. The ink on yesterday's edict is hardly dry, and already a violator has been discovered."

"Who is it?" the king asked.

"I—I can hardly say it, for he is someone you loved and trusted." After a pause, he went on. "The violator is Daniel, my lord. Though he knew of the edict, he blatantly violated it by praying to his God—not once, but three times. Obviously the man has no regard for your authority."

The king's face went white. He fought to control his regret and grief and fury—regret that he'd signed such a foolish edict, grief over the fate he'd unwittingly imposed on his friend, and fury because he could now see the conspirators' scheme.

Belok finally dared to break the silence: "My king, I see that you are deeply grieved. Please allow me to take this burden off your hands. I will have Daniel seized and—"

"Lay one finger on Daniel, and it will be you who feels the lions' fangs. Out of here! All of you!"

The conspirators scurried from the hall, and Darius called for his lawyers. He pressed them to find some obscure point of Medo-Persian law allowing royal edicts to be rescinded. But the lawyers assured him that no such provision existed.

In desperation, the king began to propose any scheme that came to mind that might save Daniel. He would send a message urging Daniel to flee. No, the lawyers said, the conspirators would be watching his doors. He would remove the lions before casting Daniel into the den. No, it would no longer be a "den of lions," as specified in the decree. He would have the lions slain and left in the den. No, that would circumvent the edict: a dead lion is not a lion but merely a carcass. Darius proposed many more schemes, all of which were quickly rejected.

The sun was almost down, and Darius was about to dismiss the lawyers when Belok and Kamur entered the hall.

Belok bowed. "Forgive our intrusion, O great king, but knowing your diligence in keeping the law, and knowing that all sentences must be executed by sundown, we came to inform you that Daniel's execution has not yet occurred. Apparently your guards have failed to carry it out."

Seeing the king's lawyers and suspecting their purpose, Belok added, "You know, my king, that the law of the Medes and Persians allows no decree signed by the king to be changed."

"I know more than you think." Darius's voice was cold. "You need not worry. Daniel will be executed precisely according to the law. And both of you will acknowledge your hand in his death by adding your signets to the seal."

Darius called in the captain of the guard, issued the command for Daniel's execution, and left the hall.

The king's den of lions was a vast cavern with a natural opening in the side of a sheer cliff. It was said to be the cave where Nebuchadnezzar had slept during his seven years of insanity. A wooden door reinforced with iron now covered the opening, which was used to allow lions into the partially wooded field for the king and his nobles to hunt. The field covered several acres and was enclosed by a high iron fence. A rough opening at the top of the cave served as a food drop to the lions below.

King Darius stood waiting in the twilight near this tunnel, chilled by the growl of half-starved lions. The guards' cart that transported Daniel arrived, and just behind it came the opulent carriage of Belok and Kamur. The moment Daniel stepped out, Darius hurried to meet him, his face wet with tears.

"Daniel, my dear friend, I've made a terrible mistake. You're facing this ordeal because of my own foolishness. I pray that you will forgive me."

"I do forgive you, my king. But save your prayer and offer it to the God of heaven on my behalf."

"Yes, I will pray that your God will deliver you from the mouths of the lions."

The guards escorted Daniel to the pit. He went without resistance, his head held high. They eased him into the shaft and released him. Immediately the roars grew frenzied, mixing with vicious snarls as the lions fought to be first to reach the morsel when it hit the floor.

Darius clapped his hands over his ears. He ordered the guards to close the door of the shaft and seal it. He pressed his signet ring into the wax and watched as Belok and Kamur stepped forward and added their signets. Darius ordered guards to remain by the stone through the night. Then, with his head down, he plodded to his carriage and returned to the palace.

The king went straight to his private chambers. Servants brought him food, but he refused to eat. They brought musicians, but he sent them away. The queen came to comfort him, but he asked her to leave. Servants offered wine to help him sleep, but he sent it back.

For the first time in his life, this mighty monarch, ruler of the Medo-Persian Empire, the largest the world had yet seen, fell on his face and prayed to the God of the Jews—the God who had no image, no face, and no name but I Am.

He prayed on his knees. He prayed on his face. He prayed while pacing around his bedchamber. No sleep came to the king that night.

* * *

When the first rays of sunlight broke the horizon, Darius had his chariot rigged and drove it himself to the lions' den. "Remove the stone!" he cried. He leaped down from his chariot and ran to the opening. "Daniel! Daniel!" He peered into the shaft. "Has your God delivered you from the lions?"

"He has, my king. God's angel stayed beside me the entire night and turned these ferocious beasts into fawning kittens."

Darius's heart soared, and words failed him.

"My king," Daniel called, "God's protection is proof of my loyalty to you. So if you will free me, I'll gladly continue in your service."

Darius gave the order, and the guards lowered a rope into the den and pulled Daniel out. He had no marks from fangs or claws anywhere on his body or clothing. The happy king put an arm around Daniel's shoulder, escorted him to his chariot, and drove him back to the palace.

An hour later, King Darius ascended his throne and ordered Belok and Kamur brought to him.

"O great and mighty king," Belok said, bowing low, "we are honored that you called us. We're ready to serve you in any way you wish."

"Since you were so eager to serve me in the matter of ridding the kingdom of Daniel, I thought it only fitting to show you what remains of his body as a memorial of your service."

"Oh, no, my king. No such token is necessary. We were only too happy to protect your throne from that troublesome Jew."

"Oh, I insist," the king responded. "It will be my pleasure to show you. Captain, please bring in the body of Daniel."

The two men turned as the captain opened the door and Daniel stepped inside. Their jaws dropped, and their eyes widened in terror. "How—how is this possible?" Kamur cried. "We saw him thrust into the den. We heard the lions fighting over him."

"Daniel's God saved him from the lions," Darius said. "Now, we will see if your gods can save you. Captain, escort these manipulators and their families to the den of lions, and cast them into it."

"No! Please, my king!" Belok shrieked. "We were only trying to do you good. Perhaps we were mistaken."

The king didn't respond. He was writing on a square of parchment.

"If you cannot forgive us, then please send us into exile." Kamur fell to his knees. "You'll never see our faces again."

Darius continued to write.

"If not exile, then imprison us." Belok was now on his face before the king. "Please! Anything but the lions' den."

Darius looked up. "I'm sorry, but I can't do that." He held up the parchment. "You see, I have already written the decree, and according to the law of the Medes and Persians, it cannot be rescinded. Captain, come forward and do your duty."

The two men were dragged from the hall as their protests reverberated from the rafters.

Just before noon, the captain reported that the executions had been carried out as ordered. "Not one of them even reached the floor of the den, my king. The lions were raging at the base of the hole, tearing flesh and snapping bones. You'd think they hadn't been fed in a week."

The king's next act was to dictate a letter, which began as follows and was distributed throughout the empire:

I make a decree that in every dominion of my kingdom men must tremble and fear before the God of Daniel. For He is the living God, steadfast forever; His kingdom is the one which shall not be destroyed, and His dominion shall endure to the end.[1]

Darius didn't replace his two governors. Instead, he reinstalled Daniel as prime minister over all the satraps of the empire. Daniel served well throughout the reign of Darius and even into the reign of Cyrus.

* * *

THE SCRIPTURE BEHIND THE STORY

As of this writing, attorney-politician James A. Baker III is eighty-five years old. For more than forty of those years, he has had a hand in politics in Washington, DC. Many so-called "career politicians" could be named, but there are few with careers as unique as Baker's. Although he'd be content to work as an attorney in Houston, he has continually been called into the corridors of power in Washington as an appointed counselor to presidents—from one administration to the next.

Baker first became involved in politics serving in the election campaigns of Richard Nixon and George H. W. Bush. When Gerald Ford succeeded Richard Nixon as president, Baker became the undersecretary of commerce, and later he became the White House chief of staff for President Reagan. Reagan then named Baker secretary of the treasury, and he became chairman of Reagan's successful reelection campaign. Baker also served on the Economic Policy Council and the National Security Council. When George H. W. Bush came into office, he named Baker secretary of state and chief of staff.

After his presidential roles, Baker served the UN secretary-general Kofi Annan as a diplomatic envoy, headed up George W. Bush's legal team during the infamous voter recounts in Florida, and served as a consultant to Congress and the Bush White House on Iraq. Along with former president Jimmy Carter, he cochaired the Federal Commission on Election Reform, was cochair of the National War Powers Commission, and is currently honorary cochair of the World Justice Project. The list of appointments and awards could go on and on.

Are you seeing a pattern here? Sometimes a person has political and relational skills that make him highly sought after by those in power. The task doesn't seem to matter: treasury, commerce, political strategy, international envoy, consensus building. The skill set includes whatever is needed to keep the machinery of politics moving forward.

My point is not to set a certain person on a pedestal but to give contemporary context to something we observe in the life of Daniel. As a conquered captive who never sought to advance his own agenda, Daniel was continually invited into places of power. In his case, these opportunities were the result of God's blessing on Daniel for his faithfulness and obedience. Even when one administration (the Babylonian Empire) gave way to another (the Medo-Persian Empire), Daniel was a constant; he was consistently sought out by various rulers to play a critical role.

At the end of Daniel 5, we saw the fall of Babylon and the rise of Darius the Mede (Daniel 5:30-31). About two years later, Daniel, by then in his eighties, was called back into the mainstream of political power in the new kingdom of Medo-Persia. He was a man of rare faith—Ezekiel, his contemporary, placed Daniel in the same circle as Noah and Job (Ezekiel 14:14, 20). Daniel's beyond-reproach character made him attractive to people in power—people who weren't always sure who could be trusted.

Daniel Is Preferred by Darius

It pleased Darius to set over the kingdom one hundred and twenty satraps . . . and over these, three governors, of whom Daniel was one, that the satraps might give account to them, so that the king would suffer no loss. Then this Daniel distinguished himself above the governors and satraps because an excellent spirit was in him; and the king gave thought to setting him over the whole realm.

DANIEL 6:1-3

Under Darius, another great world empire was established around 539 BC. Babylon's head of gold was gone, and the breast and arms of silver were established. Absolute monarchy was replaced by a system of governmental hierarchy that involved constitutional law—"the law of the Medes and Persians" (Daniel 6:8, 12, 15). The king no longer ruled simply by whim; he was subject to written law, even though he could pass these laws by unilateral decree. There was, therefore, some decrease in the monarch's absolute power.

Darius determined to reorganize the government, and 120 satraps were placed in charge of the conquered provinces and kingdoms that comprised the empire. Apparently, part of their responsibility was to collect taxes for the king. Because there was dishonesty among these lower-level officials, Darius selected three men as governors so the king "would suffer no loss" (Daniel 6:2).

Of these three governors, Darius was most impressed with Daniel and selected him to function as the prime minister over all the land. According to the description in Daniel 6, Daniel was preferred above the other governors and satraps because "an excellent spirit" was in him (verse 3). This is the same phrase that is used to describe him in Daniel 5:12. It means he had a good attitude and worked hard to fulfill his responsibilities.

Daniel continued to honor God with his life, and now God was honoring Daniel again. King Darius "gave thought to setting him over the whole realm" (Daniel 6:3). Daniel was to become the second-in-command over all the Medo-Persian Empire, a fact that didn't go unnoticed by Daniel's peers.

Daniel Is Persecuted by His Enemies

The governors and satraps sought to find some charge against Daniel.

DANIEL 6:4

We can use the metaphor introduced by the apostle John—light and darkness (John 1)—to describe Daniel's presence in Persia. Jesus came into a dark world as the Light, and the darkness did everything it could to snuff out that light. In a similar way, Daniel, by virtue of God's blessing and his irreproachable character, was a beacon of light amid the pagan ethos that governed the Medo-Persian Empire. Daniel represented an obstacle to those who wanted to profit from their positions through unethical means. Therefore, it was natural for them to hate Daniel and try to get him removed from his position.

At the core of his colleagues' hatred was their intense jealousy of Daniel's position in the kingdom. He'd risen in rank and was about to become their superior. If Darius's appointment was carried out, Daniel would have power over all governors and administrators. So they determined to get Daniel out of their way. They hoped to catch him committing some trespass he could be indicted for, but they couldn't find anything to hold against him. The more they searched, the angrier they became.

Clarence Macartney has imagined the conversation that might have taken place between Daniel's would-be accusers:

> One of them says, "Let us 'frame' Daniel. Let us forge letters and bring them to the king, stating that Daniel has been in treasonable correspondence with foreign princes and that he plans to rebel against Darius and overthrow his dynasty." But one of the others answers: "No, there is no use in trying that. Daniel has served too long and too loyally under three kings . . . for anyone to believe such a charge against him as that." Then another makes this suggestion: "Daniel has charge of the finances of the realm. Let us charge him with . . . dishonesty." But another answers, "That, too, will be in vain. No charge against the honesty of Daniel, who has handled the funds of three kingdoms will be entertained for

a moment. . . . Then the third conspirator comes forward with his suggestion: "There is only one plan that will work." "What is that?" ask the others. "We must devise some plan," says he, "by which Daniel's loyalty to the king will be brought into collision with his loyalty to God. . . . We will persuade Darius to sign a decree to the effect that for thirty days no prayer shall be made to any man or to any God save Darius. That will do the business; for if there is anything that is certain, it is that Daniel will never obey such a decree."[2]

The hatred of these men grew, for "envy . . . hates that excellence it cannot reach."[3] The final conclusion of his adversaries after their exhaustive scrutiny is summarized in Daniel 6:5: "We shall not find any charge against this Daniel unless we find it against him concerning the law of his God."

As William Heslop observes, "Never was a loftier tribute paid to mortal man than the enemies of Daniel paid to him that day. What a tremendous tribute to the trustworthiness of this public servant! The religion of Daniel operated with such power as to exclude everything in his conduct which might furnish a handle with which he might be accused and justly hurt."[4]

These men proceeded to conceive a plot based on two ingredients: falsehood and flattery.

THE FALSEHOOD

All the governors of the kingdom, the administrators and satraps, the counselors and advisors, have consulted together to establish a royal statute and to make a firm decree, that whoever petitions any god or man for thirty days, except you, O king, shall be cast into the den of lions.

DANIEL 6:7

Daniel's enemies assembled together before the king, proposing a new law: anyone who prayed to any god besides Darius for thirty days would be put to death in the lions' den. There was a lie in their proposal: not all the officials had consulted together. Daniel, the most prominent official of all, had been excluded. Naturally, the conspirators didn't mention this fact.

THE FLATTERY

Now, O king, establish the decree and sign the writing, so that it cannot be changed, according to the law of the Medes and Persians, which does not alter.
DANIEL 6:8

In effect, the proposal would make Darius "god for a month." These leaders did what they could to get the king to sign the edict, which according to law, could not be revoked once put in place. The king was considered infallible; once he put a law on the books, not even he could rescind it. In a moment he would come to regret, Darius signed the law (Daniel 6:9).

Daniel Is Persistent in Serving God

When Daniel knew that the writing was signed, he went home. And in his upper room, with his windows open toward Jerusalem, he knelt down on his knees three times that day, and prayed and gave thanks before his God, as was his custom since early days.
DANIEL 6:10

When Daniel discovered that the law had been signed by Darius, he did nothing out of the ordinary. His daily habit for years had been to pray to God toward Jerusalem three times a day—and that's exactly what he did the day he learned of the new law. In other words, he didn't change a thing. He went about his daily schedule of worship as he always did.

What can we glean about Daniel from his actions here? Clearly, he was faithful and fearless without regard to the consequences. And he was consistent. He was consistent in his *professional life*, as recognized by the king himself. He was consistent in his *personal life*—his detractors could find nothing to accuse him of. And he was consistent in his *prayer life*.

If anyone could have offered the excuse "I don't have time to pray," it would have been Daniel. Imagine the demands on his time as a governor of the mighty Medo-Persian Empire. Yet he found time—three times each day—to pray.

Daniel Is Protected by His God

The Lord didn't prevent Daniel from being thrown into the lions' den. But through all the events that transpired—the king's displeasure, Daniel's delivery to the den, and the king's depression—we see God's hand of protection over Daniel's life.

THE DISPLEASURE OF THE KING

> They answered and said before the king, "That Daniel . . . does not show due regard for you, O king, or for the decree that you have signed, but makes his petition three times a day." And the king, when he heard these words, was greatly displeased with himself, and set his heart on Daniel to deliver him; and he labored till the going down of the sun to deliver him. Then these men approached the king, and said to the king, "Know, O king, that it is the law of the

Medes and Persians that no decree or statute which the king establishes may be changed."

DANIEL 6:13-15

Darius's conscience was tormenting him. He knew the danger he had put his friend Daniel in by signing into law the preposterous thirty-day prayer ban. He worked all day trying to find a loophole in the law. He knew if he couldn't find one, he'd have to sentence Daniel to death. Persian law dictated that sentences for crimes were to be carried out on the day the crime was committed. The lower the sun set in the horizon, the louder Darius's conscience became, screaming at him to find a solution that would save the man who could save his kingdom from corruption.

THE DELIVERY OF DANIEL TO THE DEN

The king gave the command, and they brought Daniel and cast him into the den of lions. But the king spoke, saying to Daniel, "Your God, whom you serve continually, He will deliver you." Then a stone was brought and laid on the mouth of the den, and the king sealed it with his own signet ring and with the signets of his lords, that the purpose concerning Daniel might not be changed.

DANIEL 6:16-17

Old Testament scholar C. F. Keil describes a holding pen for lions that was observed in Morocco. It was underground and open to the sky, and a four-foot-tall wall surrounded the circumference of the cavern. The cavern had a wall that divided it in half, and there was a door in the wall that could be raised and lowered from above. The keepers could throw meat into one side of the cavern and raise the door to allow the lions to get to it. Lowering the door left half the cavern empty, making it suitable for cleaning. Such a cavern would fit the lions' den Daniel found himself in.[5]

Another writer has theorized what Daniel's experience might have been like during the night he spent in the lions' den:

> As the guards closed the aperture and went their way, Daniel slid gradually to the floor of the den. The big lions that had come bounding from their caverns at the inflow of light all stopped suddenly short as a steed reigned up by a powerful hand on the bridle. The initial roars died away as they formed a solid phalanx and looked toward this man who stood in their den in easy reach. There was some snorting and a little whining, and some of them turned around and went back to their caverns. Others of the great beasts yawned and lay down on the floor, but not one made a move to advance toward their visitor.
>
> "Thanks be unto Jehovah," breathed the prophet. "He hath stopped the mouths of these fierce beasts: that they will do me no harm." He sat down on the floor of the den and leaned his back against the wall to make himself comfortable for the night. Soon two cub lions moved in his direction, not stealthily or crouching as though to make an attack, but in obvious friendliness, and one lay on each side of Daniel as though to give him warmth and protection in the chilly dungeon. Presently their mother, an old lioness, crept over and lay in front of the prophet. He gently stroked their backs as they each turned their heads and licked his hand. . . . Enclosed by the lioness and her cubs, the head of the patriarch was gradually pillowed on the back of one of the cubs as the four slept soundly in perfect peace and tranquility.[6]

Many people are familiar with the Briton Rivière painting of Daniel standing in the lions' den, his back to the lions in quiet contemplation, hands behind his back. The lions are arranged in a semicircle around him, some standing still, others padding back and forth. The expression on the lions' faces is a mixture of perplexity and awe. Here is a meal standing in front of them, but they are somehow restrained from attacking, as if an invisible shield is keeping them from moving toward Daniel.

This scene stands in stark contrast to a scene no one, to the best of my knowledge, has painted: when Daniel's accusers and their families were tossed into the den the following day. The lions jumped into the air and attacked the victims before they hit the floor, crushing the people in their mighty jaws (Daniel 6:24). One scene conveys serenity and peace under the will of God; the other chaos and judgment under the will of man.

THE DEPRESSION OF THE KING

> The king went to his palace and spent the night fasting; and no musicians were brought before him. Also his sleep went from him.
>
> DANIEL 6:18

While Daniel slept like a lamb, even though he was being watched over by lions, Darius tossed and turned. He didn't eat; he couldn't sleep. He was counting the minutes until sunrise when he would discover Daniel's fate. He was probably asking himself over and over, *Why did I agree to play the role of a god for thirty days? What was I thinking?* His vanity and weak will cost him his supper and his sleep. The lions wanted to eat but couldn't; the king could eat but wouldn't. It was a unique night in Persia.

THE DELIVERANCE OF DANIEL IN THE DEN

> The king arose very early in the morning and went in haste
> to the den of lions. And when he came to the den, he cried
> out with a lamenting voice to Daniel. The king spoke, saying
> to Daniel, "Daniel, servant of the living God, has your God,
> whom you serve continually, been able to deliver you from
> the lions?"
>
> DANIEL 6:19-20

When Darius cast Daniel into the lions' den, he expressed faith
that Daniel would survive: "Your God, whom you serve continually,
He will deliver you" (Daniel 6:16). But the king's faith proved not to
be very strong, as evidenced by his anxiety through the night and by
the first words out of his mouth the next morning: "Has your God . . .
been able to deliver you from the lions?" (verse 20). Not only was the
king uncertain of God's will, he wasn't even sure God could save Daniel
from the lions. There is no sign of saving faith in Darius's life. His perspective about Daniel's God was based on Daniel's character and the
power of his God compared to the other gods in the Mesopotamian
pantheon. It was a start, but it wasn't saving faith—then or now.

The Response

> Daniel said to the king, "O king, live forever! My God sent
> His angel and shut the lions' mouths, so that they have not
> hurt me, because I was found innocent before Him; and
> also, O king, I have done no wrong before you."
>
> DANIEL 6:21-22

God shut the mouths of the lions and saved Daniel from death.
The famed London preacher Charles Spurgeon observed that it was

a good thing the lions didn't try to eat Daniel. They wouldn't have enjoyed him, since he was half grit and the other half backbone![7]

We need to ask, why did God save Daniel from death? Throughout history, many other martyrs died for their faith, some of them in Old Testament times (Hebrews 11:37-38). Some are dying for their faith today. Why didn't Daniel die?

The Rationale

My God sent His angel and shut the lions' mouths, so that they have not hurt me, because I was found innocent before Him; and also, O king, I have done no wrong before you.
DANIEL 6:22

Why did God save Daniel? The miraculous act vindicated Daniel and displayed God's power before the king. Of course, God's power could have been evident even if Daniel had been eaten by the lions. Consider again the response of Daniel's three friends before they were thrown into the fiery furnace: "Our God whom we serve is able to deliver us from the burning fiery furnace, and He will deliver us from your hand, O king. *But if not*, let it be known to you, O king, that we do not serve your gods" (Daniel 3:17-18, emphasis added). God would have been glorified by Daniel's faithfulness regardless of his fate in the lions' den, but His miraculous intervention showed beyond the shadow of a doubt that Daniel's God was real and powerful.

The Reaction

The king was exceedingly glad for him, and commanded that they should take Daniel up out of the den. So Daniel was taken up out of the den, and no injury whatever was found on him.
DANIEL 6:23

The Bible vividly portrays the king's delight in Daniel's survival. He checked him over carefully to be sure he was unharmed. Like Daniel's friends who had escaped from the furnace unscathed, Daniel came out completely uninjured. When we see how ferocious the lions were with the people who were thrown into the den later, it's obvious that Daniel was able to escape without a scratch only because of God's direct intervention.

The Reason

> . . . because he believed in his God.
>
> DANIEL 6:23

Daniel's faith cannot be discounted as a reason for God's deliverance. The Bible says that "without faith it is impossible to please [God]" (Hebrews 11:6). Jesus said, "All things are possible to him who believes" (Mark 9:23). Jesus was amazed at the faith of a Gentile soldier whose servant He healed (Luke 7:9) and also amazed at the lack of faith of those in His hometown, where their faithlessness prevented Him from working many miracles (Mark 6:6). In God's eyes, faith is critical—a principle Daniel understood.

For Daniel and his three Hebrew friends, faith was a commitment to omnipotence, not outcome. As the three friends said before being thrown in the fiery furnace, God is able to save, whether He chooses to or not. In either case, our trust is in Him and whatever outcome He deems best. That's a faith that surely pleases God.

A Sunday school teacher once asked her class why Daniel wasn't afraid when he was thrown into the lions' den. One little girl said, "Because the Lion of the tribe of Judah was in there with him!" Now that is sound theology!

Daniel Is Proved True by His God

The king gave the command, and they brought those men who had accused Daniel, and they cast them into the den of lions—them, their children, and their wives; and the lions overpowered them, and broke all their bones in pieces before they ever came to the bottom of the den.

DANIEL 6:24

The lions got their reward. Instead of one tough old Jew, they got a lot of tender, spineless Persians for breakfast. Those hungry lions ate every one of them before they hit the ground.

According to Leon Wood, the details of the lions consuming Daniel's accusers are given "to show how great the miracle of Daniel's preservation was. The lions were not old and without interest in human flesh. They were simply kept from inflicting the same sort of horrifying death on Daniel by the presiding messenger from God."[8]

C. I. Scofield, editor of the famous *Scofield Reference Bible*, was a brilliant lawyer whose career was marred by alcoholism until his conversion to Christ at the age of thirty-six. He went on to become a great Bible student, pastor, evangelist, and missionary advocate.

Scofield once gave this testimony based on the story of Daniel in the lions' den:

Shortly after I was saved, I passed the window of a store in St. Louis where I saw a painting of Daniel in the lions' den. That great man of faith, with his hands behind his back and those beasts circling him, was looking up. . . . As I stood there, great hope flooded my heart. Only a few days had passed since I, a drunken lawyer, had been converted; and no one had yet told me anything about the keeping power of Jesus Christ. I thought to myself, there are lions all about me too, such as my old habits and sins. But the One who shut the lions' mouths for Daniel can also shut them for me! I knew that I could not win the battle in my own strength. The painting made me realize that while I was weak and helpless, my God was strong and able. He had saved me, and now He would deliver me from the wild beasts in my life. O what a rest of spirit that truth brought me.[9]

Daniel was saved from the lions but not kept from them. As Christians living in a fallen world, we can expect the lions of temptation and opposition to snarl all around us. But when we put our trust in the Lion of the tribe of Judah, we do not need to fear any of them. The God who delivered Daniel is the God who is able to deliver those who, like Daniel, believe in Him.

* * *

DANIEL FOR TODAY

Daniel would rather spend time with the lions than miss his time with the Lord. What about you? Jesus told us to go into our private rooms, close the door, and pray to our Father in secret (Matthew 6:6). Daniel did this three times daily. Perhaps he prayed upon waking, again at noon when he returned to his quarters for lunch, and at bedtime before retiring. For him, prayer had become an unbreakable routine, and this was the secret to his character, his reputation, and his influence. How can we become powerful men and women of prayer?

1. Establish a daily time of prayer, and be serious about it. Too many Christians utter a hasty, "Lord, bless me!" while dashing to work in

the morning. But true power is found in true prayer, and true prayer must become a serious habit in our lives. New habits are hard to make, but once made, they're hard to break. Think through your schedule and begin to spend time in prayer each day, at a certain time and in a certain place. If you miss a day, don't give up. Stick with it until it's an unbreakable pattern.

2. Adopt a method of praying. Though no single method works best for everyone, many people like to keep praise and prayer lists or a simple prayer journal. Many follow a sequence that includes Bible reading and meditation, praise, confession, and various petitions for oneself and for others. Your practice will evolve as you pursue it, and it will grow richer and deeper as the days and years pass.

3. Don't be ashamed of praying. While we don't want to flaunt our prayers as the scribes and hypocrites did in Jesus' day (Matthew 6:5), we're thankful to have access to God's throne day and night. Our prayers form an important line of defense against that roaring lion, Satan. Daniel wasn't ashamed to be known as a man of prayer, and neither should we.

Chapter 8

THE CONQUEROR

Daniel 8:1-8, 15-22

DANIEL WOKE SUDDENLY, trembling from the vision that had come to him in the night. For a moment he thought he was in Shushan, where the vision had taken him. But as his head cleared, he realized he was at his home in Babylon.

The vision had been a terrible one to behold. A monstrous ram equipped with two enormous horns had rampaged through the nations, overwhelming everything that stood in its way, until it dominated all the lands from Lydia in the west to the easternmost reaches of civilization.

The ram seemed invincible until an equally monstrous male goat appeared from the west, armed with a gigantic horn protruding from between its eyes. The goat galloped across the earth as if it were flying. It met the ram head-on with a clash that shook the earth and reverberated through the heavens. A titanic battle ensued, and when the dust lifted, the ram lay bloody and mangled, its great horns twisted and broken.

After defeating the ram, the goat dominated the ram's entire territory and then added to it. But suddenly its horn was inexplicably broken, and four smaller ones grew in its place. None of them, however, had the power of the first.

Daniel was certain the vision carried meaning, but he couldn't find the key to it. As he pondered, a towering man suddenly appeared before him, bright as lightning and perfect in face and form. Daniel knew immediately that this man was an angel, and he fell on his face, trembling and finally fainting as the glorious sight overwhelmed him.

With a touch, the angel awakened Daniel and renewed his courage. He stood to hear what the magnificent being would say.

"I am Gabriel," the angel said. "I've been sent to make known to you the meaning of your vision. The ram's two horns signify the kings of Media and Persia. The male goat is the kingdom of Greece. The large horn between its eyes is the first king. As for the broken horn and the four that grew in its place, four kingdoms will arise out of that nation, but not with its original power."

* * *

It was 344 BC, two centuries after Daniel's vision. A twelve-year-old boy stood in the yard of the royal stables with his father, King Philip II of Macedon. They were admiring an enormous stallion, black as polished ebony. The horse was being restrained by two men, one on each side, who were gripping ropes tied to the animal's bridle. It was the finest horse young Alexander had ever seen—sleek, heavily muscled, and bright eyed, with a head as large as that of an ox.

"This magnificent beast can be yours for only thirteen talents." Philonicus was a trader from Thessaly, and King Philip purchased most of his horses from him.

"Walk him in a circle so we can see him in motion," the king said.

The two handlers, holding the ropes taut, led the horse as instructed. They had completed half the circle when the animal began to scream and buck, pawing the air with its forelegs and shaking its head wildly against the ropes. It kicked and raged, yanking the handlers around as if they were dolls. But they managed to retain their grip until the horse calmed down.

"The horses you've brought in the past have always been tamed," the king said. "Why is this one still wild?"

"No one has been able to ride him, my lord."

"Then I have no use for him. Take him away."

"Wait, Father," Alexander said. "I want that horse. Buy him, and if I fail to tame him, I'll find a way to pay for him."

"No, my king," Philonicus interjected. "This brute would kill the boy. Even my best trainers couldn't tame him."

"He won't kill me," Alexander retorted. "I must have that horse. I've never seen another like it."

After a short argument, the king relented. He bought the horse and gave it to Alexander, who named it Bucephalus, meaning "ox head."

When Alexander was watching the horse, he noticed that the animal remained calm until the handlers turned it away from the morning sun, and he determined it was distressed by its own huge shadow. Over the next several days, he won the animal's confidence by approaching slowly, talking to it in soothing tones, and stroking it gently. With a degree of trust established, he led the horse without resistance toward the sun, blindfolding the animal before leading it back to the stable.

Soon Bucephalus allowed a saddle. Shortly afterward, the horse tolerated it when Alexander mounted him. The boy began to ride the horse, always into the sun first, and then he dismounted and led him back to the stable without the blindfold, talking gently all the while. Finally, the stallion's trust in his master drove away all fear, allowing the boy to ride anytime, any direction, at any speed.

The next time King Philip came to the stable yard, Alexander mounted Bucephalus and, without a word, rode past where the king stood talking with Philonicus.

The king swelled with pride. "My son," he said, "seek out a kingdom equal to and worthy of yourself, for Macedonia is too small for you."

Little did King Philip know how prophetic those words would be.

* * *

Alexander was a prodigy from childhood. He was proficient not only in horsemanship and weaponry but also in Greek philosophy, literature, science, and medicine, having been tutored by Aristotle himself. His parents had high expectations of him. His mother, Princess Olympias of Epirus, told Alexander that he was descended from the Greek god Zeus and the mighty warrior Achilles.

Alexander's father had conquered the feuding Greek city states and fused them into a nation under his Macedonian rule. The Persian Empire was the dominant power in the world at the time, and its aggressive invasions of Greece threatened Philip's accomplishment. He set his sights on conquering the Persians and leaving the combined empires of Greece and Persia as a legacy to his son.

But it was not to be. In 336 BC, King Philip was assassinated, and his army immediately placed Alexander on his throne. He was twenty years old at the time. Intelligent, impatient, and driven, Alexander was determined to carry out his father's ambition to conquer the Medo-Persian Empire. First he solidified his rule over Greece, and then in 334 BC, he took his army across the strait of Hellespont, just off the Aegean Sea. As his ship approached the Persian shore, he threw his spear into the soil and cried, "That spear will soon conquer the whole of Asia."

Alexander first met the Persian army, led by Darius's general Memnon, at the Granicus River. Memnon's troops were massacred, allowing Alexander to march through Persian territory, taking province after province in lightning-fast battles and replacing the governors with his own men.

The alarmed Persian king, Darius III, amassed a new army of more than two-hundred thousand men, and in November of 333 BC, he led the army to meet Alexander's now reduced army of only thirty-five thousand. After a brief game of feint and counter feint, Alexander decoyed Darius's troops, leading them to a narrow plain on the Penarus River near the town of Issus.

Alexander positioned his forces across the river facing the Persians, and the next morning, he and his second in command, Parmenion, climbed a mountain to offer sacrifices to his gods to assure their victory.

As the sacrificial flames flickered into embers, General Parmenion looked out over the massive Persian encampment. "Surely you don't mean to attack now, my lord. Look at that army. It's six times the size of ours."

"Yes, but we have the gods with us," Alexander replied.

Parmenion snorted. "Gods! Waste all the bull flesh you want on your useless altars. Gods know nothing of military strategy. Even if they did, strategy means nothing against such overwhelming numbers."

"You're mistaken, Parmenion. Look—the gods are working for us already. The Persians are wedged in by the sea on their right and the mountains on their left. Their army is packed together like fish in a net. They can't maneuver in such tight quarters. Nor can they attack us in great numbers—their front is too narrow."

"How will we attack?"

"We will divide our army into two—"

"Divide our army? Surely you don't mean it! We're small already, and dividing will make us even smaller."

"I'll form a wedge-shaped force and lead half our army across the river into Darius's front line," Alexander continued. "You'll position your troops between my army and the sea to keep the Persians from flanking us in that direction. They can't outflank us on the other side because of the mountains. We'll charge simultaneously, and they'll meet us in the river. With our attack momentum and the mud bogging down their chariots, we'll split their forces down the middle and drive them back against themselves."

Parmenion nodded. "Yes, I can see your strategy now. When they retreat, they'll be too pressed by their numbers to move quickly. It's brilliant, my lord."

With his troops aligned, Alexander gave the signal to charge. The battle was fierce. Alexander was bleeding from a slash in his thigh, but he remained undaunted, leading his elite guard into the middle of the fray. Soon masses of bodies began to wash downward, forming a dam and causing the blood-red water to overflow the banks.

King Darius, watching the battle from the rear, saw the rout developing and fled into the mountains, leaving his soldiers on the field. His demoralized army turned and ran, but they were impeded by their numbers. The pursuing Greeks cut them down one after the other.

The victory at Issus gave Alexander the Syrian section of the Persian Empire, but with the escape of Darius III, he knew his hold wasn't secure. Yet his decimation of the Persian army left Egypt, the Persian's vassal state, unprotected, so he sailed along the northern African coast, conquering cities along the way, and was welcomed into Egypt as a liberator from Persian oppression.

Meanwhile, Darius III assembled and trained a new army—this one even larger than the last. In 331 BC, with Egypt secured, Alexander marched north to meet him. Darius had learned his lesson at Issus. This time he camped on the Plain of Gaugamela near the Tigris River. Masses of infantry, cavalry, and chariots equipped with razor-sharp scythes filled the plain, and fifteen huge elephants loomed above them, with Darius's lancers mounted on each one.

Alexander drew his army within hailing distance of the Persians, putting them on alert for an immediate attack. When the Greeks had set up camp, Parmenion drew Alexander aside, as he'd done at Issus. "Surely you don't mean to attack an army of that size. They now outnumber us eight to one. And they're firmly ensconced, ready for us."

"Have you forgotten we were outnumbered at Issus?" Alexander replied. "Yet we took them in a day."

"Yes, but this time Darius has picked his battleground well. It's a vast plain, where his scythed chariots can maneuver easily. Let's turn aside for now, my lord. We can build up our meager army with mercenaries and return to fight another day."

"No, we're here, and we're ready. I won't turn back."

Parmenion sighed. "Very well, my lord. You know I am with you whatever you decide. But please, I urge you: let's attack tonight using darkness for cover."

"No, that's what they expect us to do. We'll sleep tonight, while they stay awake waiting for us. Then we'll attack in the morning, when we're rested and they're exhausted."

Again Alexander divided his army into two units, the right led by him and the left led by Parmenion. But this time he had Parmenion's force remain stationary while he advanced his troops to the right. This strategy was merely a feint to draw the Persian army toward him. Darius took the bait and met Alexander's advance, enabling Parmenion to flank the Persians to the left and pinch them between the two Greek forces. Suddenly the Persians found themselves fighting on two fronts.

Alexander's cavalry led the charge, followed by his infantry. He'd instructed the infantry not to confront the scythed chariots but merely to sidestep, leaving the chariots at the mercy of the archers and javelin throwers advancing immediately behind the infantry.

Parmenion's forces held the left flank, allowing Alexander's wedge to drive forward and break through the Persian front. After a fierce battle, Alexander advanced until he caught sight of the guards stationed around King Darius's camp.

"The king!" he cried above the din. "Straight ahead! We must get the king!"

Alexander spurred Bucephalus and led the charge. His cavalry's swords hacked through Darius's elite guard. But before he reached the king, he heard cries of alarm from his left. He turned to see Parmenion's forces being driven back. Immediately he wheeled his army to aid his general, pinning the attacking Persians between his two forces. King Darius, seeing his lines breached, knew the battle was lost. The moment Alexander turned away, Darius fled with what remained of his decimated guard. With their king gone, the Persians panicked and ran, only to be cut down en masse by the pursuing Greeks.

At the end of the day, Alexander and Parmenion watched as their men looted the Persian camp, taking load after load of armor, weaponry, and chariots, and adding the fifteen elephants to the Greek army.

Alexander turned to his general. "The Medo-Persian Empire is no more. It's now part of my new Greek Empire."

The battle of Gaugamela fulfilled the prophecy God had given Daniel some two hundred years earlier. The great horned goat—the Greeks under Alexander the Great—had defeated the two-horned ram, the vast, two pronged empire of the Medes and Persians that was originally assembled in the time of Daniel by the great warrior Cyrus.

Alexander continued his campaigns of conquest, eventually extending his empire eastward, all the way to India. In thirteen years, he had conquered most of the known civilized world. He returned to Babylon and took up residence in the magnificent palace built by Nebuchadnezzar II.

* * *

Iollus, Alexander's wine pourer, watched impassively as the great feast that Medius was hosting for his friend Alexander degenerated into a drunken orgy. Many people were guzzling wine at the tables, while others played games or bellowed lurid songs about the exploits of the gods. Now and then a man would leave with one of his concubines. Alexander himself had slipped out and hadn't yet returned.

He'll be back soon, Iollus thought. *And then I'll finally avenge my father.*

Iollus's father was Antipater, one of the Macedonian viceroys whom Alexander had discharged for misconduct. The disgraced man's friends had maneuvered Iollus onto Alexander's staff by concealing his parentage.

Alexander returned to the party, reeling from the evening's massive intake of wine. The guests shouted ribald cheers: "The conqueror returns after yet another conquest." "He's the reincarnation of Hercules." "Raise your cups and drink an oblation to our new god."

Alexander, grinning foolishly, collapsed into a chair, and someone set a bowl in front of him. "Iollus," Medius called, "come fill the bowl of our new Hercules with the sweet blood of these fine Persian vineyards."

Iollus already had Alexander's wine specially prepared. He put on his usual smile, took the flask to the emperor, and filled his bowl. Alexander drank deeply and set down the empty bowl, to the raucous cheers of the guests.

Suddenly he winced in pain, clutched his heart, and collapsed to the floor. Medius ordered servants to carry him back to Nebuchadnezzar's palace to be attended by royal physicians.

Alexander awoke the next afternoon with a splitting headache and a high fever. Medius sat beside his bed, watching intently as the emperor groaned with pain. By evening Alexander felt well enough to get up and walk around, though his chest still ached.

The next morning his pain had subsided, and he awoke at his normal time, arose, and got dressed.

"Ah, my friend," Medius said, "welcome back to the land of the living. You gave us quite a scare."

Alexander said nothing, but sat at a veranda table and called for wine. Medius ordered a servant to bring food, but Alexander refused to touch it. Medius tried to engage his friend in conversation, but Alexander's responses were minimal at best. He offered to play Alexander's favorite game; Alexander declined. He offered to send for one of the slave girls, but Alexander wasn't interested. He suggested a horseback jaunt in Nebuchadnezzar's Babylonian park. Alexander shook his head and stared at his wine cup.

"Why are you so despondent?" Medius finally asked. "Look at all you've accomplished. In thirteen short years, you've conquered the civilized world. No man in history has ever approached such a feat."

"That's the trouble, Medius. All I know is conquering. I've built my life around it. And now there are no more worlds to conquer. I'm in my thirties, and I've already reached the apex of my life. Everything is downhill from here."

"Ah, but now you can enjoy what we all labor for—pleasure. Wine, women, music, food, and company. Live for pleasure, my friend. That's what life is all about."

"The pain in my chest has returned," Alexander said. "I think I'll go back to bed."

For the next week, Alexander spent more and more time in bed as the pain and fever increased daily. He became progressively weaker, and his speech grew slurred until finally he could neither get out of bed nor speak at all.

When news of his decline reached his army, his men grew distraught. Medius moved Alexander's bed to the great hall and allowed the soldiers to file by throughout the day. The emperor was barely able to raise his hand in acknowledgment. Fourteen days after the feast at Medius's home, Alexander the Great died.

Alexander had named no successor. His wife, Roxane, gave birth to a son after his death, and some of Alexander's military officers supported naming the baby as the successor. But this option never materialized, since several generals, governors, and other claimants began to vie for the throne. After a series of intrigues and assassinations, four power blocks emerged, dividing Alexander's empire into four separate kingdoms: Egypt, Seleucid Mesopotamia, Anatolia, and Macedon.

Just as Daniel's vision had prophesied, the great horn of the Greek goat was destroyed at Alexander's death, and four weaker horns sprouted up in its place.

* * *

THE SCRIPTURE BEHIND THE STORY

Both the book of Daniel and the book of Revelation frequently turn to the animal kingdom for images that convey prophetic truths. Animal metaphors work well because they're so vivid. Even in our day, we use animals to describe certain characteristics about people:

- He's as grouchy as an old bear.
- Don't trust him around your wife—he's a wolf.
- He's as wise as an owl.
- Be careful around him; he may try to outfox you.
- That clique of girls is so catty.
- He eats like a horse.
- I know I should stand up to him, but I'm a chicken.
- That woman has the memory of an elephant.
- He has the strength of an ox.
- He's as stubborn as a mule.

The traits we find in certain animals are ideal metaphors for human behavior. Correspondingly, we find animals used as metaphors in the book of Daniel.

Chapters 7–8 of Daniel give us God's viewpoint of godless Gentile governments, picturing them as wild, unclean beasts determined to dominate like the alpha male of a pack or a herd—but ultimately destined to perish.

The Reception of Daniel's Second Dream

The vision recorded in Daniel 8 came to Daniel "in the third year of the reign of King Belshazzar" (Daniel 8:1), which was around 550 BC. Daniel was approaching his seventieth birthday.

THE POSITION OF THE VISION

> In the third year of the reign of King Belshazzar a vision appeared to me—to me, Daniel—after the one that appeared to me the first time.
>
> DANIEL 8:1

This is a good place to be reminded that the book of Daniel is not arranged chronologically. Belshazzar died in the Medo-Persian invasion of Babylon recorded at the end of Daniel 5. Daniel 6 follows chronologically with events that happened under the Persian ruler Darius (Daniel 6:1). Then Daniel 7 and 8 go back almost twenty years and tell us of two visions that occurred before Belshazzar's downfall. This chapter explores the second vision—the one in Daniel 8—because the events that vision describes occurred before the events of the vision in Daniel 7. We have already addressed some of the prophecies of Daniel 7, and others will come up in a later chapter.

It's clear that when Daniel interpreted the handwriting on the wall in Daniel 5, what he learned from this vision was already in his mind.

THE PROFILE OF THE VISION

The visions in Daniel 2 and parts of Daniel 7 are parallel. Both summarize the rise and fall of four kingdoms: Babylon, Medo-Persia,

Greece, and Rome. The vision in Daniel 8 zooms in and focuses on only two of those kingdoms: Medo-Persia and Greece. These kingdoms are represented in the colossus by the chest and arms of silver and the belly and thighs of bronze (Daniel 2).

These two kingdoms are singled out in Daniel 8 because they have special relevance for the Jewish people. Medo-Persia is significant because the Persian king allowed the Jews to return to Jerusalem and rebuild its walls and Temple. Greece is relevant because during the period of history when that nation dominated, Jerusalem and the Temple were besieged again after the death of Alexander.

In Daniel 8, the original language switches from Aramaic (the language of the Gentiles) back to Hebrew, because the rest of the book deals with Israel. But that doesn't mean the importance of Daniel 8–12 is limited to Israel. Israel has been the nerve center of the earth since the time of Abraham. It has been the truth center from which a stream of divine revelation has flowed since the birth of Christ. It has been the storm center of warring nations since the days of Joshua. And it will be the peace center of the earth during the Kingdom age.

THE PLACE OF THE VISION

> I saw in the vision, and it so happened while I was looking, that I was in Shushan, the citadel, which is in the province of Elam; and I saw in the vision that I was by the River Ulai.
>
> DANIEL 8:2

Daniel was physically in Babylon but was transported in his vision to Shushan, a city some 230 miles east of the city. Shushan was at the edge of the Babylonian Empire, and it would one day become the capital of the Persian Empire. It was the home of Esther (Esther 1:1-2) and the city Nehemiah came from to rebuild

Jerusalem's walls (Nehemiah 1:1). In 1901, the Code of Hammurabi was found in Shushan. In Daniel 8, that city becomes the stage for a great drama that is symbolically presented to describe the conquests of the Medo-Persian and Greek empires.

THE PERCEIVER OF THE VISION

> It happened, when I, Daniel, had seen the vision and was seeking the meaning, that suddenly there stood before me one having the appearance of a man. And I heard a man's voice between the banks of the Ulai, who called, and said, "Gabriel, make this man understand the vision."
>
> DANIEL 8:15-16

Unlike Daniel's previous visions, this one, along with the appearance of the angel Gabriel, overwhelmed him. He "fainted and was sick for days" (Daniel 8:27). Although Daniel had understood the previous visions, he needed help interpreting this one. While he was "seeking the meaning" (verse 15)—that is, trying to understand what he'd seen—the angel Gabriel appeared to explain the symbolic imagery. Gabriel means "mighty man of God." He is often God's public relations angel, an announcer of news (Luke 1:26-28).

THE PURPOSE OF THE VISION

When the mighty angel Gabriel appeared to Daniel to help him understand the vision, he said, "Understand, son of man, that the vision refers to the *time of the end*. . . . I am making known to you what shall happen in the *latter time of the indignation*; for at the appointed time the end shall be" (Daniel 8:17, 19, emphasis added).

In general, the phrase "time of the end" or "latter time of the indignation" refers to the end of rebellion against God. The end of the rebellion of the Northern Kingdom, Israel, came when the

Assyrian army deported the Israelites. The end of the rebellion of the Southern Kingdom, Judah, came when the Babylonian armies sacked Jerusalem. As we will see later, Daniel also foresaw a final rebellion against God, which will occur at the end of the age.

The Revelation of Daniel's Second Vision

Two animals dominate Daniel's vision: a ram and a goat. These two creatures are vividly metaphoric, representing a fierce battle between two prideful generals head butting each other in mortal combat.

THE RAM

> I lifted my eyes and saw, and there, standing beside the river, was a ram which had two horns, and the two horns were high; but one was higher than the other, and the higher one came up last. I saw the ram pushing westward, northward, and southward, so that no animal could withstand him; nor was there any that could deliver from his hand, but he did according to his will and became great.
> DANIEL 8:3-4

The first animal in Daniel's vision was a ram with two horns—nothing unusual there. But Daniel saw the horns actually growing, one after the other, out of the ram's head. The second horn grew taller than the first. The two horns represent the Medes and the Persians (Daniel 8:20). The Persians joined the already existing empire of Media and grew to dominate the alliance. So the Medes existed first, then the Persians allied with them, and Cyrus, the Persian king, came to rule the Medo-Persian Empire.

Daniel saw the ram pushing "westward, northward, and southward" (Daniel 8:4), conquering all the surrounding kingdoms—including the mighty kingdom of Babylon.

THE GOAT

> As I was considering, suddenly a male goat came from the
> west, across the surface of the whole earth, without touching
> the ground; and the goat had a notable horn between his
> eyes. Then he came to the ram that had two horns.
>
> DANIEL 8:5-6

From our previous study of Daniel's visions, we know that the
Medo-Persian Empire was defeated by the Greek Empire. Therefore,
the goat that comes against the ram of Medo-Persia represents Greece.
Verse 21 affirms this fact: "The male goat is the kingdom of Greece"
(Daniel 8:21).

Geoffrey R. King explains:

> The goat is the symbol of Greece. And I'll tell you why. The
> first colony of Greece was directed by an oracle to get a goat
> for a guide and build a city, and in gratitude to that goat
> for leading them aright, they built the city and they called
> it Aegae, the goat city. And of course, you are familiar with
> the fact that the waters around Greece are to this day called
> the Aegean Sea, the goat sea. The goat has always been the
> national symbolic figure of Greece. Figures of a goat are
> found on many of the ancient Macedonian monuments.[1]

We can see how appropriate it is that Daniel 8:21 identifies the goat
as Greece. The single horn protruding from its forehead is identified
as "the first king." As we will see, history leaves no doubt whatsoever
that this king is Alexander the Great, son of Philip, king of Macedon.

Five prophecies arise out of the conflict between the goat and
ram, and the fulfillment of each is historically verifiable. The historical veracity of these prophecies underscores the importance of this

section of the book of Daniel. Scholar and pastor Rodney Stortz explains:

> It is important to understand that Alexander's rise to power was two centuries after Daniel made this prophecy—two hundred years! . . . There would be no way a human could predict this. In fact, these prophecies are so accurate that liberal scholars, those who do not believe that the Bible is God's holy and inerrant Word, suggest that Daniel must have written this book in the first century before Christ.
>
> For them that is the only explanation for the accuracy of Daniel. They do not believe this is prophecy. They think it is recorded history, because it is so accurate.[2]

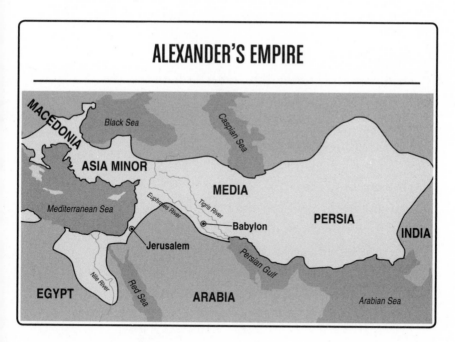

ALEXANDER'S EMPIRE

The Route to World Conquest

The Babylonians, the Medes, and the Persians all came from the east. But here was a world power coming from the west. The "male goat came from the west . . . without touching the ground," an indication of his speed (Daniel 8:5). Greece, led by Alexander the Great, conquered more nations—and at a faster rate—than any other ancient king. In thirteen years, he conquered the Mediterranean world, much of North Africa, and Mesopotamia, and he even extended his reach as far as India—never losing a battle.

The Reputation of the First King

Alexander was precocious from his youth. His mother told him his ancestors were the Greek mythological hero Achilles and the god Hercules. Tradition says that as a boy, Alexander tamed a large horse that no one else could ride—a horse that carried him into all his battles.

After a particularly significant battle (or, according to some sources, after Alexander tamed the horse), Alexander's father told him, "Oh, Alexander, my son, seek out a kingdom worthy of yourself. . . . Macedonia is too small."[3]

So Alexander followed his father's advice and decided to rule the world.

The Ruin of the Medo-Persian Empire

> He came to the ram that had two horns, which I had seen standing beside the river, and ran at him with furious power. And I saw him confronting the ram; he was moved with rage against him, attacked the ram, and broke his two horns. There was no power in the ram to withstand him, but he cast him down to the ground and trampled him; and there was no one that could deliver the ram from his hand.
> DANIEL 8:6-7

In his vision, Daniel saw the goat (the nation of Greece) and the large horn on the goat's head (Alexander the Great) leading the Greek armies. Then Daniel saw the goat soundly defeat the ram (the armies of Medo-Persia). And that's exactly what came to pass.

In 334 BC, Alexander came from the west with thirty-five thousand troops, crossed the Hellespont (now known as the Dardanelles, the strait separating Macedonia from Asia Minor), and defeated the Persian army at the Granicus River (in modern Turkey). He freed all the Greek cities of Asia Minor from the Persians.

Darius III then took personal control of his army and came face-to-face with Alexander at the Battle of Issus near Syrian Antioch in 333 BC. Darius wanted to negotiate, but Alexander swept south to occupy Egypt after taking Tyre and Gaza. He retraced his steps through Syria, and in 331 BC, he met the Persian army, now greatly enlarged, for the third time. This battle proved to be the end for the Persians. The Medo-Persian Empire was crushed forever.

As Daniel saw it, the goat "was moved with rage against [the ram], attacked the ram, and broke his two horns. There was no power in the ram to withstand him, but he cast him down to the ground and trampled him" (Daniel 8:7). This description is typical of Alexander's victories: swift and decisive.

The Remarkable Death of the King

After defeating the Medo-Persian armies, Alexander sacked several other Persian cities. He then swept toward India, but his weary army had had enough, and they returned to Babylon. Shortly afterward, Alexander died at the age of thirty-two, a victim of severe fever, which historians believe was caused by poison administered by a vengeful servant.

While his exact cause of his death is uncertain, it's certain that Alexander died heartbroken that there were no more worlds to conquer. His life was cut short at the height of his power, as Daniel's prophecy predicted: "The male goat grew very great; but when he became strong, the large horn was broken" (Daniel 8:8).

While it seems on the surface that Alexander was simply fulfilling his own dreams of conquest, in reality he was playing a role in God's prophetic plan for the Gentile kings. He was filling in the outline sketched by the Lord in the prophecies of Daniel. Alexander was not an originator; he was a copyist. He was not the writing hand; he was the pencil in it. He was not the author of the play; he was the actor on the stage.

Through these Gentile kingdoms, God was building infrastructures that would facilitate His long-term plans. The Greeks brought civilization and a universal language to the Mediterranean world. A few centuries later, the New Testament was written in Greek, making it accessible to a multitude of nations. After the Greeks, the Romans brought peace and order and paved the roads over which the gospel would be carried.

The Reorganization of the Greek Empire

> The male goat grew very great; but when he became strong, the large horn was broken, and in place of it four notable ones came up toward the four winds of heaven. . . . As for the broken horn and the four that stood up in its place, four kingdoms shall arise out of that nation, but not with its power.
>
> DANIEL 8:8, 22

Daniel's vision predicted that Alexander's empire would fragment into four parts. For twenty years following Alexander's death, it appeared that Daniel's prophecy would not be fulfilled. But history records that eventually Alexander's kingdom was divided among four of his generals:

- Cassander ruled Macedonia.
- Lysimachus conquered Thrace and most of Asia Minor.

- Seleucus took Syria.
- Ptolemy became king of Egypt and Palestine.

The veracity of the Bible is affirmed when we realize that these events, all confirmed by history, were recorded in Daniel's prophecy long before they happened.

The Resolution of Daniel's Second Vision

A GREAT PROPHECY

The Jewish historian Josephus was the most prolific compiler of Jewish history in the first century AD. One of his primary works, the twenty volume *Antiquities of the Jews*, written around AD 94, traces Jewish history from Creation forward. Josephus drew on the written and oral histories available to him. His accounts of many events in Jewish history, especially during the period between the two Testaments, have been a standard resource for nearly two thousand years.

Josephus detailed the movements of Alexander the Great in significant detail, and his record of Alexander's decision not to capture and destroy Jerusalem is especially noteworthy. Alexander was making his way down the coast of Phoenicia, destroying cities as he went. Leaving Gaza in ruins, he moved his armies toward Jerusalem. Jaddua, the high priest in Jerusalem, heard this news and was understandably distraught. He called the people to fast and pray for God's protection. In a dream, God told Jaddua that they should adorn the city, open the gates, put on their finest garments, and go out to meet Alexander as he neared the city.

When Alexander approached and saw the multitude of citizens in their finery, a multitude of priests in their white-linen garments, and the high priest in his purple and scarlet vestments, he approached and saluted them. The multitudes, in one voice, saluted Alexander in return.

Alexander's generals and officials thought he'd lost his mind. One of them asked Alexander why he condescended to give honor to the high priest of the Jews when all other people bowed to adore Alexander. Alexander's answer, recorded by Josephus, is astonishing. It reflects how God apparently worked in Alexander to accomplish His purposes for His people. Here was Alexander's reply:

> I did not adore [the high priest], but that God who hath honoured him with his high-priesthood; for I saw this very person in a dream, [wearing this] very [priestly dress], when I was at Dios in Macedonia, who, when I was considering with myself how I might obtain the dominion of Asia, exhorted me to make no delay, but boldly to pass over the sea thither, for that he would conduct my army, and would give me the dominion over the Persians; whence it is, that having seen no other in [this priestly dress], and now seeing this person in it, and remembering that vision, and the exhortation which I had in my dream, I believe that I bring this army under the divine conduct, and shall therewith conquer Darius, and destroy the power of the Persians, and that all things will succeed according to what is in my own mind.[4]

When Alexander dreamed of this priest telling him he would be victorious over the Persians, he concluded that by obeying that vision, he would "bring [his] army under the divine conduct" and conquer the Persians. Alexander recognized the Jewish high priest as the divine messenger he'd seen in his dream, and so, by honoring him, he was honoring the God who had appointed the high priest.

The story gets even better. According to Josephus, Alexander accompanied the priests and multitude to the Temple: "When he went up into the temple, he offered sacrifice to God, according to the high-priest's direction, and magnificently treated both the high-priest and the priests. And when the book of Daniel was showed him, wherein Daniel declared that one of the Greeks should destroy the empire of the Persians, he supposed that himself was the person intended."[5]

Reading this account makes us feel that we have entered a time warp. Alexander offered sacrifices to God in the Temple and was shown the very passage in Daniel 8 we are studying now—a prophecy stating that a Greek army would destroy the army of Medo-Persia. From Alexander's side of time, that was a prophesied event yet to happen, and he saw himself as the fulfillment of it. From our perspective, we see what was still in the future for him—that he actually did fulfill the prophecy.

Before leaving Jerusalem, Alexander asked the high priest what favor he could do for them in gratitude for the divine direction God had given him. The priest asked that they would be able to follow the laws of Moses—that is, exercise their Jewish religion—in the land of Israel that Alexander now controlled. He also asked that Alexander, after conquering Persia, would allow the Jews in Mesopotamia to freely exercise their religion. According to Josephus, "[Alexander] granted all they desired."[6]

Don't miss the astounding implications of these events. They give powerful evidence to the validity of this prophecy. History records that Alexander himself saw the prophecies of Daniel, which clearly shows they couldn't have been written after the fact.

Was Alexander overwhelmed and humbled to find himself the subject of biblical prophecy? And on that basis, did he go forth with confidence that Persia was already in his hand? While we can't confirm the details of Josephus's account, we can verify this: the effect biblical prophecy had on Alexander is the effect it should have on everyone who reads it. It should give us unbounded confidence that what God has prophesied will inevitably come to pass.

A GREAT PRINCIPLE

So far in this book, we have mostly addressed prophecies that have already been fulfilled—the rise and fall of four great Gentile powers. But as we will see as we continue through the book of Daniel, the prophecies in subsequent chapters deal almost exclusively with events that are yet to occur. In light of the principle spelled out above—that fulfilled prophecies give us confidence about yet-to-be-fulfilled prophecies—what should be our response to the future that Daniel reveals to us?

Daniel's response to the many visions of the future God had revealed to him guides us to the answer. He had been shown Nebuchadnezzar's dream about the coming Gentile kingdoms, as well as its interpretation (Daniel 2); he had interpreted Nebuchadnezzar's dream about his own downfall (Daniel 4); he had interpreted the handwriting on the wall at Belshazzar's feast (Daniel 5); and he had experienced God's supernatural protection in the lions' den (Daniel 6).

Given these experiences, might Daniel have been excused if he'd manifested a ho-hum attitude toward the vision of the ram and goat in chapter 8? He could have thought, *Just another vision of the future that will come to pass after I'm long gone.* But as we find in verse 27, that wasn't his response: "I, Daniel, fainted and was sick for days; . . . I was astonished by the vision." In short, Daniel hadn't become jaded by having experienced so many supernatural revelations of the future.

I can't say exactly why Daniel fainted and was ill for several days, but verse 27 gives us a clue: "I was *astonished* by the vision" (emphasis added). Daniel retained his awe that God could predict the future in such detail, including specific names, places, traits, and events.

Because of our familiarity with the miracles and prophecies and providence of God, I'm afraid it's all too easy for us to lose our awe and astonishment over how plain yet powerful the revealed Word of God is. We must never let that happen. Remember: what God has done in the past is the key to our confidence that He controls the future. May we live lives of astonishment over how God has broken into human history for our benefit—to give us a future and a hope that is absolutely certain (Jeremiah 29:11).

A GREAT PERSON

W. W. Tarn gives high praise to Alexander in his book *Alexander the Great*: "He was one of the supreme fertilizing forces in history. He lifted the civilized world out of one groove and set it in another; he started a new epoch; nothing could again be as it had been. . . . Greek culture, heretofore practically confined to Greeks, spread throughout the world; and . . . in place of the many dialects of Greece, there grew up the form of Greek known as the *koine*, 'the common speech.'"[7]

J. E. H. Thomson amplifies the importance of this new unity: "It was through the conquests of Alexander that Greek became the language of literature and commerce from the shores of the Mediterranean to the banks of the Tigris. It is impossible to estimate the effect of this spread of Greek on the promulgation of the gospel."[8]

Alexander the Great accomplished all these things and more by the time he died at the age of nearly thirty-three. But compared to the life of another who died at the same age, his record pales. It's one thing to change the world in one's day; it's another thing to change the world forever.

> *Jesus and Alexander died at thirty-three.*
> *One lived and died for self; one died for you and me.*
> *The Greek died on a throne; the Jew died on a cross;*
> *One's life a triumph seemed; the other but a loss.*
> *One led vast armies forth; the other walked alone;*
> *One shed a whole world's blood, the other gave His own.*
> *One won the world in life and lost it all in death.*
> *The other lost His life to win the whole world's faith.*

Jesus and Alexander died at thirty-three.
One died in Babylon; one on Calvary.
One gained all for self; one Himself He gave.
One conquered every throne, the other every grave.
The one made himself god, the God made Himself less;
The one lived but to blast; the other but to bless.
When died the Greek, forever fell his throne of swords;
But Jesus died to live forever Lord of lords.

Jesus and Alexander died at thirty-three.
The Greek made all men slaves; the Jew made all men free.
One built a throne on blood; the other built on love.
The one was born of earth, the other from above.
One won all this earth; to lose all earth and heaven;
The other gave up all, that all to Him be given.
The Greek forever died; the Jew forever lives;
He loses all who gets and wins all things who gives.[9]

Friedrich Flick was born in 1883, the son of a German farmer. Like Alexander, he also built a massive empire, though his was not political but financial. Flick's first job was as a clerk in a coal-mining company. He quickly became a partner in the mining company and began buying other industrial companies as well.

He was ambitious and ruthless, and through manipulation and political alliances, he soon owned more than three hundred German companies, including iron-ore and coal mines, foundries, steel mills, chemical plants, trucks, airplanes, railroad interests, and munitions plants. One of Hitler's primary financiers, he used slave labor supplied from the dictator's concentration camps. His only interest was in his business conquests, and he virtually ignored his wife and family. He was a failure as a father and eventually became estranged from his sons. In 1966 he buried his wife at 3 p.m., and two hours later, he was back at his desk working.

When Friedrich Flick died in 1972, he left a personal fortune of about two billion dollars. One of his sons held the family fortune together for a while, but the Flick empire eventually went the way of all secular empires and fell into other hands.

Like Alexander, Friedrich Flick was immensely successful by the world's standards but a miserable failure by the measure that matters. At their deaths, both men lost everything they had strived for and faced eternity empty handed.

The lesson we learn from their lives is that the human tendency to seek success on the world's terms has infected the human race since the Fall, and none of us is immune to it. Like Daniel, we must keep our focus on God and His providence, trusting that all that matters in the end is His "Well done, good and faithful servant" (Matthew 25:21).

* * *

DANIEL FOR TODAY

1. You can trust the Bible entirely, for the Bible is entirely true. The Bible verifies itself through fulfilled prophecy. Biblical prophecy was 100 percent right in the past; we can trust it 100 percent in the future. Daniel 8 provides a rich sample of biblical prophecies that have already been fulfilled to the letter. Add all the Messianic predictions fulfilled in the coming of Christ, and the evidence is overwhelming. Since the Bible's remaining predictions primarily involve the end times and the return of Christ, we can take them seriously and trust them totally. The Bible has a perfect track record. It's hard to imagine how a person who studies Daniel 8 could deny Daniel's God. "God is not a man, that He should lie, nor a son of man, that

He should repent. Has He said, and will He not do? Or has He spoken, and will He not make it good?" (Numbers 23:19).

2. It's time to study what the Bible predicts about the final days of history. Passages like those in the books of Daniel and Revelation were intended for consumption. God expects us to read and study these parts of Scripture, for He wants to prepare us for what's to come. When we neglect biblical prophecy, we're closing our eyes to the future—maybe to the immediate future! "Blessed is he who reads and those who hear the words of this prophecy, and keep those things which are written in it; for the time is near" (Revelation 1:3).

3. Having been astonished by the truths of biblical prophecy, we should prayerfully work for the Lord and faithfully go about the King's business. Take Daniel as your model for living a godly life in a pagan age, realizing you're the link between two kingdoms—living in the world but representing heaven. That's a daunting task, but it's our calling in Christ. "I, Daniel, fainted and was sick for days; afterward I arose and went about the king's business. I was astonished by the vision" (Daniel 8:27).

Chapter 9

THE MADMAN

Daniel 8:9-14, 23-27

It was the year 167 BC when Antiochus IV, king of the Seleucid Empire, rode northward along the waters of the Nile River, now brown and muddy as it branched off into the delta that fed the Great Sea. In the distance he could see the sunlit walls of Alexandria.

Antiochus turned to the man on his right. "Well, Dimitrios, we are on the verge of bringing Egypt back into my grandfather's empire."

"Indeed, my king," Dimitrios replied. "It has been an easy campaign. Luxor, Cairo, Giza, and Memphis hardly gave you any resistance. And now you have only Alexandria to conquer. You could have left half of your army in Babylon."

"You never dilute your army." The speaker was Antiochus's general, a Persian man named Gudea. "What great armies don't win in battle, they win by intimidation."

Antiochus looked over his shoulder at the army of the Seleucid Empire, marching behind him and his two fellow riders.

The general lifted his hand to signal a halt. "Look ahead, my lord.

Someone's coming." The three men shaded their eyes and peered into the distance. A group of about thirty riders approached from the north.

It soon became clear that they had no hostile intent, for none bore arms and all were attired in togas. The riders stopped twenty yards in front of Antiochus, where the leader dismounted. Using a cane for support, he hobbled toward the Seleucid invaders.

"Hail, Antiochus!" The man raised an open palm in greeting. His voice was feeble with age.

Dimitrios leaned toward Antiochus. "I know this man. He's the Roman diplomat Gaius Laenas. He served as a consul of the Roman Republic for two terms, and now he's an ambassador who is sent to Rome's trouble spots. The men behind him are undoubtedly his council."

"He's nothing but a feeble old man." Antiochus didn't try to mask the scorn in his voice. "We'll trample him as we would a mouse in our path. Gudea, signal the army to move forward."

"No, my king!" Dimitrios said. "That mouse has the power of Rome behind him. I suggest that you greet him and hear what he has to say."

With a snort, Antiochus dismounted and approached the Roman ambassador. Feigning friendship, he smiled and extended his hand in greeting. But instead of taking the proffered hand, Gaius placed in it a small papyrus scroll.

"King Antiochus," he said, "I won't offer you the conventional sign of friendship until I know whether you are a friend or a foe of Rome. You must first read this message from the Roman senate and respond with your intentions."

Gaius stood impassive as Antiochus opened the scroll. His frown deepened as he read. The Roman senate was demanding that he abandon his conquest of Egypt. Antiochus knew he wasn't ready to confront Rome, but he was enraged that the Romans had the audacity to thwart his ambitions. Yet he forced himself to speak civilly.

"I must consult with my advisers before I answer."

Without a word, Gaius Laenus took his cane and, hobbling with effort, drew a circle around the king in the sand. "Antiochus," he said, "you must give me a reply to report to the senate before you step out of this circle."

The rage bubbled up inside Antiochus. Yet he managed to hold himself in check and take the course of prudence. "I will do what the Roman Senate thinks right."

The words were obviously forced, but Gaius Laenas smiled for the first time and extended his open hand. "Greetings, friend and ally of Rome."

* * *

Gudea and Dimitrios sat in the king's tent, staring into their wine cups. Antiochus paced back and forth, ranting as he'd done every night since they'd left Egypt almost a week ago.

"Why should I bow to those Romans? I'm a descendant of Seleucus, a general in Alexander's army who won his share of the great conqueror's empire from three other generals who tried to seize it for themselves. When the four generals stalemated and divided the nations between them, not only did Seleucus get the lion's share of the territory, but he also got Babylon, the gem of the empire! Tell me, Gudea, was that not a grand feat?"

"It was, my lord." Gudea forced himself to feign interest.

"And then," Antiochus continued, "Seleucus's sons went on to conquer the lands of the other generals until they rebuilt most of Alexander's empire from Sardis to India. And as you well know, Dimitrios, if I let those Romans chip away at what my forefathers won, they'll persist until there's nothing left."

"That's right, my king," the adviser mumbled, fighting to stay awake.

"I can't let them do that!" Antiochus's voice was growing shrill.

"I'm as good as my fathers!" His fist hit the table, jolting his captive audience awake. "I won't be the one to lose what they gained."

"But, my lord," Dimitrios said, repeating what he'd told the king every night for a week, "you aren't yet strong enough to—"

At that moment, a soldier entered. "My king, a man is here who says he must see you."

"I presume this man has a name."

"He calls himself Menelaus. He—"

"Send him in. Immediately!"

Menelaus entered the tent. His robes were tattered, his beard and hair unkempt. Despite his Greek name, his features marked him as a Jew. He bowed before Antiochus.

"O great king, my lord and my benefactor. I seek your refuge and protection."

"What has happened?" Antiochus asked.

"There is rebellion in Jerusalem. Jason, whom you deposed when you appointed me high priest, has raised an army and is leading the Jews in revolt against you. He has taken over Jerusalem and the Temple. I barely escaped with my life."

For the next hour, Menelaus poured out details of the rebellion as Antiochus listened intently. When he'd heard enough, he sent Menelaus to be fed and given a place to sleep.

With eyes burning in rage, Antiochus turned to his general. "Gudea, we will delay our return to Babylon. In the morning we march toward Jerusalem. We must crush these Jews like the rebels they are."

As Gudea and Dimitrios left Antiochus's tent, the general turned to Dimitrios. "This Menelaus has done us a great favor: he has diverted the king's attention from Rome. I don't know how much longer I could have put up with his raving. He's a madman! He may call himself Epiphanes—god on earth—but he's really an *epimanes*, an absolute madman."

* * *

Ten days later, Antiochus sat on his horse at the crest of Mount Olivet, looking over the city of Jerusalem. General Gudea and the army awaited orders behind him.

"I want this city utterly ravaged. Cut down every Jew you can—young or old, male or female, virgin or married. Allow them no refuge. If they run to the Temple, pursue them and slay them on the spot."

"Do you want the entire population destroyed?"

"No, I want a remnant left to endure the misery I intend to inflict. Feed your swords on Jewish blood for three days. After that, anyone still standing will be spared, though they will soon wish that they, too, had perished."

Gudea obeyed the king. For three days, the cries of the dying, fleeing, wounded, and grieving rang through the city. When the slaughter ended, more than forty thousand Jews had been slain.

When Gudea reported the number to Antiochus, he stamped his foot. "It's not enough! Go back and capture that many more alive and exile them as slaves throughout our territories."

After Gudea had completed the task, Antiochus assembled the remaining Jews and addressed them from the steps of the Temple.

"My father, Antiochus III, treated you Jews well. He allowed you to retain your religion, your worship, your sacrifices, your Torah, and your rituals. Yet you have repaid his generosity by revolting against his empire.

"As your punishment, I now rescind my father's policy. From this day forward, you are forbidden to worship the God you call Yahweh. Every copy of the Torah will be destroyed. You will cease your Temple sacrifices. You will no longer observe your Sabbath. You are forbidden from circumcising your boys. You will no longer call certain meats unclean. You will adopt the Greek culture of the Seleucid Empire and worship the great god Zeus like the rest of my nations.

"I have reestablished Menelaus as your high priest, and he is charged with enforcing my decrees to the letter. Be assured that violators will be severely punished. As you now know, I have the power and the will to do it."

Antiochus ordered a small army to remain in Jerusalem and returned to Babylon, leaving behind a grieving contingent of Jews. Many who survived the slaughter adopted Greek culture and even began worshiping the pantheon of Greek gods. Those who didn't either fled the city or practiced their Jewish religion underground.

Menelaus and the Syrian soldiers found and killed as many of these dissenters as they could, but it soon became apparent that there were more Jews who secretly retained their religion than the overlords could control.

Menelaus reported this groundswell of resistance to Antiochus, whose antipathy for the Jews had swollen into sheer hatred. He again marched his army into Jerusalem, this time virtually destroying the interior of the city. He did, however, leave the Temple standing—but only to serve his diabolic purposes.

With the devastation of Jerusalem completed, Antiochus called in Dimitrios. "It's now time for you to set up the Temple as you've been instructed. When the task is complete, have the people gather there."

"Consider it done, my king."

* * *

Two days later, all the Jews still in Jerusalem assembled at the Temple, filling its outer courts and overflowing into the streets. Soldiers arrived and parted the crowd as Antiochus and his entourage, dressed in Greek togas, arrived on their steeds. They rode up the Temple steps, through the Court of the Gentiles, and dismounted at the great altar that stood before the Temple's most holy place. Antiochus climbed the steps to the platform around the altar, where he turned and addressed the people.

"You obstinate Jews are slow to learn. We killed and deported eighty thousand of you, but you learned nothing. Your instructions were to abandon your Jewish religion and adopt the customs of the rest of my empire. But you defied me and continued to worship a God who couldn't save your country from invasion, your people from slaughter, or your city from destruction. He couldn't even keep from being ousted from His own Temple. So I must complete your education with three additional lessons."

At his signal, four servants entered the court leading a huge, tethered pig. Great cries rippled through the astonished crowd as the sow was led up the steps and hoisted onto the altar. The servants held down the squealing animal as Antiochus drew his sword and slit its throat. The servants caught the blood in a golden Temple bowl and then lit the kindling. Black smoke began to billow upward, polluting the heavens.

"That is your first lesson," Antiochus said. "Now you will witness the second."

He descended the altar steps and strode directly to the enclosed holy place. A servant carrying the bowl of pig's blood followed. The king took the bowl and spattered the blood throughout the Temple. Then he tossed the bowl, sending it clattering, and strode to the curtain covering the Holy of Holies. This was the most sacred chamber in the Temple—the place where the Jews believed the presence of Yahweh resided. Only the high priest was allowed to enter the room—and only once a year, at the ritual of atonement.

With one sweeping movement, Antiochus flung back the curtain. The Jews who could see into the chamber gasped with horror. There, in the place where Moses' Ark of the Covenant should have resided, stood an eight-foot statue of the Greek god Zeus, bearing the facial likeness of Antiochus himself.

"This is now your god!" Antiochus cried. "From today forward, you will worship him and him alone." As he spoke, a beautiful girl attired in a translucent robe walked up beside him. "Forty of these cultic harlots have been installed in your Temple so you can participate in the rituals of your new religion. From now on, the Jewish religion no longer exists. You will worship only Zeus, the great god of the Greeks."

Antiochus's handlers brought him his steed, and the horror-stricken Jews stood in shock as he rode out of the Temple.

One of the witnesses was an elderly Jewish priest named Mattathias. He had fled Jerusalem months earlier in order to continue the Jewish rituals that Antiochus had already forbidden. Now doubly outraged, he returned to his home in Modein, reported what he had seen, and rallied the people of his village to stand firm against the decree to worship Zeus. He secured a vow that none of them would bow to the Greek gods. That vow would soon be tested.

Mattathias was praying in his home when his son Judas entered. "Father, you must come quickly," he cried. "An emissary of Antiochus has arrived. He has summoned you to the town square."

The aging priest hurried to the square, leaning on his son's arm. He was greeted by a young Greek man standing beside a crude altar. Laid across the altar was a bound goat, alive and bleating.

"Greetings, Mattathias," the man said. "I am Apelles, appointed to oversee the worship of the great god Zeus in every Judean town. You, I am told, are the most influential citizen of Modein. Therefore, I order you to sacrifice this goat according to the king's command."

"I will do no such thing." Mattathias's voice was resolute. "Even if every city in every nation under the dominion of Antiochus obeys this order, I will worship the true God alone—and so will my sons and my brothers in this town."

"Then I am ordered to cut you down, as we did to those in Jerusalem who refused the order." Apelles nodded to his commander, who reached for his sword.

Suddenly a man burst forward from the crowd and fell on his

knees before Apelles. "No! Please don't kill us. I'll offer the sacrifice for the sake of our town."

At that moment, Mattathias drew his sword and struck the man through the neck. Then he turned and drove the weapon into Apelles's belly. Both men dropped to the ground, dead.

In a flash, Judas drew his sword and rushed at Apelles's commander, catching him off guard and felling him with two mighty strokes. Mattathias's other sons already had their weapons drawn when the five remaining soldiers rushed at them. After a brief clash, all five of the Seleucids lay dead.

Mattathias knew they had just committed an irrevocable deed that would draw the wrath of Antiochus. He called to the citizens, "We must flee, or we will face certain death. Anyone who is zealous for the law of our God and for this land He's given us, come with us."

The people of Modein abandoned their possessions, taking only their weapons and whatever food and clothing their animals could carry. They followed Mattathias and his sons and found hiding places in the mountains. Word of their defiance spread quickly, and Judeans in other cities, inspired by the priest's bold actions, joined them, collecting weapons and finding refuge in hills, valleys, and desert places. Soon the sons of Mattathias built a sizable army and prepared them to meet the forces of Antiochus when they returned.

The revolt had begun—a revolt that would throw off the yoke of the cruelest tyrant the Jews had ever endured and gain their independence for the first time in four hundred years.

Antiochus IV was dealing with revolts in the eastern parts of his empire when the Jewish revolt began. He ordered his vassal, the Syrian king, to put down the rebellion. When the king failed, Antiochus headed to Israel, intending to take charge of the war. But on the way, he was struck down by a terrible illness. His body was eaten alive by parasitic worms and ulcers, which afflicted him so severely that he couldn't stand the stench of his own body.

Antiochus IV died a quick death in 164 BC, ending the infamous career of the little horn from Daniel's vision.

* * *

THE SCRIPTURE BEHIND THE STORY

Daniel's second vision, recorded for us in Daniel 8, is arranged around the extraordinary lives of three characters. In the previous chapter, we discovered the prophecy concerning one of history's greatest generals—Alexander the Great (Daniel 8:1-8, 15-22). But the remaining verses in Daniel 8 tell us of two of history's most evil dictators—Antiochus Epiphanes, who lived from 215 BC to 164 BC, and the Antichrist, whose reign is yet in the future (Daniel 8:9-14, 23-27).

The first chapter of the apocryphal book of 1 Maccabees explains the transition between Alexander, conqueror and ruler of the Greek Empire, and Antiochus, subsequent ruler of the Seleucid portion of that empire:

> When Alexander had been emperor for twelve years, he fell ill and realized that he was about to die. He called together his generals . . . and he divided his empire, giving a part to each of them.
>
> The wicked ruler Antiochus Epiphanes, son of King Antiochus the Third of Syria, was a descendant of one of Alexander's generals. . . . He became king of Syria in the year [175] B.C.
>
> When Antiochus had firmly established himself as king, he decided to conquer Egypt. . . . Antiochus was able to capture the fortified cities of Egypt and plunder the whole land.
>
> In the year [169] B.C., after the conquest of Egypt,

Antiochus marched with a great army against the land of
Israel and the city of Jerusalem.[1]

Antiochus and his cruel treatment of the Jews provide an appalling, prophetic preview of the Antichrist and the persecution he will
inflict on believers during the coming Tribulation. In Daniel 8, we see
the striking parallels between these two evil rulers. Daniel's prophecies
concerning Antiochus have been explicitly fulfilled, while the chillingly
similar but amplified atrocities of the Antichrist are yet to come.

The parallels between these two tyrants are so striking that some
scholars have called Antiochus "the Antichrist of the Old Testament."
Let's examine these parallels and determine what they mean for us.

The Cruelty of Antiochus and the Antichrist

Out of one of them came a little horn which grew
exceedingly great toward the south, toward the east,
and toward the Glorious Land.
DANIEL 8:9

The prophecy of "the little horn" was fulfilled in Antiochus
Epiphanes. His name means "God manifest."

The Seleucid Empire once covered much of Alexander's empire, but
by the time Antiochus took the throne, it had become greatly reduced.
So he embarked on a quest to regain the empire's lost territories.

Antiochus rose from insignificance and became a great power.
While on the throne, he made noteworthy conquests in the south
(Egypt), the east (Persia), and "the Glorious Land" (Israel).

THE DESCRIPTION OF HIS DEPRAVITY
According to historian Solomon Zeitlin, Antiochus holds the distinction of being "the first person in history to persecute a people

exclusively for their religious faith. Religious persecution was previously unknown in the history of civilization."[2] As history shows us, Antiochus did everything he could to completely annihilate the Jewish religion:

> The king also sent messengers with a decree to Jerusalem
> and all the towns of Judea, ordering the people to follow
> customs that were foreign to the country. He ordered them
> not to offer burnt offerings, grain offerings, or wine offerings
> in the Temple, and commanded them to treat Sabbaths
> and festivals as ordinary work days. They were even ordered
> to defile the Temple and the holy things in it. They were
> commanded to build pagan altars, temples, and shrines,
> and to sacrifice pigs and other unclean animals there. They
> were forbidden to circumcise their sons and were required
> to make themselves ritually unclean in every way they could,
> so that they would forget the Law which the Lord had given
> through Moses and would disobey all its commands. The
> penalty for disobeying the king's decree was death.[3]

Long before Antiochus arrived on the world stage, Daniel foresaw him and his wicked work. Nearly 350 years before Antiochus was born, Daniel had a vision that he would defeat the saints, defile the Temple, and destroy the Scriptures. Here's how those prophecies were fulfilled.

He Defeated the Saints

> [The little horn] grew up to the host of heaven; and it cast
> down some of the host and some of the stars to the ground,
> and trampled them.
>
> DANIEL 8:10

Leon Wood explains the imagery in this verse for us: "The host of heaven, or stars, refers to the people of God (cf. [Daniel] 12:3; Gen. 15:5; 22:17; Ex. 12:41), and the symbolism is that Antiochus would oppress God's people, the Jews, in their land."[4]

The books of 1 and 2 Maccabees tell an appalling story of two deeply committed Jewish mothers who determined to circumcise their infant boys. When Antiochus heard about it, he killed the babies and hung their dead bodies around each mother's neck. Next, he marched the mothers, all their family members, and anyone who had assisted with the circumcision through the streets of Jerusalem, up to the highest wall of the city. Then he flung them to their deaths on the rocks below. [5]

One of the most hideous stories about Antiochus is recorded in 2 Maccabees 7:

> On another occasion, a Jewish mother and her seven sons were arrested and beaten, then forced to eat pork. One of the young men said, "What do you hope to gain by doing this? We would rather die than abandon the traditions of our ancestors."
>
> This made the king so furious that he gave orders for huge pans and kettles to be heated to a boil. Then he told his men to cut off the tongue of the son who had spoken, as well as to scalp him and chop off his hands and feet while his mother and six brothers looked on. Then the king gave orders for him to be thrown into one of the pans. As a cloud of smoke streamed from the pan, the brothers and their mother encouraged one another to die bravely, saying, "The Lord God is looking on and understands our suffering."[6]

Historians tell us that during his attack on Jerusalem, Antiochus Epiphanes killed some eighty thousand Jews and sold another forty thousand into slavery.

He Defiled the Sanctuary

> He even exalted himself as high as the Prince of the host;
> and by him the daily sacrifices were taken away, and the
> place of His sanctuary was cast down.
>
> DANIEL 8:11

Antiochus didn't just think he was equal to the almighty God; he believed he and the Greek gods were superior to the living God of Israel. He was determined to extinguish the Jewish religion forever and replace it with Greek worship and culture.

Antiochus Epiphanes canceled all the Jewish festivals and instead required the Jews to celebrate Greek feasts. One of these was the celebration of Bacchanalia, which involved the worship of Bacchus, the god of pleasure and wine. He also forced the Jews to observe the Saturnalia, an ancient Roman festival dedicated to worshiping Saturn. He installed harlots in the Temple for these celebrations and forbade the observance of the Sabbath. He forced the Jews to observe all his pagan feast days and banned the practice of circumcision.

When Scripture speaks of God's sanctuary being "cast down" (Daniel 8:11), it doesn't mean the Temple was destroyed but rather that it was defiled. First Maccabees 1:21-24 records how this happened: "In [Antiochus's] arrogance, he entered the Temple and took away the gold altar, the lampstand with all its equipment, the table for the bread offered to the Lord, the cups and bowls, the gold fire pans, the curtain, and the crowns. He also stripped all the gold from the front of the Temple and carried off the silver and gold and everything else of value, including all the treasures that he could find stored there. Then he took it all to his own country. He had also murdered many people and boasted arrogantly about it."[7]

On another occasion, Antiochus brought a sow to the Temple

and, slitting its throat, sacrificed it on the sacred altar. He collected the pig's blood and sprayed it all over the inside of the Temple. This unholy sacrifice of an unclean animal on the sacred Temple altar is "the abomination of desolation" prophesied first by Daniel and later by Jesus (Daniel 11:31; 12:11; Mark 13:14). Antiochus's sacrifice was the initial fulfillment of the Daniel prophecy. The final fulfillment will occur when the Antichrist breaks his covenant with Israel, enthrones himself in the Temple, erects a profane image in the holy place, and desecrates the Temple altar with an unclean sacrifice.

In His Olivet discourse, Jesus refers to Antiochus's unholy sacrifice as typifying a comparable event that will happen in the future: "When you see the 'abomination of desolation,' spoken of by Daniel the prophet, standing where it ought not . . . then let those who are in Judea flee to the mountains" (Mark 13:14).

He Destroyed the Scripture

Because of transgression, an army was given over to the horn to oppose the daily sacrifices; and he cast truth down to the ground. He did all this and prospered.

DANIEL 8:12

Antiochus "cast truth down to the ground" by outlawing the reading of the Scriptures and burning every copy of the Torah he could get his hands on: "Any books of the Law which were found were torn up and burned, and anyone who was caught with a copy of the sacred books or who obeyed the Law was put to death by order of the king."[8]

These are just a few examples from the long history of agony the Jews endured under Antiochus Epiphanes. Is it any wonder they hated this Greek ruler and privately called him "Antiochus Epimanes," which means "Antiochus the Madman"?

THE DURATION OF HIS DESTRUCTION

After seeing the vision of Antiochus's reign of terror, Daniel asked, "How long will the vision be, concerning the daily sacrifices and the transgression of desolation, the giving of both the sanctuary and the host to be trampled underfoot?" (Daniel 8:13).

If you were a Jew who had seen a vision revealing the desolation of everything your people considered holy, isn't that the question you would ask? "How long will God let this go on?" How long would He allow such a terrible thing to happen to His people and His holy place?

In Daniel's vision, one of the holy ones answered that question explicitly: the sanctuary would be cleansed after 2,300 days (Daniel 8:14). In his commentary on Daniel, Lehman Strauss points out that "the literal expression for 'days' is 'evenings-mornings,' so that the most feasible and simplest interpretation would be a period of twenty-four hours. This means that there were to be 2,300 repetitions of the evening and morning sacrifices to be polluted at the hands of the little horn."[9]

The established date for the restoration and cleansing of the Temple under Judas Maccabeus was December 14, 164 BC. If we count back 2,300 days from that event, we arrive at fall of 170 BC—the date of the beginning of Antiochus's oppression of the Jews.

Now let's look at how this 2,300-day prophecy of persecution came to an end. The Jewish resistance to Antiochus's brutal reign began in the village of Modein, located between Jerusalem and Joppa. This town was the home of an aged priest named Mattathias. When the commissioner of Antiochus commanded Mattathias to take the lead in offering a pagan sacrifice, he responded with these words: "I don't care if every Gentile in this empire has obeyed the king and yielded to the command to abandon the religion of his ancestors. My children, my relatives, and I will continue to keep the covenant that God made with our ancestors. With God's help we will never abandon his Law or disobey his commands. We will not obey the king's decree, and we will not change our way of worship in the least."[10]

Mattathias then killed the commissioner, overturned the altar, and fled with his five sons to the hills. They became known as the Maccabees, a term believed to come from the Aramaic word meaning "hammer," a symbol of the ferocity of Mattathias's sons. Many other Jews joined the Maccabees in all-out guerrilla warfare against Antiochus.

In 164 BC, after more than two years of fighting, the Maccabean warriors finally recaptured the Temple and cleansed it from the abomination of desolation.

When the Temple was recaptured, the Maccabees wanted to light the menorah, the sacred Temple candlestick, but they could find only a small flask of the special oil required for use in the Temple—barely enough to keep the menorah lit for one day. According to tradition, the oil miraculously lasted for eight days, which gave them enough time to obtain a new supply of the purified oil to keep the menorah burning.

To commemorate this deliverance and the Temple's rededication, the Jews established the perpetual feast of Hanukkah, a word that means "dedication." The celebration is sometimes referred to as the Feast of Dedication or the Festival of Lights.

Today the Jews celebrate Hanukkah beginning on the twenty-fifth day of Kislev (in November or December on our calendar) by placing the menorah in a window or doorway where it's visible from the outside. Each day during the eight-day celebration, in late afternoon, one candle is lit until finally, on the eighth night, all eight candles are burning brightly.[11]

A commentary on the book of Daniel offers this story about God's provision for His people: "A persecutor of the Jews in Russia asked a Jewish man what he thought the outcome would be if the wave of persecution continued. The Jew answered, 'The result will be a feast! Pharaoh tried to destroy the Jews, but the result was the Passover. Haman attempted to destroy the Jews, but the result was the Feast of Purim. Antiochus Epiphanes tried to destroy the Jews, but the result was the Feast of Dedication.'"[12]

The Characteristics of Antiochus and the Antichrist

At the end of Daniel 8:22, we reach a point of transition. The first twenty-two verses have predicted the rise of the Greek Empire, its subsequent fragmentation, and the cruel oppression of the Jews under Antiochus.

In verse 23, the chapter enters a new phase. Louis T. Talbot explains:

When the vision recorded here was given to Daniel, all of it had to do with then prophetic events; whereas we today can look back and see that everything in verses 1-22 refers to men and empires that have come and gone. We read about them in the pages of secular history. But verses 23-27 of the chapter before us have to do with "a king of fierce countenance" who shall appear "in the latter time" (v. 23); and he is none other than the Antichrist who is to come. Again, while vs. 1-22 have to do with history, yet the men of whom they speak were shadows of that coming "man of sin" who is more fully described in the closing verses of the chapter.[13]

In his book *Cashless*, Mark Hitchcock writes, "There are more than 100 passages of Scripture that describe the . . . Antichrist. God doesn't want us to be preoccupied with this individual in an unhealthy, unbalanced way, but clearly God wants us to know some things about this coming prince of darkness."[14]

In the last half of Daniel 8, God gives us an introduction to the

Antichrist, describing eight characteristics that define this man of evil who will appear on the world stage during the coming Tribulation period.

HE WILL BE DYNAMIC IN HIS PERSONALITY

> In the latter time of their kingdom, when the transgressors have reached their fullness, a king shall arise, having fierce features.
>
> DANIEL 8:23

This verse portrays an individual with a bold countenance who will present himself in an arrogant manner.

John Phillips imagines what it will be like when the Antichrist comes onto the scene: "The world will go delirious with delight at his manifestation. He will be the seeming answer to all its needs. He will be filled with all the fullness of Satan. Handsome, with a charming, rakish, devil-may-care personality, a genius, superbly at home in all the scientific disciplines, brave as a lion, and with an air of mystery about him to tease the imagination or to chill the blood as occasion may serve, a brilliant conversationalist in a score of tongues . . . he will be the idol of all mankind."[15]

The Bible confirms what Phillips suggests: the Antichrist will be a gifted communicator.

- He has "a mouth speaking great things" (Daniel 7:8, ESV).
- He has "a mouth that spoke great things" (Daniel 7:20, ESV).
- "He was given a mouth speaking great things and blasphemies" (Revelation 13:5).

In one of my other books, I compare the Antichrist to some of history's greatest communicators: "Orators like Abraham Lincoln,

Winston Churchill, John F. Kennedy, Martin Luther King Jr., and yes, even Adolf Hitler, were masters at captivating and moving large audiences. But even their best and most passionate speeches will be dull compared to the rhetoric of the Antichrist."[16]

HE WILL BE DEMONIC IN HIS PROGRAM

Who understands sinister schemes . . .
DANIEL 8:23

The phrase "understands sinister schemes" refers to the ability to solve problems. "Sinister schemes" could be more literally translated as "dark sayings." Some expositors believe this is a reference to the occult. Scripture says this man of fierce countenance will present himself as a leader with a superhuman ability to solve the problems of his day. But his power will come from the invisible realms of darkness.

HE WILL BE DEVILISH IN HIS POWER

His power shall be mighty, but not by his own power.
DANIEL 8:24

When I read of the atrocities of Antiochus Epiphanes, I realize that he couldn't have been as evil as he was unless he had a special relationship with Satan, which is undoubtedly the meaning of the verse above. Surely this man was demon possessed!

The reign of Antiochus was a dress rehearsal for the reign of the Antichrist, who will also be empowered by Satan:

- "The coming of the lawless one is according to the working of Satan, with all power, signs, and lying wonders" (2 Thessalonians 2:9).

- "The dragon [Satan] gave him his power, his throne, and great authority" (Revelation 13:2).

HE WILL BE DESTRUCTIVE IN HIS PERSECUTION

He shall destroy fearfully. . . . He shall destroy the mighty, and also the holy people.

DANIEL 8:24

Antiochus's anger toward "the holy people" is a picture of the persecution the Antichrist will carry out against believers in the future: "It was granted to him to make war with the saints and to overcome them" (Revelation 13:7).

Everything I've discovered about Antiochus Epiphanes causes me to shudder, but when I consider that the Antichrist is going to be exponentially more evil than he was, I understand why Daniel "fainted and was sick for days" after he saw the vision and heard Gabriel's explanation (Daniel 8:27). How terrible will the reign of the Antichrist be? Jesus said, "Unless those days were shortened, no flesh would be saved; but for the elect's sake those days will be shortened" (Matthew 24:22).

HE WILL BE DECEITFUL IN HIS PRACTICES

Through his cunning he shall cause deceit to prosper under his rule.

DANIEL 8:25

Antiochus Epiphanes was the poster child for cunning and deceit. The apocryphal book of 1 Maccabees provides this illustration: "Antiochus sent a large army from Mysia against the towns of Judea. When the soldiers entered Jerusalem, their commander spoke to the people, offering them terms of peace and completely deceiving them. Then he suddenly launched a fierce attack on the city, dealing it a major blow and killing many of the people. He plundered the city, set it on fire, and tore down its buildings and walls. He and his army took the women and children as prisoners and seized the cattle."[17]

This gives us a preview of the deceit of the Antichrist. In order to make peace with the Jews, he will make a seven-year covenant with them at the beginning of the Tribulation period. He will gain their confidence by promising freedom to worship and observe their feast days according to their laws and traditions. Then, after three and a half years, he'll break the covenant: "He shall confirm a covenant with many for one week; but in the middle of the week he shall bring an end to sacrifice and offering. And on the wing of abominations shall be one who makes desolate, even until the consummation, which is determined, is poured out on the desolate" (Daniel 9:27).

In his second letter to the Thessalonians, Paul further describes this treacherous man: "The coming of the lawless one is according to the working of Satan, with all power, signs, and lying wonders, and with all unrighteous deception among those who perish, because they did not receive the love of the truth, that they might be saved" (2:9-10).

HE WILL BE DEFIANT IN HIS PROFESSION

> He shall exalt himself in his heart. He shall destroy many
> in their prosperity. He shall even rise against the Prince
> of princes.
>
> DANIEL 8:25

Antiochus professed to be God himself. The coins minted during his reign bore these words: *Antiochus, Theos Epiphanes*, meaning,

"Antiochus, God Manifest." Antiochus claimed to be God, again prefiguring the coming Antichrist, who will make the same claim.

Paul describes the scope of this audacious claim, calling the Antichrist the "man of sin" and the "son of perdition, who opposes and exalts himself above all that is called God or that is worshiped, so that he sits as God in the temple of God, showing himself that he is God" (2 Thessalonians 2:3-4).

HE WILL BE DEFEATED IN HIS PURPOSE

He shall be broken without human means.

DANIEL 8:25

Antiochus was determined to force the nations under his rule to adopt Greek culture and religion. He reserved his greatest fury for the Jews, who stubbornly resisted his forced idolatry. But he was defeated in his purpose by the Maccabean revolt.

Again Antiochus gives us a miniature portrait of the coming Antichrist, who will also be defeated in his ultimate purpose of bringing the entire earth under his demonic control.

HE WILL BE DESTINED TO PUNISHMENT

I watched till the beast was slain, and its body destroyed and given to the burning flame. . . . He shall be broken without human means.

DANIEL 7:11; 8:25

Even in his inglorious end, Antiochus Epiphanes illustrated the destiny of the Antichrist. When the Jews cast the image of Jupiter out of the Temple, Antiochus was enraged. He vowed to turn the city of Jerusalem into a cemetery. On his way to Jerusalem, he was suddenly afflicted with a horrible disease that caused his body to be eaten alive by ulcers and worms. His suffering was unbearable, and the stench from his own body was so vile that even he couldn't stand the smell.

Finding it impossible to fulfill his threat, he confessed that he knew he was suffering because of what he'd done to the Jews and their worship. He died in misery, a foolish man who thought he could resist God and get away with it. He was brought down supernaturally without a human hand touching him.[18]

Just as Antiochus was brought down by nonhuman means, so will the Antichrist meet his end. And just as Antiochus received severe punishment for his war against God, so will the Antichrist. He will be "cast alive into the lake of fire burning with brimstone" (Revelation 19:21). He'll share with Satan eternal punishment in the "everlasting fire prepared for the devil and his angels" (Matthew 25:41).

The Conclusion of Antiochus and the Antichrist

> The vision of the evenings and mornings which was told is true; therefore seal up the vision, for it refers to many days in the future.
>
> DANIEL 8:26

In Daniel 8, God gives us a picture of the future using the historical Antiochus as a preview of the terrors that will come under the rule of the Antichrist. The historical scope of the vision is astounding, offering details of the kingdoms yet to come under the reigns of Alexander, Antiochus, and the Antichrist—a span of thousands of years.

The angel's parting words to Daniel in verse 26 have caused some people to think he was told to keep the vision to himself. In other words, "Don't tell anyone about this—just box it up and stow it away." But that wasn't the angel's message. God was commanding Daniel to preserve the vision and its message so it could be communicated to others. Lehman Strauss explains, "Daniel was to take such precautions about the preservation and manifolding of the manuscript as might be necessary so that the document could be preserved for a long time to come. Nothing about it was intended to be kept secret."[19]

The vision was proven true when it was fulfilled in the time of Antiochus. That assures us beyond doubt that it will be proven true at the end of time as well, with the coming of the Antichrist.

When Daniel saw this grim picture of the future, he was overwhelmed, shaken to the core of his being. In Daniel 8, he says, "I, Daniel, fainted and was sick for days; afterward I arose and went about the king's business. I was astonished by the vision, but no one understood it" (verse 27).

Every time I read Daniel 8, I can't help but wonder why we aren't more emotionally affected when we hear about the coming judgment of this world. The apostles' thinking was heavily influenced by their awareness of the judgment to come in the last days. As someone has aptly said, they lived with an end-times view of the world. Their activities in the present were shaped by their acute awareness of the future.

The predictions in the book of Daniel that have already been fulfilled should serve as a reminder that the ones yet to be fulfilled will indeed come to pass. And that should impress on us the importance of living every day as if the end times may begin tomorrow.

During Dwight D. Eisenhower's term as president of the United States, he was vacationing in Denver when he learned that six-year-old Paul Haley, a Denver resident, was dying of cancer. The boy's greatest ambition was to meet his hero, the current president.

President Eisenhower had an aide find the boy's address, and the following Sunday, he was driven in the presidential limousine for an unannounced visit to the home of the dying boy. He personally knocked on the door and was greeted by Paul's stunned father,

Donald Haley, who was unshaved and dressed in old jeans and a dirty shirt.

The president asked to see the man's son, and he treated the boy royally. He shook his hand, chatted a bit, and then took Paul out for a tour of the presidential limousine. After hugging the boy and shaking his hand again, Eisenhower left.

The visit was the talk of the neighborhood for weeks. Everybody was ecstatic to hear that the president of the United States had paid one of their own a personal visit. That is, everybody but one: Paul's father, Donald. He said, "How can I ever forget standing there dressed like I was in those jeans and an old, dirty shirt and an unshaven face to meet the president of the United States?"[20]

Donald Haley wasn't prepared. We can easily forgive him, because he had no idea the leader of the free world was about to pay him a visit. But you and I have no such excuse. We know that the Name above all names is coming. Not only does Daniel prophesy of His coming, but such prophecies abound throughout the Bible, from Genesis to Revelation. And we know from reading the parallels between fulfilled and unfulfilled prophecy—like those presented in Daniel 8—that the predicted events yet to come will certainly happen. We know that Jesus Christ is coming; we just don't know when.

* * *

DANIEL FOR TODAY

The Lord is coming, so we should get moving! Our study of Daniel 8 has motivated me to serve the Lord with greater intensity, and I hope it's spurred you on as well.

1. Get excited! Believers' lives are marked by a sense of anticipation shared by no one else on earth—only those who are awaiting Christ's imminent return. That's something to get excited about. "When these things begin to happen, look up and lift up your heads, because your redemption draws near" (Luke 21:28).

2. Get busy! Jesus has a daily allotment of work for each of us to do. We have a world to reach, and every one of us has a role to fill. There's no time to waste. The closer we come to His return, the busier we become in doing His labor—and it's a joy! "Blessed is that servant whom his master, when he comes, will find so doing" (Matthew 24:46).

3. Get ready! The books of Daniel and Revelation, along with the other prophetic promises of God, compel us to live with a sense of readiness. Walk with Him today. Stay pure. Stay prayerful. If He comes before you finish reading this page, be ready to meet Him with a clear conscience and a joyful spirit. "Behold, I am coming as a thief. Blessed is he who watches, and keeps his garments, lest he walk naked and they see his shame" (Revelation 16:15).

Chapter 10

THE HERALD

Daniel 9:1-27

IT WAS THE JEWISH SABBATH, and Daniel had just returned from his customary worship with other exiles in Babylon. He was grateful that King Darius, who ruled the Persian Empire under Cyrus the Great, allowed him this weekly day of rest in accordance with the Scripture's commands. He now sat at a table in his home and, as had been his custom for seven decades, pored over one of the scrolls of the Jewish prophets, which he had bought from traveling merchants.

For the past several Sabbaths, Daniel had been reviewing Jeremiah's prophecies. Although he had read Jeremiah's words many times, he wept as he was reminded how God's people had ignored the prophet's warnings that captivity would result from their failure to follow God's law.

> Now the LORD of Heaven's Armies says: Because you have
> not listened to me, I will gather together all the armies
> of the north under King Nebuchadnezzar of Babylon,

whom I have appointed as my deputy. I will bring them all against this land and its people and against the surrounding nations. I will completely destroy you and make you an object of horror and contempt and a ruin forever. I will take away your happy singing and laughter. The joyful voices of bridegrooms and brides will no longer be heard. Your millstones will fall silent, and the lights in your homes will go out.[1]

Daniel sighed deeply. It had all happened just as Jeremiah had foretold. Now the Jews lived as captives in Babylon, their beautiful land desolate, the magnificent Temple razed, and their great city destroyed, now the lair of jackals and vultures. As he read, Daniel thought, as he had thought many times before, *How could my people have been so foolish?*

But as Daniel continued to trace his finger over the words of the scroll, his heart began to beat faster. He scanned the passage once more and then a third time as elation began to fill his soul. The words on the scroll suddenly came alive:

"Israel and her neighboring lands will serve the king of Babylon for seventy years.

"Then, after the seventy years of captivity are over, I will punish the king of Babylon and his people for their sins," says the LORD. "I will make the country of the Babylonians a wasteland forever. I will bring upon them all the terrors I have promised in this book—all the penalties announced by Jeremiah against the nations. Many nations and great kings will enslave the Babylonians, just as they enslaved my people. I will punish them in proportion to the suffering they cause my people."[2]

"Our faithful God has promised us a future and a hope," Daniel said, his voice catching in his throat. His tears of sadness were turning into tears of overwhelming joy.

Yes, God had punished His people, just as Jeremiah had warned. But here in Jeremiah's prophecy was God's reminder that after seventy years, He would restore them to their land. Daniel paused and calculated the reigns of the kings he'd served. Sixty-seven years! The time of Jeremiah's predicted return was upon them. It would occur in three short years. Eagerly, Daniel continued to read:

"In those days when you pray, I will listen. If you look for me wholeheartedly, you will find me. I will be found by you," says the LORD. "I will end your captivity and restore your fortunes. I will gather you out of the nations where I sent you and will bring you home again to your own land."[3]

The meaning of the passage was clear to Daniel: the key to the fulfillment of this prophecy—that Israel would return to its homeland—was the prayers of the people. Daniel had always been a praying man. Throughout his long years in Babylon, he prayed formally three times each day, bowing on his knees to face Jerusalem. And between those times, he prayed continually, making God his constant companion.

Had the Jews in Babylon been confessing their sins and praying for their return to Judah? Daniel suspected that most of them had not. Either way, he would pray for them. He would take the burden of the Jews' sins and place them before his God. Immediately he fell to his knees and began to pray.

Daniel praised God for His mercy. He recounted the sins of His people who had turned away from His law. He confessed that they hadn't heeded His prophets' warnings. He admitted that they'd brought reproach to God's name among the nations. He admitted that they deserved the punishment God had laid upon them and that His judgment, though severe, was just. He recounted God's mighty power when He delivered His people from slavery in Egypt and prayed that He would repeat a similar glorious feat, bringing the captive Jews out of Babylon and restoring them to their land.

He begged forgiveness for the people's sins and pleaded for God's mercy—not because they deserved it, for they certainly did not, but because of God's great love for His people. He concluded his prayer, saying, "O Lord, hear. O Lord, forgive. O Lord, listen and act! For your own sake, do not delay, O my God, for your people and your city bear your name."[4]

* * *

As Daniel began his prayer, the great angel Gabriel stood in his customary place in heaven near the throne of God. Unspeakable brightness emanated from the throne, bathing everything in heaven with warmth and light.

Suddenly a voice, mighty and thunderous, resounded from the throne: "Gabriel, My faithful messenger, please approach My throne. I have a task for you."

A thrill ran through Gabriel's entire being. He stepped forward in anticipation. "I am here, my Lord, ready to do whatever You ask."

The great voice responded, "Your fellow creature and My beloved servant Daniel, the faithful Jew in Babylon, has at this moment begun a deep and heartfelt prayer to Me. I have already prepared an answer, and I want you to deliver it immediately."

"I will do so gladly, my Lord," Gabriel replied.

The angel received God's answer to Daniel's prayer, and without hesitation, he flew away, zooming across the vast reaches of space. Experience had taught him to be wary of the demonic beings that continually lurked about, bent on disrupting all angelic assistance directed toward the fallen planet Earth.

Gabriel had begun his descent toward Babylon when he suddenly caught sight of a mass of dark beings hovering over Persia. Even from a distance, he could see that they were demons. *It seems they've increased their presence in the area,* he thought. *They must have discovered that God has something planned for Israel.* He veered around the loathsome creatures, keeping his distance, and finally reached Babylon. In the next instant, he stood in Daniel's presence, just as the man of God was finishing his prayer.

Daniel looked up, startled. He immediately recognized the majestic Gabriel as the angel who had delivered a message to him years ago concerning the late King Nebuchadnezzar. Yet he was again overwhelmed by the glory of this being's presence.

Gabriel did his best to put the trembling man at ease. "Daniel, God has sent me to tell you that you are greatly loved. He has heard your heartfelt prayer and sent me to deliver an answer. Since you have been so diligent in praying for your people, He wishes to give you a picture of their circumstances reaching far into the ages to come."

Gabriel outlined to Daniel events that would carry the Jewish nation 490 years into the future. The punishment for their sin would end, they would be restored to their city and their Temple, and their Messiah would come. But the Messiah would be cut off, and Jerusalem and the Temple would be destroyed yet again. In the far distant future, a new persecutor would arise like no other the world had seen. He would inflict terrible misery until the consummation of the glorious future awaiting God's people.

With his mission successfully completed, Gabriel vanished from Daniel's presence and returned to his place before the throne of God, eager to warn the other angels of the gathering of the enemy around Persia.

* * *

THE SCRIPTURE BEHIND THE STORY

In his book *Daniel*, Donald Campbell shares this story to illustrate the permanence of God's people throughout history:

A few years ago, a suburban area near one of our major cities was being developed as a very exclusive residential community. At first only a few Jewish people bought sites for homes; then more and more purchased lots. Other people in the community began to agitate to force the Jews out.

The minister of a nearby church announced as his sermon topic for the next Sunday, "How to Get Rid of the Jews." This caused a furor. Everyone in the area talked about it all week, and some Jews even protested to the governor of the state.

When Sunday came, the church was jammed with people. A Jewish rabbi and two reporters appeared and stalked to the front row. The pastor read his text: "Thus saith the LORD, which giveth the sun for a light by day, and the ordinances of the moon and of the stars for a light by night, who divideth the sea when the waves thereof roar. . . . If those ordinances . . . depart from before Me . . . then the seed of Israel also shall cease from being a nation before Me forever" (Jeremiah 31:35-36).[5]

This wise pastor was showing the people the immense value of the Jewish people in the eyes of God. Mistreat them, and you are treading on dangerous ground, for they are a people that God has blessed and promised a far-reaching and glorious plan for their future.

We've already seen God's plan for the Gentile nations (Daniel 2, 7). Now Daniel 9 reveals God's prophetic program for the Jews. No one who reads this chapter carefully will be able to believe that God is finished with His people, Israel. This prophetic program, which Daniel received from Gabriel, forms the backbone of Messianic prophecy—the prophecy of the seventy weeks.

Biblical scholars through the ages have noted how exceptional this chapter is in terms of biblical prophecy. Many have called it "the backbone of prophecy." H. A. Ironside says it's "the greatest of all-time prophecies."[6] H. C. Leupold writes that certain verses of this chapter "unroll a panorama of history that is without parallel even in the sacred Scriptures."[7] Philip R. Newell calls it "the greatest chapter in the book of Daniel and one of the greatest of the entire Bible."[8] Sir Isaac Newton believed we could stake the truth of Christianity on this prophecy alone.[9]

Clarence Larkin explains why Daniel 9 is foundational to all biblical prophecy:

> Daniel's seventieth week (Daniel 9:24-27), Jesus' Olivet Discourse (Matthew 24), and John's seals, trumpets, and vials (Revelation 6:1–18:24) cover the same period, and are Jewish and have no reference to the Christian Church. Daniel draws the outline in his seventieth week, Jesus roughs in the picture in His Olivet Discourse, and John fills in the details in the book of Revelation.[10]

Why did God reveal to Daniel these vital and profound prophecies? It started with a prayer Daniel felt moved to pray after making a discovery in the book of Jeremiah.

The Prayer

> I was speaking, praying, and confessing my sin and the sin of my people Israel, and presenting my supplication before the LORD my God for the holy mountain of my God.
> DANIEL 9:20

Like all true Old Testament prophets, Daniel was a man of prayer and Bible study: "There are three significant ninth chapters in the Old Testament, all of them containing a prayer of a similar nature: Ezra 9, Nehemiah 9, and Daniel 9. In each instance a servant of God was on his knees before the Word of God, earnestly interceding for the people of God. The Old Testament prophets did not sit in a passive state waiting for a revelation from God through a dream, a vision or a voice. They . . . spent time in prayer searching for the message and meaning of prophecy (1 Peter 1:10-12)."[11]

The prayer recorded in Daniel 9:4-19 is one of the greatest prayers in the entire Old Testament because it prepared the way for Daniel to receive one of the greatest prophecies in the Bible. And let's not miss the important fact that the prayer that led to the prophecy was rooted in Daniel's own personal Bible study: "In the first year of Darius . . . I, Daniel, understood by the books the number of the years specified by the word of the LORD through Jeremiah the prophet, that He would accomplish seventy years in the desolations of Jerusalem" (Daniel 9:1-2).

Daniel was reading Jeremiah's prediction that the captivity of the Jewish people would last seventy years. We can pinpoint exactly where Daniel was reading, because only three times in Jeremiah's prophecy does he mention the seventy years:

- "'This whole land shall be a desolation and an astonishment, and these nations shall serve the king of Babylon *seventy years*. Then it will come to pass, when *seventy years* are completed, that I will punish the king of Babylon and that nation, the land of the Chaldeans, for their iniquity,' says the LORD; 'and I will make it a perpetual desolation'" (Jeremiah 25:11-12, emphasis added).
- "Thus says the LORD: After *seventy years* are completed at Babylon, I will visit you and perform My good word toward

you, and cause you to return to this place" (Jeremiah 29:10, emphasis added).

We don't know how long Daniel had been in possession of these prophecies, but as John F. Walvoord says, "The implication is that Daniel had now come into the full comprehension of Jeremiah's prediction and realized that the seventy years prophesied had about run their course. The time of the vision recorded in Daniel 9 was 538 B.C., about 67 years after Jerusalem had first been captured and Daniel carried off to Babylon (605 B.C.)."[12]

As the aged Daniel read Jeremiah's prophecy and reviewed the calendar, he realized that the period of seventy years was coming to its conclusion. It was almost time for his people to be set free, and the knowledge of that imminent fulfillment drove him to his knees in prayer.

Though he was concerned about the return of his people to their homeland, Daniel focused the majority of his prayer on repentance and confession. With fasting, sackcloth, and ashes, he brought his concerns to God. He addressed God by His personal name, Yahweh. This is the only chapter in the book of Daniel where this sacred name is found, and it is used seven times. *Yahweh* is God's covenant-keeping name and was therefore the appropriate name for Daniel to use as he pleaded his case.

Daniel's prayer, one of the longest in the Bible, is a model for the public confession of national pride and sin. Daniel confessed the sins of "kings . . . princes . . . fathers and all the people of the land" (Daniel 9:6). No one—from the greatest to the least—was exempt from bearing guilt for Israel's fall.

Donald Campbell writes, "It seems no coincidence that two-thirds of this passage deals with Daniel's intercessory prayer for his people, while only a few verses reveal the timetable for the events of the end of human history. This great chapter is more than a glimpse into the future—it is a call to repentance and prayer!"[13]

Daniel concluded his prayer with this plea: "O Lord, hear! O Lord, forgive! O Lord, listen and act! Do not delay for Your own sake, my God, for Your city and Your people are called by Your name" (Daniel 9:19). *Hear, forgive, listen, act, do not delay.* "The verbs come rapidly, like hammer blows of insistence. They still are reserved in tone, continuing to show Daniel's humble spirit, but his great earnestness shines through with clarity. He wanted God to 'hear' his petition."[14]

Even though God had promised to end the captivity of His people, He'd also instructed them to pray to that end: "You will call upon Me and go and pray to Me, and I will listen to you. And you will seek Me and find Me, when you search for Me with all your heart. I will be found by you, says the LORD, and I will bring you back from your captivity" (Jeremiah 29:12-14).

As Daniel finished his prayer, he anticipated an answer concerning the seventy years of captivity his people had suffered. Remember from our discussion in chapter 1, those 70 years represented 490 years of Israel's failure to observe the Sabbath law requiring the land to lie fallow every seventh year—one year of captivity for each year of failure (2 Chronicles 36:21).

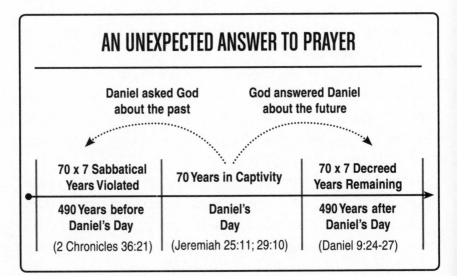

AN UNEXPECTED ANSWER TO PRAYER

Daniel asked God about the past		God answered Daniel about the future
70 x 7 Sabbatical Years Violated	70 Years in Captivity	70 x 7 Decreed Years Remaining
490 Years before Daniel's Day	Daniel's Day	490 Years after Daniel's Day
(2 Chronicles 36:21)	(Jeremiah 25:11; 29:10)	(Daniel 9:24-27)

But the aged prophet was about to get the surprise of his life. Instead of dealing with the 490 years that were behind him, God gave Daniel a look into the 490 years that lay ahead of him. Daniel asked God about the past; God was going to tell him about the future!

The Prophecy

THE MESSENGER

> Gabriel, whom I had seen in the vision at the beginning, being caused to fly swiftly, reached me about the time of the evening offering.
>
> DANIEL 9:21

Gabriel is the messenger of God who would probably win the award for "most admired angel." He always seems to be bringing important—and usually good—news. Five hundred years after Daniel, it was Gabriel who told Mary that she had been chosen to be the mother of Jesus, the Messiah (Luke 1:26-27). It was Gabriel who met Zacharias in the Temple and told him that his prayers for a son would be answered (Luke 1:11-17). Gabriel introduced himself to Zacharias, saying, "I am Gabriel, who stands in the presence of God" (Luke 1:19). Gabriel obviously stands in the right place to be reckoned a dependable liaison between God and human beings.

Even before Daniel finished his prayer, Gabriel was there with the answer. He arrived at the time of the evening offering. This would have been the middle of the afternoon, around 3:00 p.m.

Someone once recited Daniel's prayer in the Hebrew language and timed it at about three minutes. That means it took Gabriel about three minutes to get from the throne of God to Daniel's residence in Babylon. No wonder Daniel said Gabriel had been "caused to fly swiftly" (verse 21)!

The great Jewish Christian scholar Arno Gaebelein reminds us, "Heaven is not far away. There is no space and distance for God. What an encouragement to prayer this ought to be to God's people. The moment we pray in the Spirit and in His name our voices are heard in the highest heaven."[15]

The purpose of Gabriel's encounter with Daniel is spelled out clearly in the next verses: "I have now come forth to give you skill to understand. At the beginning of your supplications the command went out, and I have come to tell you, for you are greatly beloved; therefore consider the matter, and understand the vision" (Daniel 9:22-23).

Gabriel came to "inform" Daniel and "talk with" Daniel and "give Daniel skill to understand." Once Daniel heard the prophecy that was about to fall from Gabriel's lips, he would need all the skill the angel could provide.

Gabriel referred to Daniel as "greatly beloved," which is the same way Jesus referred to the apostle John, "the disciple whom Jesus loved" (John 20:2; 21:7, 20). Daniel and John also share another parallel: they are the two greatest sources of prophetic revelation in the Bible. Because of their faithfulness and obedience, God disclosed revelation to them not given to any others.

THE MESSAGE

The Timing of the Message

Gabriel began his message by introducing the timetable for the future events he was about to reveal. Some of his terminology needs to be explained for today's reader.

1. The "weeks" of Daniel's prophecy

Seventy weeks are determined for your people and for your holy city.

DANIEL 9:24

262

It's obvious that Gabriel is not referring to weeks as units of time made of seven days, which is how we commonly use the term. This would mean that the entire city of Jerusalem and the sanctuary would have been built in 490 days. This would have been impossible. The word for *week* here literally means "sevens." Daniel is told that seventy "sevens" have been determined for his people.

The question then becomes "Seven of what?" We find the answer by looking at the context the words are used in. Based on the reference to "seventy years" in Daniel 9:2, we know that Daniel has years in mind, not days. So the "seventy sevens" in Daniel 9:24 has to be "seventy groups of seven years." Biblical scholars agree on this almost unanimously.

So the angel was telling Daniel that seventy weeks of years, or seventy times seven years (a period of 490 years), is required to fulfill Israel's prophetic program.

2. The "years" of Daniel's prophecy

There is conclusive evidence to show that the prophetic year consisted not of 365 days but of 360 days, or twelve months of thirty days. According to the Genesis record, the Flood began on the seventeenth day of the second month (7:11), and it came to an end on the seventeenth day of the seventh month (8:4). This is a period of exactly five months. In Genesis 7:24 and 8:3, we are told that the Flood lasted 150 days, which corresponds to exactly five months. So the earliest known month in Bible history was thirty days in length, and twelve months of such length would be a period of 360 days, or a 360-day year.

Having explored an illustration from the first book of the Bible, let's take a look at one from the last book of the Bible. In Revelation 11:3 and 12:6, a three-and-a-half-year period is counted as 1,260 days (1,260 divided by 3.5 is 360). So while a solar year is 365 days, a prophetic year was counted as 360 days.

The Terms of the Message

> Seventy weeks are determined for your people and for your
> holy city, to finish the transgression, to make an end of sins,
> to make reconciliation for iniquity, to bring in everlasting
> righteousness, to seal up vision and prophecy, and to anoint
> the Most Holy.
>
> DANIEL 9:24

Remember, the entire prophecy has to do with Daniel's people
and Daniel's city—the nation of Israel and the city of Jerusalem. It's
important to understand that this prophecy has nothing to do with
the Gentiles. According to the angel Gabriel, the future of Israel
involves six important transactions. Three of the six are presented
negatively, and three positively. Before the seventy weeks of Daniel's
prophecy are completed, these six events must take place.

Some scholars contend that all six occurred at the Cross. They
believe that everything God planned for the Jewish people has already
been accomplished—that He has no future plans for the nation of
Israel. However, as we explore these six items, we'll see that none
of them has yet been fully experienced by the nation of Israel and
therefore must be anticipated in the future.

The first three items on the list concern the removal of sin, and
the second three concern the restoration of righteousness.

1. "To finish the transgression"

This is the first and most important item on the list of things that
must be accomplished during the seventy weeks of years. H. C.
Leupold explains the term "to finish the transgression" as meaning that "sin will come under control and will no longer grow and
flourish."[16]

For all who believe, transgression was finished at the Cross. But for Israel, which rejected Christ, the perfect consummation of the Messiah's redeeming work will not be realized until the end of the seventy weeks. Regarding this time, God says, "I will pour on the house of David and on the inhabitants of Jerusalem the Spirit of grace and supplication. . . . In that day a fountain shall be opened for the house of David and for the inhabitants of Jerusalem, for sin and for uncleanness" (Zechariah 12:10; 13:1).

2. "To make an end of sins"

This phrase points to the time when sin will be eliminated—not only in principle, but also in practice. This can't happen until the reign of Christ during the Millennium. In that day, sin will have run its course in Israel, and it will be locked up, never to do its evil work again. "They shall not defile themselves anymore with their idols, nor with their detestable things, nor with any of their transgressions; but I will deliver them from all their dwelling places in which they have sinned, and will cleanse them. Then they shall be My people, and I will be their God" (Ezekiel 37:23).

3. "To make reconciliation for iniquity"

This is a statement of atonement. Though Christ isn't explicitly mentioned in this verse, He is the One making the atonement (Daniel 9:26). Sin is ended because of the atonement of the Messiah, although the nation of Israel won't realize the effect of this atonement until the end of the seventy weeks.

4. "To bring in everlasting righteousness"

The Messiah's death not only atones for sins; it also has the power to give the nation of Israel right standing before a holy God. Leon Wood writes, "When Christ died, He provided not only for sin to be removed, but also for righteousness to be granted. . . . But again

265

it should be noted that the actual becoming righteous . . . occurs only when . . . Israel as a nation . . . [makes] appropriation at Christ's second coming in power."[17]

5. "To seal up vision and prophecy"

These words refer to the time in the future when all prophecies will be fulfilled. When Christ comes in power and establishes His Kingdom, every prophecy concerning Him will become absolute reality. Once again, this demands a time beyond the boundaries of the first sixty-nine weeks of the prophecy, which as we will soon see, ended at the time of Christ's triumphal entry into Jerusalem.

6. "To anoint the Most Holy"

Christ's Kingdom can only be established in the future, when the holy place in the Millennial Temple is anointed (or, in today's terms, completed and dedicated). The phrase "the Most Holy" is never used of a person in Scripture. It refers to the sacred place in the Temple often referred to as the Holy of Holies—where the reestablishment of religious service will take place in a future Temple (Ezekiel 41–46).

Biblical scholar G. H. Lang writes, "In the place of the Tabernacle and former temples . . . a new holy of holies shall be anointed. . . . The holy of holies of this prophecy, the innermost shrine of the grand Temple described by Ezekiel, will be no mere continuation of former sanctuaries."[18]

All six of these events Gabriel foretells in Daniel 9:24 must be ultimately fulfilled and experienced by the nation of Israel. This won't happen until the end of the 490 years of Daniel's prophecy. Since not one of these prophecies was fulfilled in the first sixty-nine weeks, there must be a future time in which they will be fulfilled.

THE METRICS

The Commencement of the Prophecy: "The Going Forth of the Command"

> From the going forth of the command to restore and build
> Jerusalem until Messiah the Prince, there shall be seven
> weeks and sixty-two weeks; the street shall be built again,
> and the wall, even in troublesome times.
>
> DANIEL 9:25

Gabriel told Daniel that the future 490 years of prophetic events would commence on a certain day. The decree to restore and build Jerusalem would signal the beginning of the seventy weeks, or 490 years, prophecy.

There were actually four decrees issued concerning the restoration of Jerusalem and the Temple. The first was by Cyrus in 538 BC (Ezra 1:1-4; 5:13-17), instigating the rebuilding of the Temple but not the city. Darius issued the second decree in 517 BC (Ezra 6:1-12). This decree was also limited to the rebuilding of the Temple. The first decree of Artaxerxes in 458 BC is sometimes thought to be the starting point for the seventy weeks of Daniel, but it, too, failed to provide for the rebuilding of Jerusalem.

Dr. Alva J. McClain, who for twenty-five years was the president of Grace Seminary in Winona Lake, Indiana, was regarded as one of the outstanding Bible scholars of his generation. With conviction, he identifies the decree that initiates the seventy-week prophetic period:

> There is only one decree in Old Testament history which . . .
> can by any possibility be identified as the "commandment"
> referred to in Daniel's prophecy. That decree is found in the

book of Nehemiah (1:1-4 and 2:1-8). . . . Nehemiah, writing by divine inspiration, records the exact date of this decree: "in the month of Nisan in the twentieth year of Artaxerxes the king" (2:1).

The date fixed by Nehemiah happens to be one of the best-known dates in ancient history. Even the latest edition of the *Encyclopedia Britannica* . . . sets the date of Artaxerxes' accession as 465 B.C.; and therefore his twentieth year would be 445 B.C. The month was Nisan, and since no day is given, according to Jewish custom the date would be understood as the first.[19]

When we convert Nisan 1, 445 BC, to our calendar, we arrive at March 14, 445 BC, as the date of the command "to restore and rebuild Jerusalem" (Daniel 9:25).

The Completion of the Prophecy: "Messiah the Prince"

From the going forth of the command to restore and build Jerusalem until Messiah the Prince, there shall be seven weeks and sixty-two weeks.

DANIEL 9:25

What was Daniel to understand concerning the completion of this prophecy? Just as there was a certain time for its commencement, there must also be a certain time for its completion. That time, according to Daniel 9:25, is the time of Messiah the Prince.

"Messiah the Prince" is a Hebrew phrase that means "the anointed One, the Ruler." The term *prince* is a title associated with kingly authority, and it's used here to describe the appearing of the Lord Jesus Christ as a prince and ruler.

But what event in the life of Jesus Christ is Daniel's prophecy pointing to? The answer that makes the most sense is the Triumphal Entry of Jesus into Jerusalem, since that was when He was presented to the Jewish people as their Messianic Prince.

Zechariah 9:9 foretold a day when Israel's king would ride into Jerusalem "on a donkey." In Luke 19, we see that prophecy fulfilled as Jesus Christ rides into Jerusalem to begin His Passion Week. Jesus' followers in Jerusalem understood the significance of that moment. They hailed Him with the Messianic praise found in Psalm 118: "Blessed is he who comes in the name of the LORD!" (verse 26; see also Luke 19:38).

Sir Robert Anderson of Scotland Yard, who well over 120 years ago wrote the classic book *The Coming Prince*, says, "No student of the Gospel narrative can fail to see that the Lord's last visit to Jerusalem was not only in fact, but in the purpose of it, the crisis of His ministry. . . . Now the twofold testimony of His words and His works had been fully rendered, and His entry into the Holy City was to proclaim His Messiahship and to receive His doom."[20]

Dr. Alva J. McClain explains how this prophecy demonstrates the truth of Scripture: "The prophecy of the Seventy Weeks has an immense evidential value as a witness to the truth of Scripture. That part of the prophecy relating to the first sixty-nine weeks has already been accurately fulfilled. . . . Only an omniscient God could have foretold over five hundred years in advance the very day on which the Messiah would ride into Jerusalem and present Himself as the 'Prince' of Israel."[21]

The Computing of the Prophecy: 69 x 7 x 360 = 173,880

Sir Robert Anderson computed the time between the decree for the walls of Jerusalem to be rebuilt and the coming of Messiah the Prince. The exact nature of his computation has stood the test for over a century and has been corroborated by many biblical scholars.

Here's a summary of his computation:

> Having found that the Weeks are composed of years, that the length of the prophetic year is 360 days, and that these years began on March 14, 445 BC, the ground is now cleared for the chronological computation. . . . In order to find the end of the Sixty-nine Weeks, we must first reduce them to days. Since we have 69 Weeks of seven years each, and each year has 360 days, the equation is as follows: 69 x 7 x 360 = 173,880 days. Beginning with March 14, 445 BC, this number of days brings us to April 6, 32 AD.[22]

And this was the day our Lord rode into Jerusalem.

The Categories of the Prophecy

1. The subdivision: "there shall be seven weeks"

> There shall be seven weeks and sixty-two weeks; the street shall be built again, and the wall, even in troublesome times.
> DANIEL 9:25

Gabriel explained to Daniel that the seventy weeks of prophetic history would be divided into three sections or periods:

- 7 weeks of years (49 years)
- 62 weeks of years (434 years)
- 1 week of years (7 years)

While scholars tend to emphasize the prophecy of the sixty-two weeks, which has already been fulfilled, and the one week, which is yet to be fulfilled, the first category (the seven weeks) is often overlooked. Gabriel told Daniel that during the first seven weeks (forty-nine years), the city would be rebuilt "even in troublesome times" (Ezra 9–10; Nehemiah 4, 6, 9, 13). Not only was Jerusalem rebuilt during that forty-nine-year period, but the Temple was also established and the canon of the Old Testament was completed.

The seven weeks of years in which the city was restored concluded in 396 BC, forty-nine years after Artaxerxes issued the decree to rebuild it in 445 BC.

2. The suspension of the prophecy: "Messiah shall be cut off"

After the sixty-two weeks Messiah shall be cut off, but not for Himself; and the people of the prince who is to come shall destroy the city and the sanctuary. The end of it shall be with a flood, and till the end of the war desolations are determined.

DANIEL 9:26

The continuation of the seventy weeks was interrupted by the rejection of Messiah the Prince, who "came to His own, and His own did not receive Him" (John 1:11). With this event, the sixty-ninth week closed and the period of what some have called "unreckoned time" began. God reckons time with the Jews only when He is dealing with them nationally, and that won't occur again until the Tribulation period, or the seventieth week of Daniel's prophecy. This means there's an indefinite period of time between the end of the sixty-ninth week and the beginning of the seventieth week. We are living in that "unreckoned" time, and it has been going on for more than two thousand years now.

The fact that prophetic time has been suspended for more than two thousand years should not cause us to doubt that it will resume with the yet-to-come seventieth week. Prophets typically saw events in the future as a series of mountain peaks in the distance. Such a perspective makes it difficult to gauge the expanse between one peak and the next. Daniel saw the sixty-ninth and seventieth weeks as separate events without knowing there would be a gap of more than two thousand years between them.

Isaiah 9:6 offers a good example of prophetic events mentioned in one verse yet widely separated in time: "Unto us a Child is born, unto us a Son is given; and the government will be upon His shoulder." That child, Christ, was born in Bethlehem more than two thousand years ago, but the government is not yet upon His shoulder—and won't be until He returns again. That verse spans more than two thousand years of history. Likewise, in Zechariah 9:9-10, we see Christ riding into Jerusalem on a donkey and having dominion from sea to sea. Those two statements occur in successive verses but are separated by, once again, more than two thousand years.

"With the Lord one day is as a thousand years, and a thousand years as one day" (2 Peter 3:8), so we should never doubt the inevitable fulfillment of prophecy based on questions of time. We trust in the certainty of what God has promised, not when it will happen.

There are many other reasons for a gap between the sixty-ninth and seventieth weeks of Daniel's prophecy. But let me remind you of one category of evidence we've already visited: the six events Gabriel said would occur in Israel's future. These include the finishing of the transgression, the end of sin, the atonement for iniquity, the bringing in of everlasting righteousness, the sealing up of the vision and prophecy, and the anointing of the most holy place (9:24). These events have not yet occurred, and they won't occur until God's program for Israel is reestablished during the seventieth week of Daniel's prophecy.

During the early days of this parenthesis between the sixty-ninth and seventieth week, two important events took place. First, Messiah the Prince was "cut off" (Daniel 9:26). The literal translation of that phrase is "to cut off and have nothing." That accurately describes the death of Jesus Christ. He died alone, deserted by His friends, ridiculed by His enemies, and seemingly forsaken by His Father.

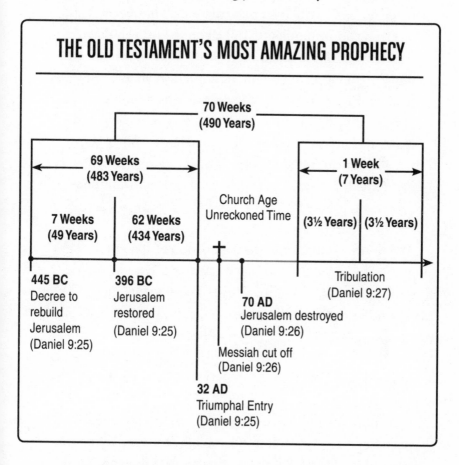

The second event predicted to occur during the beginning of the period between the sixty-ninth and seventieth weeks was the destruction of the city and the sanctuary. Jerusalem and the Temple, which were rebuilt in the time of Ezra and Nehemiah, would be destroyed again. This would take place in AD 70 at the hands of the Roman army, four decades after the crucifixion of Christ. Donald Campbell explains how this prophecy was fulfilled:

Titus Vespasian led four Roman legions to besiege and destroy Jerusalem. . . . Interestingly, General Titus ordered his soldiers to leave the temple intact, but Jesus had predicted to His disciples that "there shall not be left here one stone upon another, that shall not be thrown down" (Matthew 24:2). It is said that when a Roman soldier, on impulse, threw a flaming torch through an archway of the temple, the rich tapestries caught fire. The building soon became a raging inferno; the decorative gold melted and ran down into the cracks of the stone floors. When the remains cooled, the soldiers in their greed for wealth literally overturned the stones in search of the gold. The prophecy of Christ was grimly fulfilled.[23]

The death of Christ and the destruction of Jerusalem both occur after, not during, the sixty-nine weeks. The Temple was destroyed forty years after the death of Christ. These events do not occur in the seventieth week, for that week doesn't begin until the Antichrist makes a covenant with the nation of Israel.

THE MAN OF SIN

[The prince who is to come] shall confirm a covenant with many for one week; but in the middle of the week he shall bring an end to sacrifice and offering. And on the wing of abominations shall be one who makes desolate, even until the consummation, which is determined, is poured out on the desolate.

DANIEL 9:27

In Daniel 9:26-27, Daniel mentions two princes. The first is the Messiah Himself, Jesus Christ, who was cut off at the end of the sixty-ninth week. The second is a prince "who is to come" (Daniel 9:26). Scripture refers to this second prince using a variety of terms: the "little horn" (Daniel 8:9), a king with "fierce features" (Daniel 8:23), the "man of sin" (2 Thessalonians 2:3), "the beast" (twenty-five times in Revelation), and "the Antichrist" (1 John 2:18; 4:3). This prince will rise against the Jews during the Tribulation, just as his "people" (Daniel 9:26)—those aligned with his goal of persecuting the Jews—have done throughout history.

If there is an event to watch for that will signal the beginning of Daniel's seventieth week, or the Tribulation, it will be this: the Antichrist, seen as a world leader, will "confirm a covenant with many for one week" (Daniel 9:27). This will be a treaty with the nation of Israel, granting it protection from nations seeking its annihilation and assuring a time of religious normalcy and safety.

But this deceptively benevolent prince will break the covenant halfway through the seventieth week: "In the middle of the week he shall bring an end to sacrifice and offering. And on the wing of abominations shall be one who makes desolate, even until the consummation, which is determined, is poured out on the desolate" (Daniel 9:27).

While the first half of the seventieth week will be relatively peaceful, in the second half, the Antichrist will unleash unprecedented fury. The last three and a half years of this week constitute the Great Tribulation Jesus spoke of in Matthew 24:21 and described in detail in Revelation 4–19.

The breaking of the covenant will be accompanied by what Daniel calls "the abomination of desolation" (Daniel 11:31; 12:11). As described in our discussion of Daniel 8, this sacrilege will be the complete defamation of all that is holy in Jerusalem. It's the event Jesus warned about in His Olivet discourse:

When you see the "abomination of desolation," spoken of
by Daniel the prophet, standing in the holy place (whoever

reads, let him understand), then let those who are in Judea
flee to the mountains. Let him who is on the housetop not
go down to take anything out of his house. And let him
who is in the field not go back to get his clothes. But woe to
those who are pregnant and to those who are nursing babies
in those days! And pray that your flight may not be in winter
or on the Sabbath. For then there will be great tribulation,
such as has not been since the beginning of the world until
this time, no, nor ever shall be. And unless those days were
shortened, no flesh would be saved; but for the elect's sake
those days will be shortened.

MATTHEW 24:15-22

Jesus Christ Himself will shorten those horrific days by returning
to earth to judge the Antichrist and his armies and quell the rebellion on earth against God (Revelation 19:11-21). This will bring
the seventy weeks of Daniel to a close. The final week ends with the
second coming of Christ to earth.

MESSIAH THE PRINCE

In this vision, Daniel was not given the details of what would happen
at the end of the seventieth week. At that time, Christ will establish the
Kingdom of God on earth for a thousand years (Revelation 20:1-3).
However, two other Old Testament prophets, Isaiah and Zechariah,
saw this Kingdom coming (Isaiah 11, 61; Zechariah 9–14). But they
didn't know the exact time this would occur.

God will reestablish a relationship with His chastened and purified chosen people, and righteousness will govern the earth with
Christ, the King of kings, for a thousand years. A glorious Temple
will be built in Jerusalem, where worship will be offered to "the Lamb
of God who takes away the sin of the world" (John 1:29). "In those
days ten men from every language of the nations shall grasp the sleeve

of a Jewish man, saying, 'Let us go with you, for we have heard that God is with you'" (Zechariah 8:23). And indeed He will be.

Daniel had been a captive in Babylon for sixty-nine years, perhaps wondering all the while if God had forgotten His people. But the reminder of Jeremiah's prophecy that Israel's captivity would end in seventy years, followed by Gabriel's revelation of the triumphant seventy weeks, revived Daniel's trust in God. He realized that God was still at work in His people.

Leopold Cohn was born into the Jewish community in Berezna, Hungary, in 1862. Having lost both his parents at the age of seven, he was driven to a deep search for God. Becoming a "son of the commandment" (bar mitzvah) at age thirteen, Cohn began pursuing studies that would lead him to become a rabbi and teacher of his people. At age eighteen, he graduated from his Talmud studies with an impressive record of scholarship. He was ordained as a rabbi, got married, and continued his heartfelt study of the Law of Moses.

The focus of his studies, bordering on an obsession, was the question of the coming of the Messiah. He wanted to know when the Messiah would come and when the scattered people of Israel would be regathered to the Promised Land. His search led him to the ninth chapter of the prophet Daniel's book. It became obvious to Cohn that the Messiah should have come four hundred years after Daniel received the message of the seventy weeks from Gabriel. That meant the Messiah would have already come!

Suddenly he found the Talmud, which taught that the Messiah had not come, to be in conflict with the prophets. As he began to raise his questions with fellow rabbis, he faced ostracism and persecution. At the age of thirty, he took his family and fled to the United States, the land of religious freedom.

While walking the streets of New York City on a Sabbath afternoon, Cohn happened upon a building bearing a sign written in Hebrew: "Meetings for Jews." He was surprised to see that this

Christian church displayed a cross but also advertised a gathering for people of Jewish background. He went to the meeting, and the following week he met with the minister, who gave him a Hebrew New Testament. Cohn began to devour the book, beginning with Matthew: "This is the book of the generation of Yeshua the Messiah, the son of David, the son of Abraham" (Matthew 1:1). He read from eleven o'clock that morning until one o'clock the following morning, at which time he committed himself to Jesus of Nazareth as the Jewish Messiah.

In 1894, Rabbi Leopold Cohn founded a mission in Brooklyn, New York, to reach Jewish people with the Gospel. Today that ministry is known as Chosen People Ministries, and it has a presence in sixteen countries around the world—all because a Jewish rabbi read Daniel 9 and became convinced that the Messiah of Israel had to have come just four centuries after the prophet Daniel's revelation.

* * *

DANIEL FOR TODAY

We've just studied one of the most challenging and important prophetic passages in all of God's Word. What does it mean for us today? I believe this passage gives us at least five glittering gems to brighten our outlook and ease our concerns about the days to come.

1. Hope for the future: Reading God's prophecies is like reading the last page of a romantic novel and discovering that the guy gets the girl after all. Prophecy tells us that Christ comes to rule and reign forever.

2. Confidence in the present: When we don't fear tomorrow, we can have confidence today. The hearts of many are failing because they don't know God's prophetic story.

3. Holiness in living: The sure knowledge of Christ's appearing is motivation for us to keep ourselves pure. What children are not on their best behavior knowing their parents will soon be home?

4. Reasons to share the Good News: Our world is full of confused, despairing people who are overwhelmed by the deteriorating morality of society and the seemingly random nature of our chaotic world. For those who think all the news today is bad, prophecy provides refreshing and encouraging good news.

5. Edification, exhortation, and encouragement: In 1 Corinthians 14:3, the apostle Paul writes that God gave prophets to the church to build us up, set us straight, and keep us going. I can't think of anything our world needs more.

Chapter 11

THE ARCHANGEL

Daniel 10–11

DANIEL COULD HARDLY CONTAIN HIS ELATION. Cyrus the Great had taken control of the Medo-Persian Empire, and soon afterward he issued a decree allowing the Jews to return to their own land. More than that, he promised funds and assistance in rebuilding Jerusalem and the Temple. It was a spectacular fulfillment of the promise Daniel had discovered in the scroll of Jeremiah. Daniel longed to join the patriots who would be returning, but he was now over eighty years old and too frail to endure the grueling journey.

But as the months passed following the decree, Daniel's joy began to fade into deep concern. The Jews in Babylon hadn't responded to their release the way he had expected. He thought Cyrus's decree would inspire a surge of joy and praise from his people, and there would be a mass exodus of Jews back to their Promised Land, just as there had been from Egypt centuries before. But those who chose to return to Israel were all too few. Most of the exiles had grown accustomed to life in Babylon, choosing to remain in the comfort of their lush surroundings rather than endure the hardships of the journey back to their homeland and the rigors of rebuilding a ruined city.

To make matters worse, news from those who had returned to Jerusalem was not encouraging. The rebuilding of the city was going slowly, plagued by apathy, unsteady leadership, and attacks from hostile tribes that had settled in the vacated land. Some of the Jewish leaders had become discouraged, infecting the people with their own despair. One leader even ordered the workers to shut down the entire project and walk away.

Worst of all, in Daniel's mind, was the report that many of the returning Jews were marrying foreign wives. Daniel felt a weight of sadness settle over him. His people were headed down the same path that had led to their captivity in the first place.

Daniel took leave from his duties in Cyrus's court and went into seclusion. He fasted and prayed every day from morning to night, begging God to strengthen His people and give them the courage to accept the gift He offered—the restoration of their land and worship.

* * *

The moment Daniel began to pray, the angel Gabriel answered a summons to appear before the throne of God.

"Gabriel," the mighty voice thundered, "again My beloved servant Daniel is praying. He is in great anguish—not for himself, but for his people and their trials and discouragement. Once more I charge you to deliver My words of encouragement concerning the future of his people."

Gabriel bowed before the throne. "As always, my Lord, it is my highest honor to do as You bid me."

The angel departed instantly. It took him only a few minutes to traverse hundreds of light-years, and in moments he pierced the earth's atmosphere and shot across continents and seas, flying westward over Asia and veering toward Babylon.

Suddenly he came to a halt. Looming above the nation of Persia, directly in his path, hovered a dark, hulking figure, essentially man-like but with a hideous face and twisted limbs. The creature bulged with knotty muscles like those of an ox. Gabriel recognized the creature instantly, for he had encountered it before. It was the demonic prince that Satan had placed over the kingdom of Persia. Lurking on each side of the monstrous demon were two others, equally hideous in appearance.

"Stand aside and let me pass," Gabriel demanded.

"I will not," the demon rasped. "We know what is stirring between Babylon and Israel. Your God is trying to return the Jews to their homeland to rebuild their Holy City and their Temple, and we know why: it's all part of His preparation for the coming of their Messiah. That will never happen; we will see to it. Turn back, Gabriel. No divine help will cross our borders."

"You can't stop me," Gabriel replied. "Surely you remember our previous encounter."

The chief demon of Persia erupted in croaking laughter. "Yes, but you won't best me again. As you can see, I now have help—two of the greatest warriors in all of Satan's forces."

Gabriel drew his sword, which glowed like a live ember. He surged forward, and a titanic battle ensued. The angel's power was extraordinary—twice that of his demonic adversary. But facing the Persian monster and his two fiendish henchmen, he found himself evenly matched. Showers of sparks exploded like pulsars with each clash of their weapons, sending thunderous echoes through the heavens.

Gabriel's strokes slowly drove the demons back, but just as he was on the verge of breaking through, they rallied and held their ground. He tried to flank them to the left, but the tactic opened him to attack from the right. And when he turned to defend himself to the right, he was forced to retreat several paces.

One of the demons grew tired, and his strokes grew slow and

cumbersome. The Persian prince ordered him to drop out of the battle to recover, and in his absence, Gabriel was able to gain considerable ground. But when the refreshed demon rejoined the fray, Gabriel lost his advantage and ceded much of the ground he'd gained. This began a pattern in which the demons would rotate in and out of the battle, giving them the upper hand.

The battle raged for a day, a week, two weeks. After three weeks of continuous fighting, the warriors remained stalemated, with no significant gains by either side.

* * *

Michael, the archangel, flew through space, returning from an assignment on the far side of the Andromeda galaxy. He was headed for Earth, where his next mission had already been assigned. He was to locate and confront the demonic angel Satan had appointed as the prince of Greece. Eager to perform his duty, Michael embarked on his assignment, shooting past planets, comets, and swirling galaxies.

Through the network of angelic intelligence he had established, Michael knew trouble was brewing in the Middle East in the nations surrounding Israel. And he knew why. The demonic powers of the air had their own intelligence network, and they knew the Jews were planning to rebuild Jerusalem and the Temple. This would undo everything Satan and his demons had accomplished through their influence over King Nebuchadnezzar. They knew that if they allowed the Jews to revive as a nation of God-worshiping people, the pathway to the coming of the Messiah would be opened.

Michael smiled as he remembered the agonized howls from the demons in the Middle East when they found out they'd lost Nebuchadnezzar, previously one of their most useful humans. Just when they thought they had him securely in their clutches, he had learned humility and, in his later years, turned to God. The demons were still smarting from such a loss.

My God would do anything for Israel, the nation He loves! Michael thought. For that reason, Michael loved Israel as well—in spite of their persistent history of falling away from the glorious destiny God had planned for them. The often-beleaguered nation had seen dark days, and he knew they would face many more ahead. But Michael would do everything in his power to defend that beloved little nation from enemies who were continually determined to wipe them from the face of the earth.

As Michael neared the region of the Earth's sun, a lesser angel suddenly appeared and intercepted him.

Michael stopped and greeted the courier. "Ariel, what brings you here?"

"Great prince, I have a message from our Lord," Ariel replied. "He bids you to delay your assignment in Greece and fly immediately to the Persian border, where Gabriel is battling with the prince of that nation. He is charged to deliver a crucial message to God's servant Daniel, and he can't get through. You must join him in the battle, hold back the Persian demons, and allow Gabriel to proceed to Babylon."

Without a moment's hesitation, Michael changed his course and shot toward Persia. Breaking through Earth's atmosphere, he approached the nation's borders. Immediately, he saw flashes of light and heard thunderous clashes from the raging angelic battle.

Gabriel felt the wind of Michael's appearance and saw a shadow of fear cross the faces of the three demons. Suddenly the great Michael was beside him. Gabriel felt new strength surge through his entire being. Help had come at last—and not just any help. Michael was the mightiest of God's angels, the one who had led heaven's armies against the rebellious Satan, the one who in a titanic duel had personally hurled the rebel leader out of the heavenly realms. The story of this great feat was told often among the angels.

Michael drew his sword, as fiery as the one held by the angel in Eden, and engaged in the battle. The three demons couldn't withstand the onslaught and stumbled backward under every blow the two mighty angels inflicted. In moments, they had driven the demons apart, opening a gap between them into Persia. It was all they needed.

"Go on through, Gabriel!" Michael cried. "Fly on to Daniel, and complete the Lord's mission. These fiends will not follow you. I'll hold them here until you return."

Gabriel did as the great archangel bid him. He burst through the opening and flew directly to Daniel in Babylon.

* * *

It was the twenty-first day of Daniel's vigil of prayer and fasting. He left his room and strolled down to the Tigris River, praying as he walked.

He lay facedown on the riverbank, still immersed in prayer. After a few moments, he fell into a deep sleep. As he slept, he sensed a towering presence looming above him and heard a mighty voice speak his name. He looked up to see the form of the magnificent angel Gabriel, shining with the brightness of the sun.

Daniel lay on his face trembling until the angel touched him, sending a surge of strength through his body. "Do not fear me, Daniel, dearly loved of God, for the Lord of heaven has sent me to deliver a message of prophecy concerning times far in the future. Stand on your feet and hear."

Daniel stood, and Gabriel explained to Daniel the reason for his delay. When Gabriel finished, he related to him every word that had come from the mouth of God.

"Our Lord gave me this message the moment you began praying. It was my intention to reach you immediately, but the demonic prince over the kingdom of Persia stood in my way. He engaged me in battle and, with the aid of two warrior demons, prevented my passage. I would still be fighting if God hadn't sent

His archangel, Michael, to hold the demons at bay, allowing me to break through.

"Now that I have completed my mission, I must return to the battle and help Michael overcome the Persian demons. We can't allow them to succeed in their attempt to thwart the restoration of God's people. I bid you farewell, Daniel, friend of God, and I call His blessings on you as you continue your long and faithful service to Him."

As Daniel watched in wonder, Gabriel vanished into the air.

In seconds, the messenger angel was back at the battle site with his sword drawn. Gabriel joined his chief, and within moments, the three demons were reeling from the onslaught. Now on the defensive, their blows became feeble, until finally they were using their swords merely as shields, unable to mount any offense at all.

All at once, Michael's voice split the air: "Now, Gabriel!"

Gabriel knew exactly what the command meant. They rushed forward together, raining blows on their opponents like mighty hammers. The demons turned and ran. Michael and Gabriel pursued, and with a flurry of lightning strokes, the three demons were hurled downward toward the abyss reserved for Satan and his angels.

Michael and Gabriel wished each other Godspeed and parted ways. Gabriel returned to heaven to take his place in the presence of God, ready for another assignment. Michael resumed his flight toward Greece.

Through his intelligence network, Michael knew that the demonic spirits were stirring up strife and unholy ambition among the leaders of the Hellenic nations, setting the stage for massive persecution of the Jews. Michael's assignment was not to stop the persecution—that was part of God's plan to continue refining the Jewish nation. But he would do all he could to shorten its duration and set the stage for the coming of the Messiah.

* * *

THE SCRIPTURE BEHIND THE STORY

In order to understand Daniel 10–11, we need to view these chapters as one. Chapter 10 prepares us for the vision presented to Daniel in chapter 11.

Many scholars and commentators who have written on the book of Daniel have all but ignored the tenth chapter, treating it as incidental to the overall theme of the book. But the more I study Daniel, the more I believe chapter 10 provides the background necessary for understanding the entire prophetic message. Without a clear understanding of this chapter and its reference to demonic activity in the unseen world, the prophecies given in chapter 11, which span the history of the world from Daniel's time until the Tribulation period, will be difficult to comprehend.

Although the archangel, Michael, remains in the background of the biblical narrative of Daniel 10, he is actually the unsung hero of the story. Without his military intervention, the prophecies in Daniel 11 couldn't have been delivered or protected. When we read the now-fulfilled prophecies of Daniel 11, we are reading the very truths that Michael and the demonic prince fought over. Without Michael's intervention, we wouldn't have this section of the Bible, for Daniel never would have received it.

The Preparation for the Vision

In his book *Daniel: God's Man in a Secular Society*, Donald Campbell recounts a story about the inspiring prayer life of Andrew Bonar, one of the great preachers and writers of the last century:

> After his death, his daughter led a Welsh evangelist into her father's church in Glasgow, Scotland. She pointed out a pew in the rear where, as a small girl, she had been asked to sit

while her father went on into the empty sanctuary. After a long wait she stood up to look for him. He was seated in a pew, his head bent forward. Soon he moved to another pew, then another, and another. Sometimes she would see him carefully examine the nameplates to find the pews he desired. When she grew older she understood what her father had been doing on that day—he had been praying for his parishioners in the very spot where each worshiped.[1]

And so it was with Daniel. He was a man of prayer, and he had a burden for his people, as we saw in his prayer recorded in the previous chapter (Daniel 9:4-19). Daniel uttered that prayer after reading the words of Jeremiah concerning the release of the Jewish people from their Babylonian captivity. Jeremiah's prophecy was fulfilled when Cyrus, King of Persia, gave the Jewish captives permission to return to their homeland and rebuild the Temple.

Daniel's first concern was that not many Babylonian Jews—less than fifty thousand—returned to Jerusalem (Ezra 2). The rest chose to remain in Babylon as aliens in a land of idolatry. Daniel was also distressed over the plight of those brave pilgrims who had returned: "As the book of Ezra makes plain, the children of Israel had encountered great difficulty in getting settled in the land. Although the altar had been set up and the foundation of the temple laid (Ezra 3), the work had been suspended because of opposition by the people of the land (Ezra 4:1-5, 24). All of this was of great concern to Daniel, for his primary purpose in encouraging the expedition had been the restoration of the temple as well as the city of Jerusalem."[2]

THE DISTRESS THAT PRECEDED THE VISION

In the third year of Cyrus king of Persia a message was revealed to Daniel. . . . The message was true, but the appointed time was long. . . . In those days I, Daniel, was mourning three full weeks. I ate no pleasant food, no meat or wine came into my mouth, nor did I anoint myself at all, till three whole weeks were fulfilled.

DANIEL 10:1-3

The malaise of Daniel's people burdened him so deeply that he fasted for three weeks, mourning and praying for God to disclose His will for the nation. God answered his prayer with yet another vision—the fourth one recorded in the book of Daniel. It came to him during the third year of Cyrus's reign over Persia. Daniel was now in his eighties and had been a captive for around seventy years.

The vision is described as "true, but the appointed time was long." Numerous scholars have pointed out that this Hebrew idiom should be translated "great warfare" or "great suffering." The vision pictured dark and difficult times for Daniel's people, stretching far into the distant future.

This is almost the same situation as the one presented in Daniel 9. Daniel prayed to God about the 490 years in the past that resulted in the seventy-year captivity, and God gave him a prophecy about the 490 years that were yet in the future.

Here in chapter 10, Daniel prays to God concerning the Jews' present failure to fulfill their responsibility, and God answers by giving him one of the most comprehensive messages about the future in the entire Bible.

THE DESCRIPTION THAT PERSONIFIED THE VISION

As I was by the side of the great river, that is, the Tigris, I lifted my eyes and looked, and behold, a certain man clothed in linen, whose waist was girded with gold of Uphaz! His body was like beryl, his face like the appearance of lightning,

his eyes like torches of fire, his arms and feet like burnished
bronze in color, and the sound of his words like the voice
of a multitude.

DANIEL 10:4-6

As Daniel walked along the bank of the Tigris River with some
of his friends, he was overcome by a vision of a glorious man from
heaven. While the "man" is not identified, many scholars believe
this to be a *theophany*—a preincarnate appearance of the Lord Jesus
Christ. He is described almost exactly the way Christ is described in
Revelation 1:13-15, and Daniel's reaction is similar to the apostle
John's (Revelation 1:17).

But not all scholars agree. H. C. Leupold explains why he believes
this is not a theophany. He concludes that it "seems very strange that
Michael (v. 13) 'came to help' him. Though angels and men may
share in God's work, it is never indicated that they help Him. All of
this leads to the conclusion that the personage involved is one of the
mighty angels of God."[3]

It is probable that this is Gabriel, the same angel who appeared to
Daniel in chapters 8 and 9. One clue is that in Daniel 9:23, Gabriel
tells Daniel that he is "greatly beloved," just as the angel does in this
chapter (Daniel 10:11).

Daniel's response to the heavenly vision is given in detail. The
fasting and the mourning coupled with the vision left him with
no strength. He fell into a deep sleep with his face to the ground
(Daniel 10:8-9).

THE DELAY THAT POSTPONED THE VISION

Suddenly, a hand touched me, which made me tremble on
my knees and on the palms of my hands. And he said to
me, "O Daniel, man greatly beloved, understand the words

that I speak to you, and stand upright, for I have now been sent to you." While he was speaking this word to me, I stood trembling. Then he said to me, "Do not fear, Daniel, for from the first day that you set your heart to understand, and to humble yourself before your God, your words were heard; and I have come because of your words."

DANIEL 10:10-12

The angel told the overwhelmed Daniel not to fear and enabled him to stand so he would be fully capable of receiving the message that was about to be delivered. He told Daniel that from the moment he had begun to pray, his words had been heard in heaven. Someone has written, "The answer that is *delayed* must not be interpreted as having been *denied*."[4]

Dr. Roy L. Laurin says, "As a matter of *fact* the answer may be long in coming, but as a matter of *faith* it is ours at the time of our asking."[5]

THE DEMON THAT PREVENTED THE VISION

The prince of the kingdom of Persia withstood me twenty-one days; and behold, Michael, one of the chief princes, came to help me, for I had been left alone there with the kings of Persia. . . . Then he said, "Do you know why I have come to you? And now I must return to fight with the prince of Persia; and when I have gone forth, indeed the prince of Greece will come. But I will tell you what is noted in the Scripture of Truth."

DANIEL 10:13, 20-21

These two verses reveal an often overlooked truth. In the invisible realms rages a battle that powerfully influences events in our world. As the apostle Paul says, "We do not wrestle against flesh and blood, but against principalities, against powers, against the rulers of the darkness of this age, against spiritual hosts of wickedness in the heavenly places" (Ephesians 6:12).

When Gabriel left heaven to deliver God's answer to Daniel, Satan dispatched his own "angel"—the one responsible for the demonic control of Persia—to intercept that answer and try to thwart the work of God. When the two angels clashed, a titanic battle erupted, which continued to rage for three weeks.

The prince of Persia was obviously not a man, for no human could resist a messenger of God. This was one of Satan's demons. Evil is not an abstract concept—every evil originates in a personality. Satan ordered the prince of Persia to do whatever it took to keep God's plan in Persia from moving forward.

This record makes it apparent that Satan assigns his demons geographically. It's probable that he assigns one demon prince to head the satanic activity of each principality or government on the face of the earth. If there is a demon assigned to Persia, there is most likely a demon assigned to the territories where you and I live. It's against this army of evil princes that we are in daily conflict.

How was this battle with the prince of Persia finally won? Gabriel tells Daniel that Michael, one of the chief princes of God, was sent to help him.

Michael's name means "Who is like God?" While Gabriel's role seems essentially to be in announcing and preaching, Michael is usually involved in protecting and fighting. Michael is a royal champion of God's people, Israel. He's referred to three times in Daniel, and each time his tagline gets progressively more honorable and more personally identified with Israel:

- He is called "one of the chief princes" (Daniel 10:13).
- Then he's referred to as "your prince" (Daniel 10:21).

- Finally, he's given the name "the great prince who stands watch over the sons of your people" (Daniel 12:1).

Michael is mentioned twice in the New Testament. In Revelation 12:7, he's the leading warrior in the great heavenly battle against Satan: "There was war in heaven. Michael and his angels fought against the dragon and his angels" (Revelation 12:7, NLT). In Jude 1:9, he's called "Michael the archangel." The term *archangel* means the angel who is first, principal, or chief. Only Michael is given that title in Scripture.

Paul is probably referring to Michael when he writes of "the archangel" in 1 Thessalonians 4:16: "The Lord Himself will descend from heaven with a shout, with the voice of an archangel, and with the trumpet of God. And the dead in Christ will rise first."

The inference in this story is that, without the help of Michael, Gabriel wouldn't have been able to withstand the prince of Persia, and this prophecy intended for Daniel never would have been delivered. Apparently God assigns Michael to deal with the more difficult situations involving demonic princes. Daniel 10:20 says that after finishing with the prince of Persia, Gabriel would be challenging the prince of Greece.

THE DETAILS THAT PREVIEW THE VISION

[The angel] said to me . . . "Now I have come to make you understand what will happen to your people in the latter days. . . ." When he had spoken such words to me, I turned my face toward the ground and became speechless.

DANIEL 10:12, 14-15

When the angel told Daniel that there were still more difficult years to come for his nation, Israel, Daniel stood speechless, staring at the ground. Israel's history was a saga of one disaster after another. He must have wondered how much more suffering they could endure.

When I visited the Yad Vashem Holocaust museum in Israel and witnessed for the first time, up close, the suffering and sorrow of the Jewish people throughout history, I wept. Somehow the Lord God let His prophet Daniel see this suffering ahead of time, and the vision was so real that Daniel reacted as if these horrible things were happening as he watched.

So traumatic was this prophetic news that Daniel had to be "strengthened" three times (Daniel 10:10, 16, 18). Now, due to Gabriel's patient administration, Daniel was now ready to receive the prophecies from the angel.

The Presentation of the Vision

Daniel 11 offers a glimpse into events that were yet to come for Israel, foretold by the prophetic utterance of God and given to the angel to deliver to Daniel in response to his prayer. Someone has computed that there are as many as 135 fulfilled prophecies in these verses.[6]

John Phillips summarizes the broad sweep of this chapter: "This prophecy . . . deals with the rise and fall of empires, with alliances and intrigues, with the marching of armies, with imperial ambitions and palace plots. Daniel foresaw the turbulent years when Syria and Egypt struggled for supremacy in the Near East and when wretched Palestine was torn from the grasp of this king to that king. The prophecy reaches all the way from the heyday of the Persian Empire right down to the days of Antiochus Epiphanes and to the deployment of Roman armies on the stage of the world. Then it takes a giant leap down the centuries to the end times and gives us details about the coming reign of the Antichrist."[7]

In this message, God unfolds the detailed revelations of what would befall the nation of Israel in the centuries to come. "Daniel 11:1-2 gives the prophetic history of Persia. Daniel 11:3-20 foretells the history of Greece. Daniel 11:21-35 sets forth the history of Israel and Israel's fierce foe during Maccabean times. Daniel 11:36-45 forewarns the people of God of the last great monster and murderer, the Antichrist."[8]

The prophecies of Daniel 11 were written in 536 BC. Their fulfillment began in 530 BC, when the first of "three more kings" arose in Persia (verse 2), and verses 21-35 were fulfilled in 150 BC. The end of chapter 11 and the beginning of chapter 12 won't be fulfilled until some date in the future—a year unknown to us.

The prophecies in this chapter are so detailed that many skeptics reject the book of Daniel, claiming that no one possibly could have known coming events in such detail. John Phillips summarizes what is at stake in this discussion: "The prophecies of Daniel are recorded in such detail, and so many of them have been so meticulously fulfilled in history, that unbelieving critics have resorted to suggesting a late date for the book. According to them the book of Daniel was written after the prophecies it records took place. That would make the book a forgery, the author a fraud, and its divine inspiration a farce."[9]

People who have chosen not to believe the Bible because certain aspects of it can only be explained by supernatural rationale will have a difficult time with this chapter. Evidence leaves no room for doubt that Daniel was written before the events it predicts. Skeptics don't know what to do with this evidence, because it puts the inevitable stamp of the supernatural on the Bible.

John F. Walvoord writes, "The issue is a clear-cut question as to whether God is omniscient about the future. If He is, revelation may be just as detailed as God elects to make it; and detailed prophecy is no more difficult or incredible than broad predictions."[10] If we choose to believe that the Bible is God's Word, we accept the fact that God can reveal details of history to His people before the events occur.

The prophecies in Daniel 11 concern five rulers who were yet to come in Daniel's time. Coincidentally, the names of all five begin with the letter *A*. By looking at the reigns of these men, we will uncover the essence of the predictions outlined in Daniel 11.

THE "A" KINGS OF DANIEL 11

Ahasuerus	486–465 BC	Daniel 11:2
Alexander	336–323 BC	Daniel 11:3-4
Antiochus III (the Great)	223–187 BC	Daniel 11:10-20
Antiochus IV Epiphanes	175–164 BC	Daniel 11:21-35
Antichrist	Unknown	Daniel 11:36-45

AHASUERUS

Behold, three more kings will arise in Persia, and the fourth shall be far richer than them all; by his strength, through his riches, he shall stir up all against the realm of Greece.
DANIEL 11:2

The first prophecy the angel brought to Daniel concerned the future of the Persian government. The prophecy quickly passed over three kings that followed Cyrus. These kings were Cambyses (his son), Pseudo-Smerdis, and Darius the Great. Then came the notable fourth king, Xerxes, also known as Ahasuerus (486–465 BC). The book of Esther, in which he is a major player, tells us that Ahasuerus "reigned over one hundred and twenty-seven provinces, from India to Ethiopia" and indicates the scope of his wealth by recording a lavish 180-day feast he hosted for all his officials and servants (Esther 1:1-7). He also commanded one of the largest armies in ancient history. On one occasion, he set off to invade Greece with 2,641,000 men. But eight months later he straggled home, broken and beaten.

ALEXANDER

His Dominion

> A mighty king shall arise, who shall rule with great
> dominion, and do according to his will.
> DANIEL 11:3

The description of a mighty king in Daniel 11:3-4 fits Alexander the Great down to the smallest details. We met Alexander earlier in our study of Daniel. He ruled the kingdom represented by the section of bronze in the great colossus of Daniel 2, and he was the great horn of the goat in Daniel 8.

Alexander was one of the most remarkable men in history. He did, indeed, rule "with great dominion" and acted "according to his will." By the age of thirty-two, he had gained control of the entire known world, from Europe to India. Near the end of his life, he was crying in his tent because there was nothing left to conquer. He became a drunkard and a carouser, and although the cause of his death is a mystery, he may have died as a result of either acute alcoholism or treacherous poisoning.

His Defeat

> When he has arisen, his kingdom shall be broken up and
> divided toward the four winds of heaven, but not among

his posterity nor according to his dominion with which he ruled; for his kingdom shall be uprooted, even for others besides these.

DANIEL 11:4

When Alexander had "arisen," that is, when he was at the zenith of his career, he died. His only possible heirs were a brother with a mental disability, an illegitimate son, and the unborn child of his pregnant wife. All were murdered within a matter of months, leaving no posterity. Daniel tells us that this leader's great empire was "broken up and divided toward the four winds of heaven" (Daniel 11:4). History confirms that prophecy, telling us that it split into four parts, each ruled by one of his generals.

His Descendants

After a chaotic power struggle filled with intrigue, assassinations, and a succession of wars, two of the four divisions of Alexander's empire rose to dominance: Egypt and Syria. They were significant to the prophecy because of their location in relation to Israel. Egypt is directly to the south and Syria is to the north, and the fighting between these warring empires would affect Israel for years to come.

Daniel 11:5-20 prophesies years of fighting between these two nations, and it's astounding to realize how accurately these prophecies were fulfilled. For example, look at Daniel 11:6: "At the end of some years they shall join forces, for the daughter of the king of the South shall go to the king of the North to make an agreement . . . but she shall be given up, with those who brought her, and with him who begot her."

History records that King Ptolemy II of Egypt gave his daughter Berenice to Antiochus II of Syria in order to seal an alliance between the two nations. But in time, Antiochus's first wife, an evil and power-hungry woman named Laodice, poisoned Antiochus and murdered Berenice and her son. The prophecy in verse 6 was explicitly fulfilled.

As we read on, we find that additional prophecies were fulfilled in history: "From a branch of her roots one shall arise in his place, who shall come with an army, enter the fortress of the king of the North, and deal with them and prevail. And he shall also carry their gods captive to Egypt, with their princes and their precious articles of silver and gold; and he shall continue more years than the king of the North" (Daniel 11:7-8). To avenge the murder of his sister Berenice, Egypt's Ptolemy III attacked and defeated Syria, carried their gods and other valuables back to Egypt, and executed Laodice.

ANTIOCHUS THE GREAT (ANTIOCHUS III)

Daniel 11:10 introduces us to Antiochus III of Syria, whose wars against Egypt were marked first by a series of defeats followed by a series of victories (verses 10-16).

If you know your history, you'll recognize the story of Cleopatra in verse 17: "He shall also set his face to enter with the strength of his whole kingdom, and upright ones with him; thus shall he do. And he shall give him the daughter of women to destroy it; but she shall not stand with him, or be for him."

John Phillips explains that "Antiochus III gave his own daughter Cleopatra, then only eleven years of age, in a treacherous marriage to Ptolemy V of Egypt, a boy of twelve. He hoped his daughter would help him complete his control over Egypt. However, she sided with her husband and defeated her father's plans."[11]

History also tells us that Antiochus III tried to attack Egypt's coastal cities but was rebuffed by the rising Roman armies. In anger, he returned home and plundered his own land. When he attacked the temple of Jupiter to steal its treasures, his people rose up and murdered him. His body was never found. Consider how this perfectly fulfills Daniel's prophecy: "After this he shall turn his face to the coastlands, and shall take many. But a ruler shall bring the reproach against them to an end; and with the reproach removed, he shall turn back on him. Then he shall turn his face toward the fortress of his own land; but he shall stumble and fall, and not be found" (Daniel 11:18-19).

Seleucas IV, the son of Antiochus III, inherited his father's war debts, so he sent a tax collector to plunder the Temple in Jerusalem. Notice again how history affirms Daniel's prophecy: "There shall arise in his place one who imposes taxes on the glorious kingdom" (Daniel 11:20).

ANTIOCHUS EPIPHANES (ANTIOCHUS IV)

> In his place shall arise a vile person, to whom they will not
> give the honor of royalty; but he shall come in peaceably,
> and seize the kingdom by intrigue.
>
> DANIEL 11:21

The period we have just covered in Daniel 11:5-20 spans nearly 150 years and involves a long succession of rulers. But in verses 21-35, the pace slows and we view just one decade, 175 to somewhere around 164 BC, and concentrate on one ruler.

We met Antiochus Epiphanes in an earlier chapter. He is the "antichrist of the Old Testament" and a picture of the future Antichrist of the Tribulation period.

Antiochus Epiphanes was among the wickedest men who ever lived. He had no claim to the Syrian throne, but he deceived and finagled his way into power through bribes and gifts, just as Daniel had predicted: "He shall enter peaceably, even into the richest places of the province; and he shall do what his fathers have not done, nor his forefathers: he shall disperse among them the plunder, spoil, and riches; and he shall devise his plans against the strongholds, but only for a time" (Daniel 11:24).

Then, as Daniel prophesied, Antiochus stirred up a battle against "the South" (Egypt), but he couldn't win on the battlefield: "Both these kings' hearts shall be bent on evil, and they shall speak lies at the same table; but it shall not prosper, for the end will still be at the appointed time" (Daniel 11:27).

The two stalemated kings agreed to a peace treaty, which both quickly broke. After yet another failure, Antiochus vented his anger on Israel: "Forces shall be mustered by him, and they shall defile the sanctuary fortress; then they shall take away the daily sacrifices, and place there the abomination of desolation" (Daniel 11:31).

Antiochus IV invaded Jerusalem, raping and murdering women and slaughtering children on sight. He erected an image of Zeus in the Jewish Temple and demanded that the Jews worship it. He stopped all the Jewish sacrifices and sacrificed a pig on the altar. He flung its blood throughout the Temple and force-fed the pork to the priests. The Temple was desolate; no Jew could go there because Antiochus Epiphanes had made it an abomination.

But as Daniel prophesied, a small band of Jewish patriots inspired a rebellion and turned things around: "Those who do wickedly against the covenant he shall corrupt with flattery; but the people who know their God shall be strong, and carry out great exploits" (Daniel 11:32).

The apocryphal book of 1 Maccabees tells the story of a family of brave Jews who led a revolt against Antiochus IV, finally bringing his reign to an end. (We explored the details of their uprising in chapter 9 of this book.)

At this point there's a break in the action in Daniel 11. John Phillips explains, "A clear-cut break in this remarkable prophecy occurs between Daniel 11:35 and 11:36. The prophetic history is continuous right down to the days of Antiochus Epiphanes (Antiochus the God). Then it leaps over the ages (as does the prophecy of Dan. 9:25-26) and comes back into focus at the time of the Antichrist, of whom Antiochus was a type."[12]

THE ANTICHRIST

Once again Antiochus Epiphanes (Daniel 11:21-35) is depicted adjacent to the Antichrist (Daniel 11:36-39). Many scholars believe that the entire second half of the book of Daniel is just a preamble to these verses. All the evil rulers we have studied in Daniel 11 tell us that the ultimate evil ruler is ascending. This final ruler can't be Antiochus Epiphanes, as some would have us believe. Note the words at the end of verse 35: "the time of the end." There's a break from the discussion of Antiochus Epiphanes, whose atrocities have already been recorded. What is about to be discussed concerns another despot, more evil than Antiochus.

I've written extensively about the Antichrist in three previous books: *What in the World Is Going On?*,[13] *The Coming Economic Armageddon*,[14] and *Agents of the Apocalypse*.[15] We have also discussed this final Gentile ruler in chapters 9–10 of this book. As we draw near to the close of Daniel's prophecy, we're given one more look at the man of sin.

Our previous investigations of the Antichrist have focused on his characteristics, while Daniel chapter 11 is more about his career. Rather than exploring every verse in this extended passage, I'll offer this list—the Old Testament's final description of the Antichrist:

1. **He will do what he desires:** "The king shall do according to his own will" (Daniel 11:36).
2. **He will deify himself:** "He shall exalt and magnify himself above every god" (Daniel 11:36).
3. **He will defy the true God:** "He . . . shall speak blasphemies against the God of gods" (Daniel 11:36).
4. **He will disregard all religion:** "He shall regard neither the God of his fathers nor the desire of women, nor regard any god; for he shall exalt himself above them all" (Daniel 11:37).

5. **He will devote himself to the military:** "He shall honor a god of fortresses" (Daniel 11:38).

6. **He will declare war against foreign powers:** "He shall act against the strongest fortresses with a foreign god, which he shall acknowledge, and advance its glory; and he shall cause them to rule over many, and divide the land for gain" (Daniel 11:39).

7. **He will defend himself against other nations:** "The king of the South shall attack him; and the king of the North shall come against him like a whirlwind, with chariots, horsemen, and with many ships; and he shall enter the countries, overwhelm them, and pass through" (Daniel 11:40).

8. **He will defeat some early enemies:** "He shall also enter the Glorious Land, and many countries shall be overthrown; but these shall escape from his hand: Edom, Moab, and the prominent people of Ammon" (Daniel 11:41).

9. **He will develop great wealth:** "He shall have power over the treasures of gold and silver, and over all the precious things of Egypt; also the Libyans and Ethiopians shall follow at his heels" (Daniel 11:43).

10. **He will be defeated, and no one will come to his aid:** "He shall come to his end, and no one will help him" (Daniel 11:45).

As we conclude our study of the Antichrist, John Walvoord offers an overview of this passage of Scripture: "Taken as a whole, Daniel 11:36-45 is a description of the closing days of the times of the Gentiles, specifically, the great tribulation with its world ruler, world religion, and materialistic philosophy. In spite of its satanic support, the world government fragmentizes into sectional disputes and a great world war which climaxes with the second advent of

Christ. This brings the times of the Gentiles to a close with the destruction of the wicked rulers who led it."[16]

In a single chapter of the Bible, we have just covered an entire era of history that was accurately predicted in detail long before it happened. One writer has said, "The book of Daniel is especially fitted to be a battleground between faith and unbelief."[17] It doesn't allow a neutral position; either it is divine or it is fraudulent, written after its ostensibly prophetic predictions were already history.

There is considerable evidence that demonstrates Daniel is not fraudulent. Among that proof is the fact that the book was known to exist long before the destruction of the Temple in AD 70—an event Daniel predicted. The Jews never would have accepted a fraudulent book as Scripture. The most authoritative endorsement of Daniel is that of Jesus Himself, where He quotes "Daniel the prophet" (Matthew 24:15), giving the book's veracity His stamp of approval.

If God is able to create the entire universe, surely He'd have no trouble giving us accurate pictures of events long before they happen. We have no reason to doubt that the future is as accessible to Him as the past is to us.

Yes, we can choose whether to believe or disbelieve, but our choice doesn't affect reality. Truth doesn't adjust itself to accommodate our preferences. Daniel is true whether we believe it or not. God gave us Daniel 11 to demonstrate in one little section of prophecy that when He says something is going to happen, it will happen exactly as He says it will.

Biblical scholar Dr. E. Schuyler English tells the story of a man from Long Island who satisfied a lifelong dream by buying a high-quality barometer:

> When he unpacked the instrument, he was dismayed to find that the needle appeared to be stuck, pointing to the section marked "Hurricane." After shaking the barometer vigorously,

the man wrote a scorching letter to the store from which he had purchased the instrument and, on his way to his office in New York the next morning, mailed the protest. That evening he returned to Long Island to find not only the barometer missing, but his house also. The barometer's needle had been right—there was a hurricane![18]

Truth is truth, whether or not we choose to believe it.

* * *

DANIEL FOR TODAY

1. Discover the power of praying God's promises. Daniel prayed the promises of God that were recorded by Jeremiah, and God heard and answered his prayer. According to Dr. Everek R. Storms, God makes 7,487 promises to people throughout the Bible. How did he know this? On his twenty-seventh reading of the Bible, he counted each one of them, a project that took him a year and a half to complete.[19]

When I was growing up, my parents used to keep a box full of God's promises from Scripture on the kitchen table. Every evening before we ate, each of us would pull one of those promises from the box and read it aloud.

Almighty God has given His children many promises, and He delights in having us remind Him of those promises, just as Daniel did. What are your needs? What are your goals and dreams? If you explore the Word of God, you will find your promise from God. Why not begin the search today?

2. Remember, God's delays are not God's denials. For twenty-one days, Daniel poured out his heart to God in prayer and fasting.

During those twenty-one days, it must have seemed to Daniel as if God weren't listening. Little did Daniel know that God had heard his prayer from the very moment he began to pray: "From the first day that you set your heart to understand, and to humble yourself before your God, your words were heard" (Daniel 10:12).

We can become easily discouraged when our prayers seem to go unheard, but Daniel reminds us to be persistent in praying. Likewise, Jesus Himself encouraged us to "pray and not lose heart" (Luke 18:1), and the apostle Paul told us to pray "with all perseverance" (Ephesians 6:18).

Take up the challenge to pray with perseverance. Don't quit, faint, or yield in bringing your requests to God. He is listening—and the answer to your prayer may be closer than you realize.

3. Never underestimate or overestimate the power of Satan. More than in any other book of the Bible, Daniel gives us a behind-the-scenes look at the activity of our adversary, the devil. In Daniel 10 we learned that Satan is organized geographically—that he has demons assigned regionally. These demons were so powerful that they delayed the answer to Daniel's prayer for twenty-one days.

We don't understand all that happened in the heavenly realm during that time, but this scene does provide us with a glimpse of the battle every Christian is involved in—a battle not "against flesh and blood, but against principalities, against powers, against the rulers of the darkness of this age, against spiritual hosts of wickedness in the heavenly places" (Ephesians 6:12).

While we must not underestimate Satan's power, we must not overestimate it either. In Christ, God has provided us with the strength and resources to overcome our adversary:

Be strong in the Lord and in the power of His might. Put on the whole armor of God. . . .

Stand therefore, having girded your waist with truth, having put on the breastplate of righteousness, and having shod your feet with the preparation of the gospel of peace; above all, taking the shield of faith with which you will be able to quench all the fiery darts of the wicked one. And take the helmet of salvation, and the sword of the Spirit, which is the word of God; praying always with all prayer and supplication in the Spirit, being watchful to this end with all perseverance and supplication for all the saints.

EPHESIANS 6:10-11, 14-18

Chapter 12

THE END

Daniel 12

DANIEL STOOD ON THE BANK OF THE TIGRIS RIVER, listening intently to the angel Gabriel, who towered above the water. The glorious creature continued to unfold the future of the people of Israel.

Daniel's heart grew heavy as Gabriel described the terrible conquests that would ravage Israel in future years. The angel had told him to stand up and be strong, but now the darkness of the future caused the prophet's knees to tremble, and he felt like he was about to collapse.

But just when Daniel thought he could bear no more, the angel began to relate better news. Yes, Israel would experience a time of great tribulation, but God's people would be delivered. The severity of the persecution would produce brave, wise Jewish teachers and evangelists who would turn many people to God.

As Gabriel spoke, Daniel began to see in his mind's eye one of those brave Jewish men who would work diligently to bring God's people back to Him.

* * *

Rabbi Abel Ebrahim made his way through the dark streets of Jerusalem. He avoided streetlights, kept to the shadows, and took shortcuts through alleyways, always on the lookout for dictator Judas Christopher's police officers. Beneath his coat, he carried a well-worn Bible, one of the few that had escaped confiscation.

Navigating the city was difficult now, no matter the time of day. Even in daylight, few ventured out between 10:00 a.m. and 6:00 p.m. The heat was deadly, and many had died from even an hour's exposure. No one dared to go out at night because of Christopher's strictly enforced curfew. Many who did were never seen again.

The heat and the brutal police force weren't the only dangers. It hadn't rained in Israel for almost three years. The searing heat had dried up the rivers, and the lakes that remained were little more than stagnant, scum-infested pools. Earthquakes and showers of molten sulfur were now commonplace. Volcanic ash filled the atmosphere, turning the sun into a lurid red ball, killing crops, trees, and vegetation and forming a canopy that held in the merciless heat.

To make matters worse, the world was filled with political upheaval. Parts of Christopher's coalition of nations had begun to crumble. Rebel armies had begun to attack Christopher's forces in the northern part of Israel and were moving toward Jerusalem. Rabbi Ebrahim could hear the distant rumble of bombs and the shriek of missiles even now.

He reached the old section of the city and turned down the narrow lane that led to his destination. He entered an apartment building, silently ascended the stairway, and found the door to the home of Yosef and Anna Matthias. They were observant Jews who had been members of Abel's synagogue before it was forced to disband. The couple had recently lost a child to illness, and this tragedy only added to their struggles in their faith. Ever since Judas Christopher had desecrated the newly built Temple with an image of himself, they'd been wrestling to understand why God would allow His people to experience such harsh persecution.

Abel tapped on the door, using a prearranged signal of two knocks and a pause followed by three additional knocks. The door opened a crack before widening enough to admit Abel.

"Shalom, Rabbi," Yosef said in a subdued voice. "We weren't sure you'd make it. The police doubled their watch after finding a small group of Christians meeting nearby."

"I know." Abel's face darkened. "I knew them well."

Anna served cups of bitter coffee, and the three of them sat at the kitchen table. "We sent for you because our friends said you had answers to why all these horrors are devastating our people."

"Believe me, we're ready for answers," Yosef added.

"By God's grace, I have found answers in the books of our own prophets—Jeremiah, Ezekiel, Daniel, and others. I'm eager to share them with you. Yosef, would you please get out your Tanakh?"

"We no longer have one." Yosef looked at the table. "We—we destroyed it when little Reva died."

"I understand," Abel said gently. "It's okay; I have what I need with me." He reached inside his coat and took out his Bible.

"But that's a Christian Bible!" Anna said.

"Yes, but it includes the Tanakh—what Christians call the Old Testament. I want you to see something I found that will help you understand." As he turned to the book of Daniel, he said, "You know how accurately Daniel's final prophecy foretold the disasters that would be brought on Israel by a succession of kings—Ahasuerus, Alexander, Antiochus the Great, and Antiochus Epiphanes."

"Yes," Yosef replied. "Everything happened precisely as Daniel predicted."

"Not quite everything," Abel said. "As you know, the last parts of Daniel's prophecy have remained a mystery to us Jews. Nothing about that last king fits anything in history—the 'abomination of desolation' in the Temple, the three and a half years of unprecedented persecution of Israel, the battles of the kings of the South and the North. And the blaspheming king who honors no god but sets himself up as the king above all kings." Abel paused and sipped from his coffee cup, grimacing as he swallowed.

"I know; it's awful," Anna said.

"But it's better than the water," Abel replied.

"You're right," Yosef said. "Not only about the coffee, but about the prophecy. We've never understood Daniel's final predictions, and I suppose we never will."

"We didn't understand them because they hadn't occurred yet," Abel said. "The fact is, we are living in those predicted times right now. Let me show you what I mean."

For the next three hours, the rabbi compared the prophecies of Daniel with those of the apostle John in the book of Revelation, showing how the two books agree and how precisely their prophecies fit the events they were now enduring. He ended by reading the angel's prophecy of ultimate triumph for the Jewish people:

At that time your people shall be delivered,
Every one who is found written in the book.
And many of those who sleep in the dust of the earth shall awake,
Some to everlasting life,
Some to shame and everlasting contempt.
Those who are wise shall shine
Like the brightness of the firmament,
And those who turn many to righteousness
Like the stars forever and ever.[1]

"I can see it now." Anna's eyes widened in awe. "Everything you said fits together like a jigsaw puzzle. We are now living in those times Daniel wrote of."

"I don't know why we never saw it before!" Yosef exclaimed. "When we look at what's going on around us, it seems obvious, doesn't it?"

At that moment, a distant whine filled the air, followed by the boom of an exploding bomb.

"The war is getting closer," Yosef said. "I fear it will soon reach Jerusalem."

"But remember what we just read," Abel replied. "Those who remain faithful to God will triumph in the end. Don't you want to be one of those victorious ones?"

"We certainly do!" Yosef said. "What should we do?"

"I lead a small group of Jews who have come to believe that Jesus, the one who was crucified and rose again, is indeed our Messiah. Join us. We meet late on Saturday nights in the basement of the abandoned factory near the Eastern Gate."

The couple promised to be there. They prepared a bed for Rabbi Ebrahim, and after a short night's rest, he left early the next morning.

* * *

When Rabbi Ebrahim's little church of Jewish believers met the following Saturday night, the war had moved closer to Jerusalem. A few missiles had even fallen on the city, causing widespread destruction and a number of deaths.

Only twelve people made it to the assembly that week. The group's numbers constantly fluctuated, as converts tended to disappear almost as quickly as they became part of the church. Few of the losses were defections, however. Some of the believers were discovered and arrested, and others died due to natural disasters.

Rabbi Ebrahim introduced Yosef and Anna to the other believers, and after baptizing them, he began his sermon of encouragement. He often had to raise his voice over the clamor of planes and exploding bombs. He was halfway through his message when an explosion shook the walls, raining plaster from the ceiling. More explosions followed, and fighter jets shrieked directly overhead. The congregation could hear screams of panic erupting from the streets.

"The enemy is upon us!" Abel cried. "We must leave immediately. Go out through the Eastern Gate and run for the hills near the Dead Sea. Don't take anything with you—just get out of the city as fast as you can."

The rabbi unbolted the door, and the group streamed into the night, which was now lit by staccato bursts of gunfire and exploding bombs. They joined others who were flooding into the streets, all running toward the Eastern Gate.

As they ran, they heard a volley of gunfire behind them. Abel, bringing up the rear of his group, saw one of his people drop to the ground. He stopped and bent over the man. He was dead. Abel had no choice but to hurry on and rejoin the others.

Suddenly a woman ran past him, hurrying back toward the city. He looked closer and saw that it was Anna. He turned and ran after her.

"Anna, what are you doing?" he called.

"My baby!" she cried. At that moment she stumbled over a loose stone and sprawled to the ground.

Abel reached her and helped her up. She was bleeding profusely from a gash in her head. She struggled to wrench free of his grip.

"My baby," she cried again. "Her photo is in my purse. It's all I have left of her. Please, let me go!" But before she could struggle any further, she collapsed onto the ground.

Abel scooped her up and began running toward the mountains with the rest of the group. Just when he thought he couldn't take another step, he heard a voice ahead of them.

"Anna! Anna! Where are you?" It was Yosef.

"We're here," Abel managed to get out through gasps.

Yosef appeared out of the darkness and took Anna in his arms, and they hurried toward the mountains again. Abel, reeling from exhaustion, couldn't keep up. Eventually he sank to his knees, panting heavily.

As he struggled to stand, a round of gunshots rang out behind him. He fell face down, his body riddled with bullets.

* * *

"Abel, wake up. It's time for you to rise." Abel heard the voice, pure and full of love, pulling him out of the darkness.

"Get up." The call came again, clearer this time.

"Abel." He felt a gentle hand on his shoulder. "Get up. I have work for you to do."

The rabbi finally opened his eyes and looked into the face of a Man he had never seen but somehow knew he would love forever.

At once he realized who the Man was, and such joy surged within him that he could hardly speak. "You . . . you are . . ."

The Man smiled. "Yes, I am Jesus, your Messiah. Welcome to the Millennium. Now I have work for you." He took the rabbi's hand and drew him to his feet.

Abel looked all around him. The parched, harried world he had known was gone, and he saw a lush land of grassy meadows and thriving trees filled with birds. Before him flowed a river, which fed into a pristine lake.

"Come, walk with Me."

Abel fell in step with his Messiah, and they began walking toward a city beyond the lake. Its walls gleamed in the sun like burnished gold. "That looks like . . ."

"Yes, it's Jerusalem—no longer the ravaged and troubled city you knew, but cleansed and set right as the capital of My Kingdom for the next thousand years. When we arrive, I'll explain the task I have for you."

"What will You have me do?"

"I will answer that later. But you will love the task. And as you accomplish it, you will shine among My people like a star forever and ever."

* * *

The vision faded, and Daniel again found himself on the bank of Babylon's Tigris River in the presence of the mighty Gabriel.

Gabriel spoke: "Daniel, you must record everything I have told you. Then you must seal up the book until the time of the end."

"But, sir, what is the point in writing these words if they are to be sealed from view?"

"They are sealed not to prevent access but for preservation. Believers in the future will search this book and find knowledge to help them through the horrific struggles that will come to God's people in the last days."

Just then two lesser angels appeared, one on each side of the river. The angel on the near bank spoke: "When will all these prophecies be fulfilled?"

Gabriel lifted his arms to heaven and swore an oath by the name of God Himself that the words he said were as lasting and true as if they were engraved in everlasting stone. "These terrible times will last three and a half years, and when the evil of Israel has been completely shattered, all the prophecies I have uttered will be fulfilled."

"I still don't understand," Daniel said. "Please explain to me how all these events will end."

"These words are not for you to understand. They are reserved for the people of the last days. Be content to know that the righteous ones of Israel will be vindicated and saved after their suffering is over. And no one will completely understand the words of this book until that time."

"But sir . . ."

"Go on with your normal business, Daniel. You know all you need to know, and you still have work to do before you leave the earth. Rest assured that you are deeply beloved by God, for you have served Him faithfully throughout difficult times in a godless land. Your reward will be great in the new Kingdom that is to come."

THE SCRIPTURE BEHIND THE STORY

Reading the book of Daniel up to this point has been like reading a mystery novel and wondering how it will end. With Daniel 12, we now come to the end. The first part of the chapter tells us about the prophecies of the end, and the second part tells us about the end of the prophecies. Both are about "the time of the end" or, as they are popularly called, the end times.

The first three verses of chapter 12 continue the vision given to Daniel concerning the Antichrist and the coming of a time of trouble for Israel (Daniel 11:36-45).

John F. Walvoord summarizes the events that will characterize that era:

> The entire section from Daniel 11:36 to 12:3 constitutes a revelation of the major factors of the time of the end which may be summarized as follows: (1) a world ruler, (2) a world religion, (3) a world war, (4) a time of great tribulation for Israel, (5) deliverance for the people of God at the end of the tribulation, (6) resurrection and judgment, and (7) reward of the righteous. All of these factors are introduced in this section. Added elsewhere in the Scriptures are the additional facts that this time of the end begins with the breaking of the covenant by 'the prince that shall come' (Dan 9:26-27); that the 'time of the end' will last for three and one-half years (Dan 7:25; 12:7; Rev 13:5); that the time of the end is the same as the time of Jacob's trouble and the great tribulation (Jer 30:7; Mt 24:21).[2]

The Prophecies of the End
The first three verses of Daniel 12 review and affirm four major prophecies concerning the future of Israel.

ISRAEL WILL BE RAVAGED

> At that time Michael shall stand up, the great prince who
> stands watch over the sons of your people; and there shall be
> a time of trouble, such as never was since there was a nation,
> even to that time.
>
> DANIEL 12:1

The phrase "at that time" ties chapter 12 to the last verses of chapter 11—the period of time marked by the Antichrist's reign of terror and known as the Great Tribulation. The last verses of Daniel 11 lead up to this summary statement about the Great Tribulation in Daniel 12:1. Jeremiah refers to this period as "the time of Jacob's trouble" (Jeremiah 30:7).

Verse 1 connects the Great Tribulation with the standing up of Michael, the archangel of God. To understand what this means, we must turn from Daniel 12 to Revelation 12: "War broke out in heaven: Michael and his angels fought with the dragon; and the dragon and his angels fought, but they did not prevail, nor was a place found for them in heaven any longer. So the great dragon was cast out, that serpent of old, called the Devil and Satan, who deceives the whole world; he was cast to the earth, and his angels were cast out with him" (verses 7-9).

When Satan is cast down to the earth, the Great Tribulation will be initiated against Israel. Again the book of Revelation explains: "Rejoice, O heavens, and you who dwell in them! Woe to the inhabitants of the earth and the sea! For the devil has come down to you, having great wrath, because he knows that he has a short time" (Revelation 12:12).

There are many passages that describe what will happen during this time of tribulation for Israel:

- From the prophet Zechariah: "I will gather all the nations to battle against Jerusalem; the city shall be taken, the houses rifled, and the women ravished. Half of the city shall go into captivity" (Zechariah 14:2).
- From the prophet Jeremiah: "We have heard a voice of trembling, of fear, and not of peace. Ask now, and see, whether a man is ever in labor with child? So why do I see every man with his hands on his loins like a woman in labor, and all faces turned pale? Alas! For that day is great, so that none is like it; and it is the time of Jacob's trouble" (Jeremiah 30:5-7).
- From the Lord Jesus Christ: "Then there will be great tribulation, such as has not been since the beginning of the world until this time, no, nor ever shall be. And unless those days were shortened, no flesh would be saved; but for the elect's sake those days will be shortened" (Matthew 24:21-22).

When the prophet Daniel says "at that time," he is referring to this period of war, famine, darkness, disease, and demons. *At that time*, the earth will experience wholesale slaughter, the collapse of heavenly bodies, the destruction of one third of the earth and sea, and scorching sunlight that will burn people to death. It will be an era the likes of which our world has never seen and cannot comprehend. Horrors will be unleashed on the earth in the breaking of the seals, the blowing of the trumpets, and the emptying of the bowls of judgment described in Revelation 6–19.

ISRAEL WILL BE RESCUED

At that time your people shall be delivered, every one who is found written in the book.

DANIEL 12:1

The Book of Life is mentioned a number of times in the Bible (e.g., Exodus 32:32-33; Psalm 69:28; Daniel 12:1; Philippians 4:3; Revelation 3:5; 13:8; 17:8; 21:27; 22:19). Some first-century cultural background will help us understand the nature of this book.

The cities of John's day had a register that listed the names of every citizen in the city. If a person committed crimes or otherwise defiled his standing in the city, he could be called before a tribunal and his name removed—literally blotted out—from the city's registry. Such a person would no longer be considered a citizen of that city and would be forced to move elsewhere.[3]

I believe this is the concept behind the Book of Life. It is a book originally containing the name of every person ever born into this world. As author Henry Morris says:

> One can speculate that beside each person's name as entered in the book at time of conception will be recorded the time of his "age of accountability," the date of his conversion to Christ as His Savior, and evidence demonstrating the genuineness of that conversion. However, if there are no entries for the last two items by the time that person dies, the entire record will be blotted out (Revelation 3:5), and an awful blank will be left in the book at the place where his name would have been. Exhibiting this blank spot in the book will be the final and conclusive evidence that the person being judged must be consigned to the lake of fire.[4]

In Daniel 12:1, the names written in the book are godly Jews, the believing remnant on the earth at the end of the Tribulation. These Jews will be rescued out of the Tribulation period. In Ezekiel 20:33-38, God says He will purge Israel of rebellious, disobedient Jews, leaving a remnant of the committed. Zechariah 13:8-9 says, "In all the land . . . two-thirds in it shall be cut off and die, but one-third shall be left in it: I will bring the one-third through the fire, will refine them as silver is refined, and test them as gold is tested. They will call on My name."

In some of the last words of the Old Testament, Malachi refers to the time when the Lord will preserve the godly Jewish remnant: "A book of remembrance was written before Him for those who fear the LORD and who meditate on His name. 'They shall be Mine,' says the LORD of hosts, 'On the day that I make them My jewels. And I will spare them as a man spares his own son who serves him.' Then you shall again discern between the righteous and the wicked, between one who serves God and one who does not serve Him" (Malachi 3:16-18).

God will use the Tribulation period to sift the faithful Jews from those who are unfaithful. Those left at the end of that time will be a righteous nation that will reign with Him for a thousand years in His Kingdom on the earth: "The saints of the Most High shall receive the kingdom, and possess the kingdom forever, even forever and ever. . . . Then the kingdom and dominion, and the greatness of the kingdoms under the whole heaven, shall be given to the people, the saints of the Most High. His kingdom is an everlasting kingdom, and all dominions shall serve and obey Him" (Daniel 7:18, 27).

ISRAEL WILL BE RESURRECTED

Many of those who sleep in the dust of the earth shall awake, some to everlasting life, some to shame and everlasting contempt.
DANIEL 12:2

This verse is not a proof text for a general resurrection; not everyone will be resurrected at the same time. By the end of the Tribulation period, all the righteous dead will have been resurrected to life. But the resurrection of the unrighteous won't occur until a thousand years later, at the end of the Millennium (Revelation 20:5, 13-14).

In Daniel 12:2, then, we notice a one-thousand-year time gap between the resurrection of the just ("Many of those who sleep in the dust of the earth shall awake, some to everlasting life") and the resurrection of the unjust ("some to shame and everlasting contempt").

The important point being made in Daniel 12, however, has to do with the resurrection of those who die during the Tribulation period as a result of their faithfulness to the Lord. John tells us in the book of Revelation that these martyrs will be raised up at the end of the Tribulation period and will reign with Christ for a thousand years: "I saw the souls of those who had been beheaded for their witness to Jesus and for the word of God, who had not worshiped the beast or his image, and had not received his mark on their foreheads or on their hands. And they lived and reigned with Christ for a thousand years. . . . Blessed and holy is he who has part in the first resurrection. Over such the second death has no power, but they shall be priests of God and of Christ, and shall reign with Him a thousand years" (Revelation 20:4, 6).

ISRAEL WILL BE REWARDED

> Those who are wise shall shine like the brightness of the firmament, and those who turn many to righteousness like the stars forever and ever.
>
> DANIEL 12:3

The word *wise* in this passage is describing teachers—individuals who have insight into the times and impart it to others. Out of the Tribulation period will rise some courageous individuals who will instruct people from the Word of God. They will encourage and strengthen God's people during this terrible time.

The Tribulation will also produce courageous evangelists—"those who turn many to righteousness"—who will be instrumental in bringing many to faith in Jesus the Messiah.

These faithful teachers and evangelists will be rewarded first with "everlasting life" (Daniel 12:2). This is the first mention of this term in the Old Testament. Along with everlasting life, we are told that they will "shine like the brightness of the firmament . . . like the stars forever and ever" (Daniel 12:3).

A saying about the gospel puts it this way: "If you want to plant something that will last a year, plant a flower. If you want to plant something that will last a lifetime, plant a tree. But if you want to plant something that will last forever, plant the gospel in someone's life."

The End of the Prophecies

Now that we've addressed the prophecies of the end, we come to the end of the prophecies. Daniel 12:5-13 is the conclusion to the book, and in these verses Daniel confesses that he doesn't understand much of what God has said (Daniel 12:8). What an encouragement for us! If Daniel didn't understand it all, we don't need to feel incompetent that we don't either.

Actually, we may understand this book better than Daniel did because we have the perspective of history. Daniel didn't have the advantage of reading the Olivet discourse, which came from the lips of our Lord. He didn't have John's revelation to offer further clarity to the end times. Daniel had the words of some of the prophets but not all of them, as we do. Yet even with all our resources, there are still some things we don't understand. But we don't need to be discouraged!

Peter says,

Of this salvation the prophets have inquired and searched carefully, who prophesied of the grace that would come

to you, searching what, or what manner of time, the
Spirit of Christ who was in them was indicating when He
testified beforehand the sufferings of Christ and the glories
that would follow. To them it was revealed that, not to
themselves, but to us they were ministering the things which
now have been reported to you through those who have
preached the gospel to you by the Holy Spirit sent from
heaven—things which angels desire to look into.

I PETER 1:10-12

Peter says that while the prophets knew they were writing prophecies describing events yet in the future, they didn't always understand
what the Holy Spirit gave them to write. They studied their own
words to try to figure out what they meant. We, however, have the
additional testimony of the New Testament writers to add light and
understanding to what confused Daniel.

FINAL DISCUSSIONS WITH THE ANGELS

The Discussion about Time

As Daniel stood on the bank of the Tigris River, three angels appeared.
One stood on the same side of the river as Daniel, and another stood
on the other side. The third angel, who stood above the waters of the
river and is described as "a man clothed in linen," was most likely
Gabriel, whom Daniel had met once before on the bank of the Tigris
(Daniel 10:4, 10, 16, 18).

One of the angels, probably the one on the same side as Daniel,
asked Gabriel a question: "How long shall the fulfillment of these
wonders be?" (Daniel 12:6). In other words, "How long will the
Antichrist be allowed to oppress the people of God during the Tribulation period?"

Then came the answer: "I heard the man clothed in linen, who was above the waters of the river, when he held up his right hand and his left hand to heaven, and swore by Him who lives forever, that it shall be for a time, times, and half a time; and when the power of the holy people has been completely shattered, all these things shall be finished" (Daniel 12:7).

Before Gabriel answered the question, he raised both hands to heaven and swore "by Him who lives forever." In ancient times, raising one hand in an oath was a way of showing the seriousness and importance of a promise (Genesis 14:22; Deuteronomy 32:40). Raising both hands conveyed even greater significance. And since God was the One by whom the oath was verified, there could be no greater solemnity attributed to what the angel was about to communicate.

Gabriel answered that the time of the Antichrist's reign would be for "a time, times, and half a time." "A time" equals one unit, "times" equals two units, and "one-half time" equals one-half a unit. The time of the Antichrist's atrocities against the Jews would be one plus two plus one-half, or three and a half years, which equals the last half of the seven years of tribulation for the Jews.

Joseph Seiss removes any doubt as to the length of time Gabriel is indicating:

> In not less than six different places, and in almost as many different ways, is this declared in the prophecies, including both Testaments. It is for "*a time and times and the dividing of time*" (Dan. vii. 25)—"It shall be for *a time, times, and a half*" (xii. 7)—"the holy city shall they tread under foot *forty and two months*" (Rev. xi. 2)—"the woman fled into the wilderness, *a thousand two hundred and three-score days*"—for "*a time, and times, and half a time*" (xii. 6, 14)—"and power was given him to continue *forty and two months*" (xiii. 5). All

these passages refer to one and the same period of oppression and trouble under the Antichrist, and in each instance the measure is three and a half years. . . . Our Lord ministered on earth three and a half years, and the Antichrist shall enact his Satanic ministry for the same length of time."[5]

The last part of Gabriel's answer was that all these dire prophecies would be fulfilled "when the power of the holy people has been completely shattered." The "end of wonders" will continue as long as it takes for the power of the Jews to be broken.

The Discussion about Tribulation

The question Daniel asked was different from the one the angel asked: "What shall be the end of these things?" (Daniel 12:8).

The angel's question was about "when"; Daniel's question was about "what." Daniel was begging to know more, saying, in essence, "What last things will happen before the very end? Please, give me more details."

But the details weren't for Daniel to know. Gabriel told him, "Go your way, Daniel, for the words are closed up and sealed till the time of the end" (Daniel 12:9). Daniel wouldn't get a complete answer to this particular question, but Gabriel did relieve his anxiety by adding a note of hope: "Many shall be purified, made white, and refined, but the wicked shall do wickedly; and none of the wicked shall understand, but the wise shall understand. And from the time that the daily sacrifice is taken away, and the abomination of desolation is set up, there shall be one thousand two hundred and ninety days. Blessed is he who waits, and comes to the one thousand three hundred and thirty-five days" (Daniel 12:10-12).

After being appalled by the calamitous prophecies concerning his people, Daniel must have been relieved to hear this assurance of their ultimate, glorious future. The angel explained that while the sufferings would harden some in their wickedness, those same afflictions would result in a remnant being purified and cleansed.

The banning of the Jews' daily sacrifices in Daniel 12:11 refers to the middle of the Tribulation period, when the Antichrist will break his covenant with the nation of Israel and set up an idol in the Temple.

Verses 11 and 12 are filled with mystery. Having established in his prophecy the importance of 1,260 as the number of days that mark the Great Tribulation, the angel now introduced two additional numbers that seem to have no reference point. First, he told Daniel that from "the abomination of desolation" there "shall be one thousand two hundred and ninety days" (Daniel 12:11). That's thirty more than the established number of 1,260 days.

Before we can even digest that variance, an additional number is introduced: "Blessed is he who waits, and comes to the one thousand three hundred and thirty-five days" (Daniel 12:12).

Here the angel announced the first blessing in the book of Daniel and then confuses us by adding another 45 days to the 30 days he already added to the 1,260 days. Now we are left to decipher the meaning of 75 total days that have never been spoken of the rest of biblical prophecy.

Why would the angel add seventy-five days to the end of the Tribulation period and bless those who wait for those days to expire? What's the significance of these extra days? Here's an explanation from Leon Wood: "It may be the time necessary for setting up the governmental machinery for carrying on the rule of Christ. The true and full border of Israel (from the River of Egypt to the Euphrates, Genesis 15:18) will have to be established, and appointments made of those aiding in the government."[6]

The blessing for those who wait for these things to happen will be the privilege of being present at the very beginning of the Millennium, the thousand-year reign of Christ.

FINAL DIRECTIONS TO DANIEL

This section of Daniel 12 devotes three verses to the final instructions the angel gave to Daniel.

He Is Instructed to Protect the Prophecy

> You, Daniel, shut up the words, and seal the book until the time of the end; many shall run to and fro, and knowledge shall increase.
>
> DANIEL 12:4

Daniel was told to seal up the prophecy—but not so that no one could read it. He was told that the prophecy was for the end times and that it must be secured so it would be available when it was needed most. While some of these prophecies weren't applicable to Daniel in his time or to us in our time, a time is coming when the words of this book will be the most important words on Earth.

Joseph Seiss writes, "Just as valuable official documents intended to direct and inform successive generations are carefully engrossed and secured and held inviolable against all tampering, that they may be preserved entire and transmitted uncorrupted to all whom they concern, so and in this sense and spirit was Daniel to shut up and seal the words of this Book."[7]

The angel's expression "many shall run to and fro, and knowledge shall increase" is often misinterpreted to mean that international travel will increase exponentially and that knowledge will be made available through technology in the end times. But the correct interpretation has nothing to do with the material advances of the final days.

The phrase "run to and fro," when connected with a book, means "to let one's eyes run to and fro"—that is, to diligently peruse the words on the page. According to H. C. Leupold, those alive during the Tribulation "will read, reread, and check on what they have read, and so ponder these words diligently. . . . And in the process of such earnest searching, 'knowledge shall be increased.' In the light of the developments of the last times, the purpose of the book and its meaning will become increasingly clear."[8]

While nations are plotting against each other, while much blood is being shed all over the world, people will be searching for answers to why there is such great suffering and sorrow.

Jesus said that in the time of Tribulation, people will be reading the book of Daniel, and he urges them to take what they read very seriously:

> "When you see the 'abomination of desolation,' spoken of
> by Daniel the prophet, standing in the holy place" (whoever
> reads, let him understand), "then let those who are in Judea
> flee to the mountains. Let him who is on the housetop not
> go down to take anything out of his house. And let him
> who is in the field not go back to get his clothes. But woe to
> those who are pregnant and to those who are nursing babies
> in those days! And pray that your flight may not be in winter
> or on the Sabbath. For then there will be great tribulation,
> such as has not been since the beginning of the world until
> this time, no, nor ever shall be."
>
> MATTHEW 24:15-21

Daniel was instructed to make sure the book would be available to those who would need it later, in the Tribulation period.

He Is Instructed to Proceed with His Life

> He said, "Go your way, Daniel, for the words are closed up
> and sealed till the time of the end."
>
> DANIEL 12:9

The angel told Daniel not to waste time delving more deeply into these prophecies; they simply wouldn't be fully understood until they came to pass. In the meantime, Daniel had his own work to do; he was to accept the mystery of what he had been given and get on with his life.

Leon Wood applies this principle to Christians today: "So often today, too, Christians want to know more details regarding some doctrine, especially concerning the last things, than God has revealed in His Word; but they also should rest content with what God has chosen to make clear."[9]

He Is Instructed to Prepare for the Future

Go your way till the end; for you shall rest, and will arise to your inheritance at the end of the days.

DANIEL 12:13

For the third time in just thirteen verses, the angel spoke personally to Daniel and instructed him to go about his duties and responsibilities. He was told to protect the prophecy and proceed with his life, and now he was being told to prepare for the future.

One writer has paraphrased "go your way till the end" as "keep on living until the time of the end." If this is the meaning of these words, they become even more motivational when we remember that Daniel was now in his eighties.

Daniel was told that in due time he would "rest" (as in death), and afterward, that he would "arise" (as in resurrection). At that time, he would receive his inheritance. Since Daniel's resurrection is scheduled to take place at the end of the Tribulation period, we can assume that part of his inheritance will be reigning with Jesus during the Millennium along with those who survive that time of trouble and those who have been martyred and raised back to life.

Daniel spent all his days in a foreign culture, away from his home in Palestine. Now God was promising him that someday he would receive his part of the redistribution of the land. Daniel's inheritance was safe and secure.

Daniel lived a long and productive life. But as we come to the end of his story, it's apparent that for him, as it should be for any follower of Christ, the best is yet to come.

* * *

DANIEL FOR TODAY

As we come to the end of the book of Daniel, we, too, can follow these three directions that were given to Daniel in the last chapter of his prophecy.

1. Protect the prophecy. Daniel was told to seal up the prophecy and preserve it for a future day when it would be needed. That instruction was given to Daniel more than 2,500 years ago. We have been blessed to study the book of Daniel because it has been preserved.

And now it's our turn. How can we preserve the words of Daniel's prophecy? We can read them, study them, determine to understand them, and obey them. We can teach our children the importance of understanding the prophetic sections of Scripture, and we can encourage our pastors and teachers to explain these truths to us.

Someday soon the Lord is going to return for His saints, and immediately the prophecies we've studied in Daniel will begin to unfold as the seven years of the Tribulation begin.

Future events cast their shadows before they become reality. In other words, the events of the Tribulation will be unloosed after the Rapture, but to those who know their Bibles, the buildup to those events will be evident before then. So as God's people, we must be vigilant.

> This is all the more urgent, for you know how late it is; time is running out. Wake up, for our salvation is nearer now than when we first believed. The night is almost gone; the day of salvation will soon be here. So remove your dark deeds like dirty clothes, and put on the shining armor of right living. Because we belong to the day, we must live decent lives for all to see. Don't participate in the darkness of wild parties and drunkenness, or in sexual promiscuity and immoral living, or in quarreling and jealousy. Instead, clothe yourself with the presence of the Lord Jesus Christ. And don't let yourself think about ways to indulge your evil desires.
>
> ROMANS 13:11-14, NLT

2. Proceed with your life. In response to one of Daniel's questions, Gabriel told him the answer would be revealed at the appointed time—and that was all he needed to know. Daniel wasn't to waste time in pursuit of the answer but rather to get on with his life.

While prophecy is important and should never be neglected, neither should it become an obsession to the exclusion of our service to the Lord. Daniel was told not to sit by and wait for the fulfillment of prophecies but to "go his way" and serve the Lord.

The angel told Daniel that those who teach the Word and share the gospel would "shine . . . like the stars forever and ever" (Daniel 12:3). As I read that verse, I'm reminded of something I wrote in the introduction to the book of Daniel in *The Jeremiah Study Bible*. It challenged me then, and it still does now:

> Contemporary culture loves the idea of "stars." We have star musicians, singers, actors, athletes, and others who

become stars simply because they are wealthy or glamorous. This sort of stardom hangs by the most tenuous of threads; yesterday's "stars" are often today's has-beens. The book of Daniel, however, speaks of the genuine version: "Those who are wise shall shine like the brightness of the firmament, and those who turn many to righteousness like the stars forever and ever" (12:3).

Most of us will probably never live to see our names in lights. But if we pursue and apply the wisdom of God's Word and—as best we know how—live our lives to point others toward Christ, we will somehow reflect God's beauty and glory, lighting up the skies of the new heaven.[10]

3. Prepare for the future. Daniel was told to "go his way till the end, for he would rest, and arise to his inheritance at the end of the days." In other words, he was promised something far better in the future. And so are we. Like Daniel, we are promised a glorious future if we put our trust in our Lord and persevere. Like the teachers and evangelists of the end times, we have the potential to shine like stars in the new Kingdom of Jesus Christ.

As we close our extended study of the book of Daniel and the agents of Babylon, I can think of no better way to summarize all we've learned than by quoting my friend Warren Wiersbe:

> Mention the name of Daniel among people who read the Bible and you will get a variety of responses. Prophecy students will say, "An inspired interpreter!" Businesspeople will reply, "He was also an efficient administrator." A youth pastor might say, "A model young man," and the prayer warriors will add, "But don't forget he was a faithful intercessor."
>
> These assessments are true, but behind them is the most

important characteristic of all: Daniel was a conqueror. In fact, he was a "more-than-conqueror" kind of person who believed God and became an overcomer. George Washington Carver said that success is measured not only by where people end up in life but also by how much they had to overcome to get there. Daniel had to meet and overcome many enemies and obstacles in order to survive and continue serving the Lord and His people in a pagan kingdom. "The story of Daniel is fascinating," said G. Campbell Morgan, "because it reveals the possibilities of godliness in the midst of the circumstances of ungodliness."

Daniel was a teenager when he was taken to Babylon in 605 BC, and he served successfully for at least sixty years under four different Gentile rulers. While Jeremiah was helping the poor remnant in Judah and Ezekiel was encouraging the exiles in Babylon, Daniel was at the center of political power bearing witness of the one true and living God. He was serving the Lord by witnessing to the lost, advising the king, and writing the book that today teaches God's people. He did his work faithfully, and God honored him.[11]

Epilogue

MARCHING TOWARD THE BEGINNING

Near the end of C. S. Lewis's acclaimed novel *Perelandra*, Dr. Elwin Ransom, a British scholar who has been taken to the planet Venus to fulfill God's purpose, is speaking with a native Perelandrian, Tor, who is the new king of the planet. Tor has just explained to Ransom about the coming time when all God's creatures will be changed into heavenly ones with eternal bodies and leave the planets they inhabit to live with God.

"And that," said Ransom, "will be the end?"

Tor the King stared at him.

"The end?" he said. "Who spoke of an end?"

"The end of your world, I mean," said Ransom.

"Splendour of Heaven!" said Tor. "Your thoughts are unlike ours. About that time we shall not be far from the beginning of all things."[1]

Most Christians use the term "end times" when referring to the prophetic events described in the books of Daniel and Revelation. There's nothing wrong with that phrase; it accurately describes the cessation of world history and the chaos that will precede that end. But the pervasive use of the term may tell us something about our focus. "End times" puts the focus on the tragedy, loss, and apocalyptic horrors that will accompany the final destruction of earthly kingdoms. Such a focus can fill our hearts with dread, anxiety, and fear. To focus on the end times stops us short of where our attention should be, which is on what will happen next—what Lewis's King Tor called the "beginning of all things." This shift in focus replaces fear and anxiety with hope and joy.

This beginning of all things deserves our attention because it is actually the culminating purpose of world history. From the moment man and woman fell from created perfection in Eden, everything God has done in relation to humankind has been designed to bring about this new beginning. It's the purpose of God's promise of redemption to Adam and Eve in Genesis 3. It's the meaning behind Israel's preparation to bear the light of God to the world. It's the meaning behind the coming of Christ and of the implanting of God's Holy Spirit within the hearts of those who believe in Him. It's the meaning of the Christian church, a community dedicated to preparing the hearts of men and women to desire and anticipate this new beginning.

The beginning of all things is also the centerpiece of the book of Daniel. In Daniel 7:9-14, we read about Daniel's vision of God, the Ancient of Days, seated in majesty and glory on His heavenly throne. He is surrounded by a host of millions of angels, and the royal court of heaven is seated before Him. Daniel watches as God opens the books of judgment and brings about the final doom of the Satan-inspired beings that are inflicting havoc and misery on the earth in the end times. Then Daniel sees the climactic event of the vision:

Behold, One like the Son of Man,
Coming with the clouds of heaven!
He came to the Ancient of Days,
And they brought Him near before Him.
Then to Him was given dominion and glory and a kingdom,
That all peoples, nations, and languages should serve Him.
His dominion is an everlasting dominion,
Which shall not pass away,
And His kingdom the one
Which shall not be destroyed.

DANIEL 7:13-14

This is the moment everything written in the book of Daniel is pointing toward. Indeed, it's the moment everything in the Bible and all history is pointing toward. It's the beginning of all things, the moment when God hands to His Son, Jesus the Messiah, the crown and scepter of the new Kingdom of God on earth—a Kingdom where "there shall be no more death, nor sorrow, nor crying. There shall be no more pain, for the former things have passed away" (Revelation 21:4).

As someone has aptly said, history is actually "His story." While the account of humanity's journey from Eden to the end times makes it seem that the forces of evil are continually dominating the earth and winning the battle against humanity, at the end of history, it will be clear that God was in control the whole time.

* * *

THE INVISIBLE AGENT

In this book, I have written about the various agents of Babylon who have been moving history toward the beginning of all things. In reality, there has always been only one Agent throughout the entire process—an invisible Agent who is in reality the Agent of agents: God Himself.

The presence of God in the prophecies of Daniel is astounding. His sovereignty is on display in each story and each chapter.[2] Although He appears to be offstage in the book of Daniel, His is the supreme mind working above all the other agents, using their free will to accomplish His eternal purpose.

You may wonder how God can use evil agents such as Antiochus Epiphanes—people who don't know God or reject Him outright. The answer is that every person alive eventually serves God in some way, whether intentionally or not. God never originates evil, but He uses it as an instrument to accomplish His ultimate purpose. In the Old Testament we read of how Joseph's jealous brothers sold him into slavery in Egypt. About twenty years later, when the brothers unexpectedly faced Joseph, now the regent of a powerful nation, they were terrified that he would avenge his maltreatment. But this is what he told them:

> I am Joseph your brother, whom you sold into Egypt. But now, do not therefore be grieved or angry with yourselves because you sold me here; for God sent me before you to preserve life. For these two years the famine has been in the land, and there are still five years in which there will be neither plowing nor harvesting. And God sent me before you to preserve a posterity for you in the earth, and to save your lives by a great deliverance. So now it was not you who sent me here, but God; and He has made me a father to Pharaoh, and lord of all his house, and a ruler throughout all the land of Egypt.
>
> GENESIS 45:4-8

Joseph's brothers committed a terrible evil. They did it of their own free will; God didn't compel them. But God's providence works to use every event, good or evil, to move history toward His desired end—the beginning of all things, when He will turn His Kingdom over to His beloved Son. No one thwarts God; all serve His ultimate purpose, whether wittingly or unwittingly. This explains how God, the Agent above all other agents, could use those who didn't acknowledge Him, such as Belshazzar, Alexander, and Antiochus, for His purposes.

Though it may not seem so when evil seems to engulf our lives, God is indeed in control. Not a sparrow falls without His knowing it.

* * *

THE INVINCIBLE AGENT

Daniel, the apostle John, and Jesus Christ Himself all foretold that one more world kingdom would rise before the end. That kingdom will be in some way a rebirth of the old Roman Empire, but it will have at its heart the anti-God spirit of Babylon. While Rome and Babylon were relentless in their persecution of God's people, this coming kingdom will multiply that evil to unprecedented proportions. As Jesus said, "Unless those days were shortened, no flesh would be saved; but for the elect's sake those days will be shortened" (Matthew 24:22).

In Daniel 7, the prophet Daniel he tells us plainly that this evil kingdom will arise and that God will bring it down in final judgment through the agency of the invincible Christ, who will establish His eternal Kingdom on earth (Daniel 7:13-14, 26-27). Indeed, a primary purpose of the book of Daniel is to inform us of Christ's ultimate victory and the ensuing beginning of all things. It's as if Daniel is saying, "When you look at world history, both past and future, it may seem gloomy and disheartening. But let me assure you, these traumas will someday end, and there will follow a new and eternal beginning full of goodness, truth, justice, and righteousness."

We can see signs that this prophesied end of history may well be on the horizon. The indulgent and licentious rejection of biblical standards we now see in the Western world, coupled with the rise of oppression against Christians and the increasing godlessness and autocratic control of governments around the world, are signs that storm clouds are gathering and that the shadows of future prophetic events are beginning to darken the present. We are not told when it will happen, but the signs suggest that it could be very soon.

While we don't know *when* this world as we know it will come to an end, we know from the prophecies of Daniel and others *what* will happen: Christ, the invincible Agent, will appear; He will cleanse the world of its evil; and He will set up His perfect Kingdom, which will completely reverse the ravages inflicted on the earth by the Fall.

The important thing to remember about Christ's coming is not that it will mark the end of world history—the end times—but that it will signal the beginning of all things. It is the time toward which all history has been marching. It is the time that God, always the invisible Agent in human affairs, has been engineering with love, providence, judgment, and protection from the moment of the Fall. It will be a glorious morning when we as humans realize and fulfill the purpose of our being—when we become fully all that God intended us to be and live in complete joy and harmony with Him and nature throughout all eternity.

THE AGENT OF AGENTS

THE BOOK OF DANIEL is cast with some of the most intriguing individuals in the Bible. While Daniel often receives the most attention, he is, in reality, a supporting actor to the true Hero of the story: Almighty God. God is the Agent who towers above every other agent, and His presence is evident from the first verse to the last—sometimes in the most surprising ways.

Here are more than one hundred instances where Almighty God appears in the book of Daniel. Read them and be encouraged, for we have an awesome God!

DANIEL 1

- He is the God who gave King Jehoiakim into the hands of King Nebuchadnezzar (Daniel 1:1).
- He is the God who brought Daniel into favor with the chief of the eunuchs (Daniel 1:9).

- He is the God who gave Daniel and his friends knowledge and skill in all literature and wisdom (Daniel 1:17).

DANIEL 2

- He is the God of heaven from whom Daniel and his companions sought mercies concerning the king's dream (Daniel 2:18).
- He is the God who revealed the secret of the king's dream (Daniel 2:19).
- He is the God whose name Daniel blessed forever and ever (Daniel 2:20).
- He is the God of wisdom and might (Daniel 2:20).
- He is the God who changes the times and the seasons (Daniel 2:21).
- He is the God who removes kings and raises up kings (Daniel 2:21).
- He is the God who gives wisdom to the wise and knowledge to those who have understanding (Daniel 2:21).
- He is the God who reveals deep and secret things (Daniel 2:22).
- He is the God who knows what is in the darkness (Daniel 2:22).
- He is the God with whom light dwells (Daniel 2:22).
- He is the God of Daniel's fathers (Daniel 2:23).
- He is the God who gave Daniel wisdom and might (Daniel 2:23).
- He is the God who made known to Daniel what he had asked (Daniel 2:23).
- He is the God who revealed to Daniel King Nebuchadnezzar's demand (Daniel 2:23).

- He is the God of heaven who gave King Nebuchadnezzar a kingdom, as well as power, strength, and glory (Daniel 2:37).
- He is the God who made King Nebuchadnezzar the ruler over the children of men, the beasts of the field, and the birds of heaven (Daniel 2:38).
- He is the God of heaven who will set up a Kingdom that will never be destroyed (Daniel 2:44).
- He is the Stone cut out of the mountain that broke in pieces the iron, the bronze, the clay, the silver, and the gold (Daniel 2:45).
- He is the God who made known to King Nebuchadnezzar what would come to pass (Daniel 2:45).
- He is the God of gods, the Lord of kings, and a revealer of secrets (Daniel 2:47).

DANIEL 3

- He is the God whom Shadrach, Meshach, and Abed-Nego served (Daniel 3:17).
- He is the God who was able to deliver these men from the fiery furnace (Daniel 3:17).
- He is the fourth Man walking in the midst of the fire (Daniel 3:25).
- He is the God of Shadrach, Meshach, and Abed-Nego (Daniel 3:29).

DANIEL 4

- He is the Most High God who worked signs and wonders for King Nebuchadnezzar (Daniel 4:2).
- He is the God of great signs, mighty wonders, and an everlasting Kingdom (Daniel 4:3).

- He is the God whose dominion is from generation to generation (Daniel 4:3).
- He is the Spirit of the Holy God who dwelled in Daniel (Daniel 4:8-9).
- He is the Most High God who rules in the kingdom of men and gives it to whomever He chooses (Daniel 4:17).
- He is the Spirit of the Holy God who made known to King Nebuchadnezzar the interpretation of his dream (Daniel 4:18).
- He is the Most High God whose decree came upon King Nebuchadnezzar (Daniel 4:24).
- He is the Most High God who lives forever (Daniel 4:34).
- He is the Most High God whom King Nebuchadnezzar blessed, praised, and honored (Daniel 4:34).
- He is the God whose dominion is an everlasting dominion (Daniel 4:34).
- He is the God whose Kingdom is from generation to generation (Daniel 4:34).
- He is the God before whom the whole earth is reputed as nothing (Daniel 4:35).
- He is the God who works according to His will in the army of heaven and among the inhabitants of the earth (Daniel 4:35).
- He is the God whose hand no one can restrain and to whom no one can say, "What have You done?" (Daniel 4:35).
- He is the King of heaven, whom King Nebuchadnezzar praised, extolled, and honored (Daniel 4:37).
- He is the God whose works are truth and whose ways are just (Daniel 4:37).
- He is the God who is able to put down those who walk in pride (Daniel 4:37).

DANIEL 5

- He is the Holy God whose Spirit was in Daniel (Daniel 5:11).
- He is the Spirit of God who was in Daniel, giving him light, understanding, and excellent wisdom (Daniel 5:14).
- He is the Most High God who gave King Nebuchadnezzar a kingdom and majesty, glory, and honor (Daniel 5:18).
- He is the Most High God who rules in the kingdom of men and appoints over it whomever He chooses (Daniel 5:21).
- He is the Lord of heaven against whom Belshazzar lifted up his heart (Daniel 5:23).
- He is the God who held Belshazzar's breath in His hand, whom Belshazzar had not glorified (Daniel 5:23).
- He is the God whose fingers wrote on the wall of Belshazzar's banquet hall (Daniel 5:24).
- He is the God who numbered Belshazzar's kingdom and finished it (Daniel 5:26).
- He is the God who weighed Belshazzar's kingdom in the balance and found it wanting (Daniel 5:27).
- He is the God who gave Babylon to the Medes and Persians (Daniel 5:28).

DANIEL 6

- He is the God to whom Daniel knelt three times a day (Daniel 6:10).
- He is the God to whom Daniel was praying when he was found by the king's representatives (Daniel 6:11).
- He is the living God whom Daniel served continually (Daniel 6:20).
- He is the God who sent His angel to shut the mouths of the lions so that they could not hurt Daniel (Daniel 6:22).

- He is the God of Daniel before whom every member of Darius's kingdom must tremble in fear (Daniel 6:26).
- He is the living God and steadfast forever (Daniel 6:26).
- He is the God whose Kingdom will not be destroyed and whose dominion will endure to the end (Daniel 6:26).
- He is the God who delivers and rescues (Daniel 6:27).
- He is the God who works signs and wonders in heaven and on earth (Daniel 6:27).
- He is the God who delivered Daniel from the power of the lions (Daniel 6:27).

DANIEL 7

- He is the Ancient of Days whose garment is white as snow (Daniel 7:9).
- He is the God whose throne is a fiery flame (Daniel 7:9).
- He is the God before whom a fiery stream flows (Daniel 7:10).
- He is the God before whom thousands and thousands ministered and ten thousand times ten thousand stood (Daniel 7:10).
- He is the God who is One like the Son of Man (Daniel 7:13).
- He is the God who is the Ancient of Days (Daniel 7:13).
- He is the God who has dominion and glory and a Kingdom over all peoples, nations, and languages (Daniel 7:14).
- He is the God whose dominion will not pass away and whose Kingdom will not be destroyed (Daniel 7:14).
- He is the God who makes a judgment in favor of the saints of the Most High when it is time for them to possess the Kingdom (Daniel 7:22).
- He is the God whom all dominions will serve and obey (Daniel 9:27).

DANIEL 8

- He is the God who sent Gabriel to help Daniel understand his vision (Daniel 8:16).
- He is the God who will break the Antichrist without human means (Daniel 8:25).

DANIEL 9

- He is the God who made Darius king over the realm of the Chaldeans (Daniel 9:1).
- He is the God who specified through Jeremiah the prophet that He would accomplish seventy years in the desolations of Jerusalem (Daniel 9:2).
- He is the God, the Lord, to whom Daniel prayed with fasting, sackcloth, and ashes (Daniel 9:3).
- He is the God who is the Lord (Daniel 9:4).
- He is the God who is great and awesome and who keeps His covenant with those who love Him and keep His commandments (Daniel 9:4).
- He is the God whose prophets spoke to Israel's kings, princes, fathers, and all the people of the land (Daniel 9:6).
- He is the God to whom righteousness belongs (Daniel 9:7).
- He is the God who drove the inhabitants of Jerusalem and all Israel far off because of their unfaithfulness to Him (Daniel 9:7).
- He is the God, the Lord, to whom belong mercy and forgiveness (Daniel 9:9).
- He is the God who sets His laws before His people (Daniel 9:10).
- He is the God of the Law of Moses, the servant of God (Daniel 9:11).

- He is the God who poured out the curse and the oath written in the Law of Moses because Israel sinned against Him (Daniel 9:11).
- He is the God who confirmed His words, which He spoke against Israel and its judges by bringing upon them a great disaster (Daniel 9:12).
- He is the God, the Lord, who kept the disaster in mind and brought it upon Israel (Daniel 9:14).
- He is the God, the Lord, who is righteous in all the works He does (Daniel 9:14).
- He is the God of Israel, the Lord, who brought His people out of the land of Egypt with a mighty hand and made Himself a name (Daniel 9:15).
- He is the God, the Lord of righteousness, to whom Daniel prayed (Daniel 9:16).
- He is the God who heard the prayer and supplications of His servant Daniel (Daniel 9:17).
- He is the God, the Lord, who caused His face to shine upon His sanctuary (Daniel 9:17).
- He is the God who inclines His ear and hears, and who opens His eyes and sees our desolations, not because of our righteous deeds, but because of His great mercies (Daniel 9:18).
- He is the God, the Lord, who forgives, listens, and acts (Daniel 9:19).
- He is the God who caused Gabriel to fly swiftly to Daniel (Daniel 9:21).
- He is the God who sent Gabriel to give Daniel skill in understanding the vision (Daniel 9:22).
- He is the God who sent Gabriel to tell Daniel that he was greatly beloved (Daniel 9:23).

- He is the God who determined seventy weeks for Daniel's people and for the holy city to finish the transgression, to make an end of sins, to make reconciliation for iniquity, to bring in everlasting righteousness, to seal up vision and prophecy, and to anoint the Most Holy (Daniel 9:24).

DANIEL 10

- He is the God who revealed a message to Daniel in the third year of Cyrus, king of Persia (Daniel 10:1).
- He is the God whose message to Daniel caused him to mourn for three full weeks, during which time Daniel ate no pleasant food and drank no wine (Daniel 10:3).
- He is the God who sent to Daniel a certain man clothed in linen, whose waist was girded with gold of Uphaz (Daniel 10:5).
- He is the God whose great vision turned Daniel's vigor to frailty (Daniel 10:8).
- He is the God who sent an angel to Daniel to remind him that he was greatly beloved (Daniel 10:11).
- He is the God who sent an angel to embolden Daniel and help him understand (Daniel 10:12).
- He is the God who heard Daniel's prayer (Daniel 10:12).
- He is the God who sent an angel to touch Daniel and strengthen him (Daniel 10:18).
- He is the God whose angel spoke great words of encouragement to Daniel (Daniel 10:19).

DANIEL 11

- He is the God who knows the future and fulfills His prophecies (at least 135 in Daniel 11:1-35 alone).

DANIEL 12

- He is the God who will deliver all those whose names are found written in the book (Daniel 12:1).
- He is the God who will awaken many of those who sleep in the dust of the earth, some to everlasting life, some to shame and everlasting contempt (Daniel 12:2).
- He is the God who will make the wise shine like the brightness of the firmament, and those who turn many to righteousness like the stars forever and ever (Daniel 12:3).
- He is the God who lives forever (Daniel 12:7).
- He is the God whose words are closed up and sealed till the time of the end (Daniel 12:9).
- He is the God who will purify, make white, and refine many (Daniel 12:10).
- He is the God who blesses those who wait and come to the 1,335 days (Daniel 12:12).
- He is the God who promised to raise up Daniel to his inheritance at the end of the days (Daniel 12:13).

ACKNOWLEDGMENTS

MORE THAN ANY PREVIOUS PROJECT, the message of this book weighed heavily upon my heart. Some of the most profound and disturbing visions in the entire Bible come to us in the pages of Daniel. I felt like I could sympathize in some small way with Daniel when he wrote that "no strength remained" in him after receiving the revelation he did from Almighty God (Daniel 10:8).

At the same time, nothing could have lifted my spirits higher and placed in my heart more confidence in Almighty God than the stories and truths contained in the book of Daniel. To see how Daniel and his friends responded to the adversity in their lives is nothing less than inspiring. More important, tracing the hidden sovereignty of God in each chapter strengthened my resolve to continue living for Him in the days ahead.

I am thankful for the wonderful team God has provided around me. Without them, *Agents of Babylon* would not have made it to publication.

Barbara Boucher is my administrative assistant at Shadow Mountain Community Church. She is the one who coordinates my work at the church with my responsibilities at Turning Point so I can be faithful to the assignments God has called me to at each.

Diane Sutherland protects and organizes my schedule at Turning Point. Never has her job been more challenging, and never has she done it with greater excellence. Thank you, Diane, for your servant heart!

Paul Joiner is the executive producer and creative director at Turning Point. His leadership, professionalism, and creativity never cease to amaze me. This time he set a standard that I cannot imagine ever again being equaled.

Rob Morgan and William Kruidenier each helped with the research and devotional content, and it means so much to me to have friends of this caliber who invest in our work. My research assistant, Beau Sager, holds all the various pieces of our writing projects together. His careful editing and research and especially his verification of all the quotes in this book were done with the quiet excellence he brings to whatever he does. Thank you, Beau, for the valuable insights you provided to the finished product.

This was the third book for which Tom Williams has written the narrative. Tom took the notes from my study of the book of Daniel and turned them into narratives that help us experience the truth of Scripture in new ways. Tom, it is great fun working with you!

The team at Tyndale House, under the direction of vice president Ron Beers, has been a pleasure to work with.

My agent, Sealy Yates, is the best at what he does. Sealy, I hope the message of this book will encourage you as much as it did me.

Each year as Turning Point radio and television explodes around the world with the message of the gospel, my oldest son, David Michael, continues to lead the great team of people here at the Turning Point headquarters. He understands the biblical principle that in order to "lengthen the cords," you have to "strengthen the stakes" (Isaiah 54:2). David, you cannot imagine what a joy it is for me to walk with you in this great endeavor.

As I finish this book and write these acknowledgments, my wife, Donna, and I are celebrating our fifty-second wedding anniversary. During these fifty-two years, I have written more than fifty books. That gives you insight into the kind of loving and patient wife God gave me. We are both amazed at His blessing on our ministry, and we rejoice that we have been able to share every single step of the journey together.

Finally, and most important, to Daniel's God—to the Most High God—thank You for the opportunity to glorify Your name and serve Your people in the writing of this book.

NOTES

CHAPTER 1. THE HOSTAGE

1. Stephen R. Miller, *Daniel*, The New American Commentary 18 (Nashville: Broadman & Holman, 1994), 58.
2. Stan Phelps, "Cracking into Google: 15 Reasons Why More than 2 Million People Apply Each Year," *Forbes*, August 5, 2014, http://www.forbes.com /sites/stanphelps/2014/08/05/cracking-into-google-the-15-reasons-why-over -2-million-people-apply-each-year/.
3. Leon J. Wood, *A Commentary on Daniel* (Grand Rapids, MI: Zondervan, 1973), 33.
4. Ibid., 32.
5. John F. Walvoord, *Daniel: The Key to Prophetic Revelation* (Chicago: Moody, 1971), 43.

CHAPTER 2. THE INSOMNIAC

1. H. A. Ironside, *Lectures on Daniel the Prophet* (New York: Bible Truth Press, 1920), 25.
2. Wood, *A Commentary on Daniel*, 44.
3. Geoffrey R. King, *Daniel: A Detailed Explanation of the Book* (London: Henry E. Walter, 1966), 49.

4. Miller, *Daniel*, 81.

5. Ibid., 82.

6. Walvoord, *Daniel: The Key to Prophetic Revelation*, 52.

7. Joseph A. Seiss, *Voices from Babylon* (Philadelphia: Castle, 1879), 49.

8. Miller, *Daniel*, 84.

9. Wood, *A Commentary on Daniel*, 59.

CHAPTER 3. THE COLOSSUS

1. Herodotus, *The History of Herodotus*, Book 1.183.

2. Plutarch, "On Contentedness of Mind."

3. Herbert Carl Leupold, *Exposition of Daniel* (Minneapolis: Augsburg, 1949), 119.

4. Walvoord, *Daniel: The Key to Prophetic Revelation*, 66.

5. Ibid, 71.

6. William G. Heslop, *Diamonds from Daniel* (Grand Rapids, MI: Kregel, 1976), 46.

7. Ibid.

8. Ibid.

9. C. I. Scofield, *The Scofield Reference Bible* (New York: Oxford University Press, 1945), 901.

10. Flavius Josephus, *Antiquities of the Jews*, book XI, chapter 8, paragraph 5.

11. David Jeremiah, *What in the World Is Going On?* (Nashville: Thomas Nelson, 2008), 56.

12. Leupold, *Exposition of Daniel*, 119.

CHAPTER 4. THE FIRE MEN

1. Heslop, *Diamonds from Daniel*, 57.

2. Walvoord, *Daniel: The Key to Prophetic Revelation*, 81.

3. Ibid., 83.

4. Wood, *A Commentary on Daniel*, 83.

5. Walvoord, *Daniel: The Key to Prophetic Revelation*, 87.

6. John Calvin, *Commentaries on the Four Last Books of Moses Arranged in the Form of a Harmony*, vol. 2 (Edinburgh: Calvin Translation Society, 1853), 108.

7. Leupold, *Exposition of Daniel*, 153.

8. Geoffrey Anketell Studdert Kennedy, *The Hardest Part* (London: Hodder and Stoughton, 1919), 110–11.

9. King, *Daniel*, 85.

10. Walvoord, *Daniel: The Key to Prophetic Revelation*, 90.

11. Arno C. Gaebelein, *Daniel: A Key to the Visions and Prophecies of the Book of Daniel* (Grand Rapids, MI: Kregel, 1968), 47.

CHAPTER 5. THE WOLF-MAN

1. Daniel 4:1-3.
2. C. S. Lewis, *Mere Christianity* (New York: Macmillan, 1960), 108–109.
3. Wood, *A Commentary on Daniel*, 99.
4. C. F. Keil, *The Book of the Prophet Daniel* (Edinburgh: T. & T. Clark, 1877), 216.
5. Charles W. Colson, *Born Again* (Grand Rapids, MI: Baker, 2008), 65.
6. Graham Scroggie, quoted in King, *Daniel*, 109.

CHAPTER 6. THE FINGERS OF GOD

1. David Jeremiah with Carole C. Carlson, *The Handwriting on the Wall* (Dallas: Word, 1992), 98.
2. Leupold, *Exposition of Daniel*, 214.
3. Seiss, *Voices from Babylon*, 145–46.
4. Walvoord, *Daniel: The Key to Prophetic Revelation*, 119.
5. Wood, *A Commentary on Daniel*, 150.
6. *Herodotus*, vol. 1, trans. Henry Carey (New York: Harper, 1889), 190–91.
7. Walvoord, *Daniel: The Key to Prophetic Revelation*, 131.

CHAPTER 7. THE LION KING

1. Daniel 6:26.
2. Clarence E. Macartney, *Trials of Great Men of the Bible* (Nashville: Abingdon-Cokesbury, 1946), 97–98.
3. James Thomson, "Spring," in *The Seasons: A Poem* (New York: Clark, Austin & Co., 1854), 14.
4. Heslop, *Diamonds from Daniel*, 87.
5. C. F. Keil, *Biblical Commentary on the Book of Daniel* (Grand Rapids, MI: Eerdmans, 1955), 171.
6. James Robert Graham, *The Prophet-Statesman*, quoted in Donald K. Campbell, *Daniel: God's Man in a Secular Society* (Grand Rapids, MI: Discovery House, 1988), 96–97.
7. Charles Spurgeon quoted in King, *Daniel*, 197.
8. Wood, *A Commentary on Daniel*, 174.
9. Robert J. Morgan, *From This Verse* (Nashville: Thomas Nelson, 1998), June 5.

CHAPTER 8. THE CONQUEROR

1. King, *Daniel*, 127.
2. Rodney Stortz, *Daniel: The Triumph of God's Kingdom* (Wheaton, IL: Crossway, 2004), 134.
3. Plutarch, *Alexander*.
4. Flavius Josephus, *Antiquities of the Jews*, book XI, chapter 8, paragraph 5.
5. Ibid.

6. Ibid.

7. W. W. Tarn, *Alexander the Great*, vol. 1 (Cambridge: Cambridge University Press, 1948), 145–46.

8. J. E. H. Thomson, "Alexander, the Great," in *International Standard Bible Encyclopedia*, vol. 1, ed. James Orr (Grand Rapids, MI: Eerdmans, 1957), 93.

9. Charles Ross Weede, quoted in *The Speaker's Quote Book* (Grand Rapids, MI: Kregel, 2009), 69–70.

CHAPTER 9. THE MADMAN

1. 1 Maccabees 1:5-7, 10, 16, 19-20, GNT.

2. Solomon Zeitlin, *The Rise and Fall of the Judean State*, vol. 1 (Philadelphia: Jewish Publications Society, 1962), 92.

3. 1 Maccabees 1:44-50.

4. Wood, *A Commentary on Daniel*, 213.

5. 1 Maccabees 1:60-61; 2 Maccabees 6:10.

6. 2 Maccabbees 7:1-6.

7. 1 Maccabees 1:21-24.

8. 1 Maccabees 1:56-57.

9. Lehman Strauss, *The Prophecies of Daniel* (Neptune, NJ: Loizeaux Brothers, 1978), 242–43.

10. 1 Maccabees 2:19-22.

11. "Hanukkah," History.com, accessed June 11, 2015, http://www.history.com /topics/hanukkah.

12. Campbell, *Daniel: God's Man*, 125.

13. Louis T. Talbot, *The Prophecies of Daniel* (Wheaton, IL: Van Kampen, 1954), 143.

14. Mark Hitchcock, *Cashless* (Eugene, OR: Harvest House, 2009), 104.

15. John Phillips, *Exploring Revelation: An Expository Commentary* (Grand Rapids, MI: Kregel, 2001), 166.

16. David Jeremiah, *The Coming Economic Armageddon* (New York: FaithWords, 2010), 115.

17. 1 Maccabees 1:29-32.

18. 1 Maccabees 6:1-17.

19. Strauss, *The Prophecies of Daniel*, 250.

20. Adapted from Billy Graham, *World Aflame* (New York: Doubleday, 1965), 206–207.

CHAPTER 10. THE HERALD

1. Jeremiah 25:8-10, NLT.

2. Jeremiah 25:11-14, NLT.

3. Jeremiah 29:12-14, NLT.

4. Daniel 9:19, NLT.

5. Campbell, *Daniel: God's Man*, 134–35.
6. H. A. Ironside, *Daniel: An Ironside Expository Commentary* (Grand Rapids, MI: Kregel, 2005), 86.
7. Leupold, *Exposition of Daniel*, 376.
8. Strauss, *Prophecies of Daniel*, 253.
9. Isaac Newton, *Observations upon the Prophecies of Daniel and the Apocalypse of St. John* (London: J. Darby and T. Browne, 1733).
10. Clarence Larkin, *The Book of Daniel* (Philadelphia: Rev. Clarence Larkin, 1929), 197.
11. Strauss, *Prophecies of Daniel*, 256.
12. Walvoord, *Daniel: The Key to Prophetic Revelation*, 202.
13. Campbell, *Daniel: God's Man*, 148.
14. Wood, *A Commentary on Daniel*, 242.
15. Arno Gaebelein, *The Prophet Daniel* (Grand Rapids, MI: Kregel, 1955), 129.
16. Leupold, *Exposition of Daniel*, 412.
17. Wood, *A Commentary on Daniel*, 250.
18. G. H. Lang, *The Histories and Prophecies of Daniel* (Grand Rapids, MI: Kregel, 1973), 132.
19. Alva J. McClain, *Daniel's Prophecy of the Seventy Weeks* (Grand Rapids, MI: Zondervan, 1969), 18–19.
20. Sir Robert Anderson, *The Coming Prince* (London: Hodder and Stoughton, 1909), 121–23.
21. McClain, *Daniel's Prophecy*, 5.
22. Ibid., 19–20.
23. Campbell, *Daniel: God's Man*, 143–44.

CHAPTER 11. THE ARCHANGEL
1. Quoted in Campbell, *Daniel: God's Man*, 153.
2. Walvoord, *Daniel: The Key to Prophetic Revelation*, 240.
3. Leupold, *Exposition of Daniel*, 447–48.
4. Strauss, *The Prophecies of Daniel*, 302.
5. Ibid., 302.
6. Mark Hitchcock, *The Amazing Claims of Bible Prophecy* (Eugene, OR: Harvest House, 2010), 55.
7. John Phillips, *Exploring the Future: A Comprehensive Guide to Bible Prophecy* (Grand Rapids, MI: Kregel, 2003), 37–38.
8. Heslop, *Diamonds from Daniel*, 166.
9. Phillips, *Exploring the Future*, 26.
10. Walvoord, *Daniel: The Key to Prophetic Revelation*, 253.
11. Phillips, *Exploring the Future*, 43.
12. Phillips, *Exploring the Future*, 39.
13. David Jeremiah, *What in the World Is Going On?* (Nashville: Thomas Nelson, 2008).

14. David Jeremiah, *The Coming Economic Armageddon* (New York: FaithWords, 2010).
15. David Jeremiah, *Agents of the Apocalypse* (Carol Stream, IL: Tyndale, 2014).
16. Walvoord, *Daniel: The Key to Prophetic Revelation*, 280.
17. E. B. Pusey, quoted in James Montgomery Boice, *Daniel: An Expositional Commentary* (Grand Rapids, MI: Baker, 2003), 13.
18. Quoted in Campbell, *Daniel: God's Man,* 169.
19. "Religion: Promises," *Time*, December 24, 1956.

CHAPTER 12. THE END

1. Daniel 12:1-3.
2. Walvoord, *Daniel: The Key to Prophetic Revelation*, 281–82.
3. See David Jeremiah, *Agents of the Apocalypse*, 258–59 for my commentary on the Book of Life.
4. Henry M. Morris, *The Revelation Record: A Scientific and Devotional Commentary on the Book of Revelation* (Carol Stream, IL: Tyndale, 1983), 433.
5. Seiss, *Voices from Babylon*, 310–11, emphasis added.
6. Wood, *A Commentary on Daniel*, 328–29.
7. Seiss, *Voices from Babylon*, 306.
8. Leupold, *Exposition of Daniel*, 534–35.
9. Wood, *A Commentary on Daniel*, 325.
10. David Jeremiah, "Daniel: Book Introduction," in *The Jeremiah Study Bible* (Nashville: Worthy, 2013), 1118.
11. Warren W. Wiersbe, *Life Sentences* (Grand Rapids, MI: Zondervan, 2007), 192.

EPILOGUE. MARCHING TOWARD THE BEGINNING

1. C. S. Lewis, *Perelandra* (New York: Simon & Schuster, 1944, 1972), 182.
2. See the appendix, "The Agent of Agents."

ABOUT THE AUTHOR

DR. DAVID JEREMIAH serves as senior pastor of Shadow Mountain Community Church in El Cajon, California. He is the founder and host of Turning Point, a ministry committed to providing Christians with sound Bible teaching relevant to today's changing times through radio and television, the Internet, live events, and resource materials and books. A bestselling author, Dr. Jeremiah has written more than fifty books, including *Captured by Grace, Living with Confidence in a Chaotic World, What in the World Is Going On?, The Coming Economic Armageddon, God Loves You: He Always Has—He Always Will, What Are You Afraid Of?, Agents of the Apocalypse*, and *A.D. The Bible Continues: The Revolution That Changed the World*.

Dr. Jeremiah's commitment to teaching the complete Word of God continues to make him a sought-after speaker and writer. His passion for reaching the lost and encouraging believers in their faith is demonstrated through his faithful communication of biblical truths.

A dedicated family man, Dr. Jeremiah and his wife, Donna, have four grown children and twelve grandchildren.

stay connected to the teaching series of

DR. DAVID JEREMIAH

· · · · · · · ·

Publishing | Radio | Television | Online

FURTHER YOUR STUDY OF THIS BOOK

• • • • • • • •

Agents of Babylon Resource Materials

To enhance your study on this important topic, we recommend the correlating audio message album, study guide, and DVD messages from the *Agents of Babylon* series.

Audio Message Album

The material found in this book originated from messages presented by Dr. David Jeremiah at the Shadow Mountain Community Church where he serves as senior pastor. These ten messages are conveniently packaged in an accessible audio album.

Study Guide

This 128-page study guide correlates with the *Agents of Babylon* messages by Dr. Jeremiah. Each lesson provides an outline, overview, and application questions for each topic.

DVD Message Presentations

Watch Dr. Jeremiah deliver the *Agents of the Apocalypse* original messages in this special DVD collection.

· · · · ·

COMPLETE YOUR STUDY

ON BIBLE PROPHECY

With These Additional Titles from
DR. DAVID JEREMIAH

New York Times Best Seller
Agents of the Apocalypse
by Dr. David Jeremiah

Are we living in the end times? What if the players depicted in the book of Revelation were out in force today? And if they were, would you know how to recognize them?

In *Agents of the Apocalypse,* noted prophecy expert Dr. David Jeremiah does what no Bible teacher has done before. He explores the book of Revelation through the lens of its major players: the exile, the martyrs, the 144,000, the two witnesses, the dragon, the beast from the earth, the beast from the sea, the Victor, the King, and the Judge.

Skillfully crafted to engage both the heart and the mind, each chapter opens with an engaging, biblically based dramatization that brings prophecies to life as never before. As Dr. Jeremiah presents these agents in the context of their unique times and places in the end times, he weaves a rich tapestry of the temperaments, motives, and conspiracies that Scripture tells us will precipitate earth's final days. Then, in each chapter, Dr. Jeremiah provides a detailed study called "The Scripture behind the Story," which explores some of Revelation's most cryptic passages, explaining how to interpret them and—most important—how they apply to the malevolent forces at play in the world today.

The stage is set, and the curtain is about to rise on earth's final act. Will you be ready?

What in the World Is Going On?

Many theories try to depict the end times, and the Bible itself is filled with prophecies explaining this subject. In this book, Dr. Jeremiah identifies ten essential prophecies in the Bible to help us gain an understanding of the mysteries of the future.

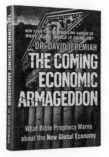

The Coming Economic Armageddon

The chaotic global financial market and widespread debt surround us daily. In this book, Dr. Jeremiah explores these economic disasters and answers questions like "How did we get to this place?" and "Are the last days of Earth's history fast approaching?" to help us better prepare for the future.

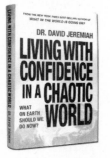

Living with Confidence in a Chaotic World

It is an undeniable truth that there is turmoil and trouble in our world today; however, it is possible to live confidently in the midst of the chaos by practicing ten biblical principles that God has provided for us. *Living with Confidence in a Chaotic World* is your personal guide to discovering and enjoying a confident life in the midst of chaos.

To order these books, call us at 1-800-947-1993 or visit us online at www.DavidJeremiah.org.

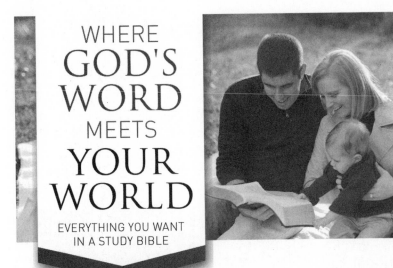

WHERE GOD'S WORD MEETS YOUR WORLD

EVERYTHING YOU WANT IN A STUDY BIBLE

WHAT IT SAYS. WHAT IT MEANS. WHAT IT MEANS FOR YOU.

More than 100,000 people are currently using *The Jeremiah Study Bible.* The comments we are receiving from our readers have been a great encouragement. This study Bible contains a wealth of information that will help you understand what the Bible says, what it means, and what it means for you.

The Jeremiah Study Bible is comprehensive, yet easy to understand. Over 40 years in the making, it is deeply personal and designed to transform your life. No matter your place or time in history, Scripture always speaks to the important issues of life. Hear God speak to you through studying His Word in *The Jeremiah Study Bible.*

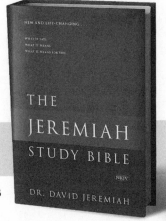

www.DavidJeremiah.org/JSB

STAY CONNECTED

· · · · · · · ·

Take advantage of two great ways to let
Dr. David Jeremiah give you spiritual direction every day!
Both are absolutely free!

① *Turning Points* Magazine and Devotional

each magazine features:
- A monthly study focus
- 48 pages of life-changing reading
- Relevant articles
- Special features
- Devotional readings for each day of the month
- Bible-study resource offers
- Live-event schedule
- Radio & television information

Request your free subscription today!

CALL: (800) 947-1993
CLICK: DavidJeremiah.org/Magazine

② Your Daily Turning Point E-Devotional

Start your day off right! Find words of inspiration
and spiritual motivation waiting for you on
your computer every morning! You can receive
a daily e-devotional from Dr. Jeremiah that will
strengthen your walk with God and encourage
you to live the authentic Christian life.

Request your free e-devotional today!

CLICK: DavidJeremiah.org/Devo

BOOKS WRITTEN BY DAVID JEREMIAH

· · · · · · · ·

Escape the Coming Night
Turning toward Joy
The Handwriting on the Wall
Invasion of Other Gods
Angels: Who They Are and How They Help…What the Bible Reveals
The Joy of Encouragement
Prayer: The Great Adventure
God in You
Until Christ Returns
Stories of Hope from a Bend in the Road
Slaying the Giants in Your Life
My Heart's Desire
Sanctuary
The Things That Matter
The Prayer Matrix
31 Days to Happiness: Searching for Heaven on Earth
When Your World Falls Apart
Turning Points with God
Discover Paradise
Captured by Grace
Grace Givers
Why the Nativity?
Signs of Life
Life-Changing Moments with God
Hopeful Parenting
1 Minute a Day: Instant Inspiration for the Busy Life
Grand Parenting: Faith That Survives Generations
In the Words of David Jeremiah
What in the World Is Going On?
The Sovereign and the Suffering
The 12 Ways of Christmas

What to Do When You Don't Know What to Do
Living with Confidence in a Chaotic World
The Prophecy Answer Book
The Coming Economic Armageddon
Pathways: Your Daily Walk with God
What the Bible Says About Love, Marriage, and Sex
I Never Thought I'd See the Day!
Journey: Your Daily Adventure with God
The Unchanging Word of God
God Loves You: He Always Has–He Always Will
Discovery: Experiencing God's Word Day by Day
What Are You Afraid Of?
Destination: Your Journey with God
Answers to Your Questions about Heaven
Answers to Questions about Spiritual Warfare
Answers to Questions about Adversity
Quest: Seeking God Daily
Ten Questions Christians Are Asking
Understanding the 66 Books of the Bible
A.D. The Bible Continues: The Revolution That Changed the World
A.D. The Bible Continues: The Book of Acts
Agents of the Apocalypse
Discovering God

To order these books, call us at 1-800-947-1993 or
visit us online at www.DavidJeremiah.org.

CP0995

DAVID JEREMIAH FOR THE NEXT GENERATION

The Barnyard Bunch and Friends book

This book includes twelve different stories featuring the animals in the *Barnyard Bunch*. Each story stands alone and can be read or listened to once a month or all in one sitting. Follow along with the audio CD or listen in the car while traveling to school or going to the store. Each story has a specific lesson to learn and a special verse to memorize.

ALSO AVAILABLE ONLINE

The Barnyard Bunch and Friends online

Visit the *Barnyard Bunch and Friends* website each month to read and listen to a new story from your friends at Happy Meadow. Kids will discover a new truth from God's Word every month and a memory verse to accompany that truth.

Airship Genesis: The Legendary Bible Adventure online

This interactive website features the audio episodes of *Airship Genesis: The Legendary Bible Adventure*—an action-packed dramatic audio series designed to show children the adventures that can be found inside the Bible.

Visit us online at www.DavidJeremiah.org/KIDS.

African
Art
in
Needlework

Other Books by Leslie Tillett:

The Fall of the Aztecs
American Needlework 1776/1976
Wind on the Buffalo Grass
The Zoophabet Needlework Book